LUTHERAN QUARTERLY BOOKS

Editor

Paul Rorem, Princeton Theological Seminary

Associate Editors

Timothy J. Wengert, The Lutheran Theological Seminary at Philadelphia
Steven Paulson, Luther Seminary, St. Paul
Mark C. Mattes, Grand View College, Des Moines, Iowa

Lutheran Quarterly Books will advance the same aims as *Lutheran Quarterly* itself, aims repeated by Theodore G. Tappert when he was editor fifty years ago and renewed by Oliver K. Olson when he revived the publication in 1987. The original four aims continue to grace the front matter and to guide the contents of every issue, and can now also indicate the goals of *Lutheran Quarterly Books:* "to provide a forum (1) for the discussion of Christian faith and life on the basis of the Lutheran confession; (2) for the application of the principles of the Lutheran church to the changing problems of religion and society; (3) for the fostering of world Lutheranism; and (4) for the promotion of understanding between Lutherans and other Christians."

For further information, see www.lutheranquarterly.com.

The symbol and motto of *Lutheran Quarterly,* VDMA for *Verbum Domini Manet in Aeternum* (1 Peter 1:25), was adopted as a motto by Luther's sovereign, Frederick the Wise, and his successors. The original "Protestant" princes walking out of the imperial Diet of Speyer in 1529, unruly peasants following Thomas Müntzer, and from 1531 to 1547 the coins, medals, flags, and guns of the Smalcaldic League all bore the most famous Reformation slogan, the first Evangelical confession: The Word of the Lord remains forever.

Living by Faith: Justification and Sanctification, by Oswald Bayer (2003).

Harvesting Martin Luther's Reflections on Theology, Ethics and the Church, essays from *Lutheran Quarterly,* edited by Timothy J. Wengert, with foreword by David C. Steinmetz (2004).

A More Radical Gospel: Essays on Eschatology, Authority, Atonement, and Ecumenism, by Gerhard O. Forde, edited by Mark Mattes and Steven Paulson (2004).

The Role of Justification in Contemporary Theology, by Mark C. Mattes (2004).

The Captivation of the Will: Luther vs. Erasmus on Freedom and Bondage, by Gerhard O. Forde (2005).

Bound Choice, Election, and Wittenberg Theological Method: From Martin Luther to the Formula of Concord, by Robert Kolb (2005).

A Formula for Parish Practice: Using the Formula of Concord in Congregations, by Timothy J. Wengert (2006).

Luther's Liturgical Music: Principles and Implications, by Robin A. Leaver (2006).

The Preached God: Proclamation in Word and Sacrament, by Gerhard O. Forde, edited by Mark C. Mattes and Steven D. Paulson (2007).

Theology the Lutheran Way, by Oswald Bayer (2007).

A Time for Confessing, by Robert W. Bertram (2008).

The Pastoral Luther: Essays on Martin Luther's Practical Theology, edited by Timothy J. Wengert (2009).

Preaching from Home: The Stories of Seven Lutheran Women Hymn Writers, by Gracia Grindal (2011).

The Early Luther: Stages in a Reformation Reorientation, by Berndt Hamm (2013).

The Life, Works, and Witness of Tsehay Tolessa and Gudina Tumsa, the Ethiopian Bonhoeffer, edited by Samuel Yonas Deressa and Sarah Hinlicky (2017).

A Time for Confessing

Robert W. Bertram

edited by Michael Hoy
with a Foreword by Edward H. Schroeder

Fortress Press
Minneapolis

A TIME FOR CONFESSING

Interior contents have not been changed from prior editions.

Paperback ISBN: 978-1-5064-2707-2
eBook ISBN: 978-1-5064-2708-9

The paper used in this publication meets the minimum requirements of American National Standard for Information Sciences — Permanence of Paper for Printed Library Materials, ANSI Z329.48-1984.

Manufactured in the U.S.A.

Contents

Foreword, *by Edward H. Schroeder*   vii

Editor's Preface   xvi

1. Augsburg: A Modern "Time for Confessing"   1

2. *Confessio:* Self-Defense Becomes Subversive   23

3. Black Churches in the Civil Rights
   Movement as a Confessing Movement:
   Confessio as Disencumbering the Gospel   39

4. "Confession" against Apartheid: When Faith Is Ethos   57

5. Bonhoeffer's "Battle(s) for Christendom":
   His "Responsible Interpretation" of Barmen   65

6. A Philippine Revolution: From Patients to Agents   96

7. A Time for Confessing; or,
   When Is the Church a Confessional Movement?   132

APPENDIX   Postmodernity's CRUX:
A Theology of the Cross for the Postmodern World   150

   Theses on "C Is for Criticism"   150

   Theses on "R Is for Revelation"   159

   Theses on "U Is for Universality"   172

   Theses on "X Is for Christ-ening"   184

Bibliography of Robert W. Bertram by Michael Hoy   206

Index of Names and Subjects   217

Index of Lutheran Confession References   219

Index of Scripture References   220

Foreword

Bob Bertram is perhaps the most unpublished major Lutheran theologian of the twentieth century. When I say "unpublished," I mean he never wrote a book, although there were book-length manuscripts in his computer when he breathed his last. So it's high time that we his students, his "living letters," do something about it — at the very least with those manuscripts.

Unpublished, of course, doesn't mean un-public. Bob theologized "in public" for all his adult life. Where my life first intersected Bob's theology "in public" was well over half a century ago in 1949 in the classroom at Valparaiso University. He was a Young Turk prof, age 28, and, at 18, I was just young. My baccalaureate major was philosophy, and that's where Bob was teaching — alongside colleagues Jaroslav Pelikan and Richard Luecke, equally youngish and possibly even more Turkish. At Valparaiso in those days, university and church politics being what they were, serious theology was being taught in the philosophy department. This trio of hot shots (also competent philosophers for the required courses) were hustling theology under such camouflage titles as Recent Religious Philosophies, Representative Christian Thinkers, or Philosophy of Christian Theology. And all this in a university linked to the Missouri Synod!

In the rest of that half-century Bob moved on to the classrooms and intra-churchly conversations of Concordia Seminary in St. Louis, Christ Seminary-Seminex, the Crossings Community, and a concluding decade at the Lutheran School of Theology in Chicago.

So there are thousands of us living letters. But we're not the only public for whom he theologized, though he probably honed his distinctive teaching method with us regulars who appeared before him several times a week for a whole semester. At one Seminex commencement a graduating senior, saying thanks to each faculty member, identified Bob's own version of Socrates' method thus: "And to Blessed Bob Bertram, who always took us on the scenic route. Yet if we paid attention, we did get to the destination just before the bell rang."

Bob had publics beyond the classroom. "On journeyings often," he put his theology out in public — at conferences of all sorts, church consultations, presentations at professional academic meetings, with the Faith and Order Commission of the World Council of Churches, the Lutheran World Federation, the U.S. Lutheran-Catholic Dialogue, his long years as co-chair of ITEST, the Institute for Theological Encounter with Science and Technology. The Crossings webpage, www.crossings.org, has archived almost 100 of these "Works by Bob Bertram."

Not that his theology never got into print. Some of these essays did get published in Festschrifts, conference proceedings, and various journals. But Bob never got around to putting a string of them together into a book by the time he died at 82 in March 2003, not that he didn't have that in mind.

Thus these major manuscripts in his computer. One reason for them staying in the computer — so some of us think — was his perfectionism. No version of a frequently-revised chapter was quite good enough. So he would tweak it and try it out again on a new audience the next time he was asked to speak. But even that tweaked version, he would decide, needed more tweaking.

Such self-doubt regarding his prose even plagued Bob's doctoral dissertation at the University of Chicago. Not till 1963 (at age 42), after 15-plus years of "working on it," did Bob hand it in to his committee (Paul Tillich and Jaroslav Pelikan) and get the degree. I remember hearing Pelikan himself once say, "We told Bob, just hand in the Chicago telephone directory, and we'll give you your degree!" Granted, it is a *magnum opus*, though not quite as big as the phonebook. Its title? "The Human Subject as the Object of Theology: Luther by Way of Barth." Its egghead-sounding agenda? "The grammar of theological predication."

One might say it set the direction for Bob's half-century of public theologizing. Bob opens his case noting Karl Barth's complaint that the human-centeredness of modern theology, of which Feuerbach was the arch-proponent and Schleiermacher was not far behind, came straight from Luther. Barth says, "Luther emphatically shifted the interest from what God is in himself to what God is for man." One might say that Barth's immense theological production was dedicated to correcting Luther's mistake. Well, Bob "cross-examines" Barth's challenge, waltzing his readers through pages and pages of exegesis of Luther's two great classic works — *Bondage of the Will* and *Galatians Commentary* — to show that Barth is actually correct. For Luther, theology is indeed about "what God is for man." But that is not to be lamented — pace Barth — but rather celebrated "for us and for our salvation."

One of Bob's dissertation chapters on Luther's own venture into the grammar of theological predication (heisted from Paul's Galatians) has generated a Bertram *bon mot*. In academic prose the issue is this: how our sins (rightly predicated to us) become rightly predicated to Christ, and how Christ's righteousness (rightly predicated to him) rightly becomes predicated to us sinners. Bob's shortcut shibboleth for that was "the sweet swap," his American translation of Luther's classic *"fröhlicher Wechsel."* You can still hear it in the theological vocabulary of his students everywhere.

Bob's theological work might be seen as a lifelong set of variations on that *cantus firmus*. Over and over again he piped that tune — though largely unknown (or sung off-key) in modern theology (Lutheran or otherwise) — demonstrating its currency, its "winsomeness" (one of his favored terms) to us moderns as music to our ears.

Another phrasing for Luther's theological Aha! according to Bob — both back in the sixteenth century and still today — is "the proper distinction between God's law and God's gospel." Bob might already have learned that even before his years of Luther-probing at the University of Chicago; it could have been in his DNA. How so? His maternal grandfather, William H. T. Dau, had translated the Missouri Synod patriarch's classic work into English: C. F. W. Walther's *The Proper Distinction between Law and Gospel*. Bob's father, a Germanics professor, later translated Werner Elert's dogmatics (in which the law/gospel distinction is the fundamental axiom for Lutheran theology) into English. Though Bob could read and speak German, and thus didn't need these translations, might such Lutheran theology have been transmitted at the family table (or even from mother's milk)? We'll never know.

Whatever its provenance, sweet-swap theology of the cross and law-gospel hermeneutics are what Bob was up to all the time. And for most of Bob's subsequent teaching years I was not too far away.

After being his student in the late 1940s I returned as greenhorn instructor to Valparaiso University in the late fifties, just as a "real" Theology Department had been finessed through university politics, with Bob as the chair and thus my boss. There Bob led the department — some, not all — into a curricular venture grounded in this double axiom of sweet-swap and law-gospel. The ancient Latin proverb proved true for us: *docendo discimus* — by teaching we learned. And so did our students. They said so.

In 1963 Bob moved to Concordia Seminary, the Missouri Synod's major seminary, as professor of systematic and historical theology. A few years later I was called to teach there too, and the hurricane brewing in the synod — substantively about this doublet of cross-theology and law-gospel lenses for reading the Bible — soon made landfall. The consequence was Seminex, originally Concordia Seminary in Exile, where the expelled faculty and students recouped and lived out for ten years the cross-theology and biblical hermeneutics that had so aggravated our antagonists.

Bob's final chapter in this volume takes that event as a "time for confessing" that we learned not from books, but from lived experience. I'm convinced that were it not for Seminex none of the chapters in this book would have been written. Although Bob became the theological interpreter — for insiders and outsiders — of what was happening, it was not right away that he (or we) got clarity on what was happening to us and on what we ourselves were doing.

One example was our understanding of the word "exile." Early on we thought it was linked to the Hebrew Scriptures — the people of God exiled from their homeland, but anticipating "some day" to come back home again, home to Missouri. Then one day at morning devotions, senior professor "Doc" Caemmerer, pioneer gospel-guru for most of us on the faculty when we were his students at Concordia Seminary, preached on the text of Hebrews 11, Abraham as an "exile" — a thousand years before the Babylonian captivity. Doc showed us that Abraham's exile was not "from a country to which he longed to return, but from a better country, one up ahead, where he'd never been before." Exile in the New Testament is not like exile in the Old, returning to a place that once was home. Exile for Christians is heading toward a promised future, something brand new up ahead, "a city which God has prepared for them."

So looking back to Missouri soon faded into looking forward to something better. Even the ELCA, the Evangelical Lutheran Church in America, that eventually came over the horizon, "better" for sure than the old homeland for Seminexers, is still a ways away from that city God has prepared.

But we didn't come into exile with any consensus about it being a "time for confessing." Partly that derived from the widespread ignorance for most of us about Article X of the Formula of Concord. We'd all learned in seminary that it was about that funny term, adiaphora, things neither commanded nor forbidden in Scripture. It seemed to be ho-hum stuff. But had any of us learned that it *really* was about coercive authority in the church and how cross-theology and law-promise hermeneutics are called to respond in such a time as this? I don't remember anyone talking this way early on in our community. We hadn't really caught what that article's key Latin terms — *tempus confessionis, status confessionis* — were talking about. In a word, they were talking about us!

Here's how the title of this book came to be.

Three years into Seminex, 1977, was the 400th anniversary of the Formula of Concord. Bob gave a lecture — on Article X — at a major conference celebrating those four centuries. In that essay he showed us that *tempus confessionis*, "times for confessing," are crunch-moments in church history, not just everyday occasions for Christian witness. And the crunch is heightened in the second Latin term, *status confessionis*. Said Bob, that means being on the witness stand, on trial, out in public, before the authorities. You are in the dock, accused of "bad" faith and under orders to "fess up," to testify (*martyria* in Greek, with the overtones included), seeking to show your critics that the faith they call bad is indeed the faith that Christ commends.

Where Bob first got wind of this in FC X, I don't know. My hunch is that it may have come through his depth probe into Bonhoeffer's writings, and then early on in Seminex's history the visit of Bonhoeffer's biographer and onetime student Eberhard Bethge to our community. There had been some talk among us before our cataclysm struck of an "exile seminary," and where any precedents might be. A few of us knew of Bonhoeffer's "exile" seminary hidden away in Finkenwalde during the Third Reich, and that prompted more serious investigation. We knew that our church opponents were a far cry from the Gestapo that threatened Finkenwalde — though now and then we wondered.

We learned from Bethge that — of all things! — FC X was fundamental to the confessing that Bonhoeffer himself learned — and did — during the time of the Third Reich. It was also a cornerstone piece of the

Finkenwalde curriculum during Bethge's student days there. At a conference in 1984 commemorating the fiftieth anniversary of the Barmen Declaration, the anchor-piece of the Confessing Church in the Third Reich, someone asked Bethge if he'd ever experienced anything close to Finkenwalde since his own student days there. "Yes, once," he said, "at Seminex. Especially the singing, the singing." Chapter 5 in this book shows what Bob learned about times for confessing from Bonhoeffer and from FC X — and what he sought to show the rest of us.

Bob's paradigm, with its "six clues" for times for confessing, also got a boost in our core-course teaching in systematic theology at Seminex. In the final curriculum revision there were only two required courses in systematics. They were "Christian Confession: Classical," the ecumenical creeds and the confessing done at Augsburg, and "Christian Confession: Contemporary," twentieth-century movements beginning with the Confessing Church in Germany, our own experience in the Missouri Synod, and the confessing in liberation theology movements of our day. The "classical" and "contemporary" confessing examined in those two courses parallel the table of contents of this book. Bob's six clues arise from these data.

The clue of "martyria" discussed in Chapters 1 and 2 comes from the classical confessions. "Adding items to the gospel" — Bob calls it "gospel-plussing" — Chapter 3's focus, took us to M. L. King's "Letter from Birmingham Jail." South African confessors contra apartheid in Chapter 4 signaled the ecumenical clue, confessing as an appeal to the whole church. Misaligned church authority is the clue Bob unpacks in Chapter 5, the Bonhoeffer chapter. The Philippine confessing movement, the topic of Chapter 6, is clued to "an appeal for and to the oppressed."

Bob's final chapter on "ambiguous certitude" is about us Missouri confessors. It was probably the last of the half dozen to come into focus, as Bob (and we all) kept trying to explain our actions to our friends, our well-meaning supporters. Many of them were the dear Missourians who kept us financially alive with nearly one million dollars coming our way during each of our ten years of seminary in exile. But even as generous patrons they kept asking why "giving up the seminary campus" and letting ourselves get sacked — "You wouldn't have had to do that!" — was being "faithful to our calling and faithful to our Lord." What was certitude to us was highly ambiguous to them — and sometimes to us as well. Bob concludes the sextet with that look at ourselves at the end — not a bang, but not a whimper either. We didn't always know what we were doing.

Over and over again in this text you will hear Bob zeroing in on "the one gospel-and-sacraments." He's taking that term from the Augsburg Confession (1530) where this one gospel-and-sacraments, spelled out with its native New Testament substance, becomes the criterion for the yea and nay of these Augsburg confessors — all of them laymen! — in their own time on the witness stand.

It might appear that Bob's life's work in theology was largely inside the walls of the seminary and the church. "Au contraire" (as he himself liked to say, when we didn't get it), he was regularly out beyond those borders in conversation with (another favored phrase) "God's dear worldlings." See that list of his works on the Crossings webpage for examples outside the churchly envelope: "Ethical Implications of Military Leadership," "Church and Economic Order," "How to Be Technological, though Theological: An Answer for 'Fabricated Man.'"

The last of those three comes from his quarter-century as co-chair of ITEST, the Institute for Theological Encounter with Science and Technology. His co-chair, Robert Brungs, S.J., was a physicist. ITEST kept Bob constantly crossing his Lutheran theology not only with the Roman Catholic heritage of most of the ITEST members, but also with no-nonsense first-echelon international professionals in science and technology.

Come to think of it, most of this book is really not confined to inner-churchly conversation, but unfolds in the public arena, most often the conflict-laden public arena of politics — the American civil rights movement, apartheid in South Africa, the struggle of the churches in Hitler's Third Reich, the Philippine revolution against Marcos. And in every one Bob shows us Christians out there in the thick of it hearing and following Christ's call to take the witness stand.

In conclusion, let me mention two other items in this same genre of theology crossing the world "out there." The first was in-house in Seminex, but it addressed a strictly-speaking "secular" agenda: How to organize our communal life where "dear worldly" elements of finance, grades, hiring and firing, contracts, laws and municipal codes, responsibility, and sanctions all are in play alongside (in, with, and under) the "one gospel-and-sacraments" of our faith and worship life. Bob was chosen to compose our "Internal Governance Document." When Seminex began, there was no handbook; there wasn't even a "mother church" to whom we belonged. So we started from scratch and — no surprise — Bob got the job. What he came up with was a tour de force of law-gospel architecture for our life together.

One plank in that Internal Governance actually came from the "*regula*" of the Dominican monastic order in the Middle Ages, to wit, their axiom that in the community "the decision-makers shall be the consequence-takers, and the consequence-takers shall be the decision-makers." Our ancient tradition in Missouri had been "benign hierarchy." Thus the governing board of Concordia Seminary were not trustees, but the "Board of Control." But if you are sharing common life according to that axiom of the Dominican *regula*, especially in its Lutheran recasting, you can't have hierarchy, even benign hierarchy.

Even more complex than political democracy which may have some affinity to the Dominican axiom, we were doing it with a Lutheran foundation. We were learning to march simultaneously to two drums, even though both sets of sticks were in the hands of one and the same Drummer, one set in his left hand and the other in the right. That was new for all of us. It had to be learned, and thus at the outset it was sometimes messy and patently not "efficient." Besides that there are always slow learners, and some folks don't like what they learn.

Bob's Internal Governance Document articulating our common life according to the hermeneutics of law and gospel was one of a kind. It probably still is. Bob worked hard to teach it to us, for it was really our own theology applied institutionally to our own selves. With the students the learning came easier. Little wonder, we had been "explaining" its theological infrastructure to the students in their courses in systematic theology. But with our fellow faculty, our track record was not so good. Eventually it got modified out of existence. Bob occasionally referred to it as "Seminex's best-kept secret." Some day someone ought to do a doctoral dissertation on this blessed failure.

The second item where Bob palpably — and organizationally — crossed over to "God's dear worldlings" with his Lutheran theology was in the Crossings Community. Its roots go all the way back to that theology curriculum he pioneered along with a bunch of us at Valparaiso University in the late 1950s. Here the point of the law-and-gospel's relevance was the secular callings these students (scarcely any of them seminary-bound) were envisioning and preparing for. The curriculum made their own secular worlds part of the study program.

During the days of Seminex Bob re-visioned the paradigm into a theology venture for grown-ups, folks already working out in the world. The goal was for them to learn to practice "the Crossings matrix." The process is a three-step one. First to have the dear worldlings do some "tracking" of their own personal "text" out there in the world of daily work. Second came using the law-gospel lenses for getting some "grounding" in a biblical text that showed up regularly in the Sunday liturgy. The final step was "crossing" those two "texts" with each other, so that the law-gospel of the biblical text took flesh in the text of the worldling's own life. If curious, you'll find a fuller treatment — Bob's own — on the Crossings webpage.

Summa. Among international Lutheran scholars Bob was not a voice crying in the wilderness. You'll see that in the chapters that follow. He was in conversation with theologians around the world. For his brand of Lutheranism he had theological allies in the Luther Research Congress, where he was a regular attender and presenter beginning already in the 1960s. He was a major presenter at the 1971 congress gathering that took place in St. Louis. His drumbeat for *sola fide* (faith alone) — and not *sola gratia* (grace alone), Barth's preference — as *the* center of the sixteenth-century Reformation debate was shared by others. *Sola fide* orbits the same *solus Christus* (Christ alone) center as does sweet-swap theology of the cross and law-gospel hermeneutics.

In drawing confessing movements to orbit this center, Bob offers us his life's work. Though each of these chapters show how others were doing it on their own witness stands, Bob pulls them together to this center — even to the point where he will show us that the mostly Roman Catholic confessing movement in the Philippines was running on the fuel of *sola fide!* That may sound like a stretch, but he says the evidence is there. See for yourself.

Bob's discovery of the "six clues" for times for confessing and his mastery in using them to help us see these seemingly disparate movements as united, yes, even centered, in the "one gospel and sacraments" is a feisty proposal. Yet it is typical of his theological chutzpah all through the years. Even more, if valid, it's a milestone in ecumenical — and evangelical — theology.

"A voice from heaven says: 'Blessed are the dead who from now on die in the Lord.' 'Yes', says the Spirit, they will rest from their labors, and their works do follow them" (Rev. 14:13). Blessed Bob's now at rest, and from his work that follows him, we too are blessed.

EDWARD H. SCHROEDER
St. Louis, Missouri
September 17, 2005

Editor's Preface

Three years ago, Robert W. Bertram asked if I would see to the future publication of certain works which he had "on the back burner." They remained on the back burner because Bob always placed teaching and preaching the gospel over writing about it, let alone publishing. Since he was such a beloved teacher, mentor, and friend for decades, I never could say no to him. This was especially true in the last days of his life (he was faithful to the end).

The present volume combines two of those works: *A Time for Confessing* and *Postmodernity's CRUX*. *A Time for Confessing* represents the weightier contribution from Bertram's theology from the exile of Seminex in 1974 to the early 1990s. Several of its chapters were delivered as papers at various conferences during those years. Chapter Two was published earlier in *dialog: A Journal of Theology,* vol. 26, no. 3 (Summer 1987), pp. 201-8. Chapter Seven was first delivered as an address at Valparaiso University in 1977, and published the following year in the university's journal (edited by David G. Truemper), *The Cresset: Confession and Congregation, Occasional Papers III,* pp. 78-85. These are republished with permission.

A Time for Confessing is a legacy of Bertram's reflections on the important topic of *status confessionis.* Bertram understands "times for confessing" to be those unique moments or events when the authority of the gospel is being supplanted by an "alien" gospel, and when Christians disobey the secular authorities, including the church's own, in order to testify to the integrity of the church's confession of the one gospel of Jesus the

Christ as "authority enough" for the church's unity. The opening chapter serves as Bertram's own introduction to "times for confessing"; those that follow examine in greater detail the six characteristics or features which define times for confessing, utilizing different historical case studies as examples. These six characteristics and their corresponding case studies explore how the confessors are themselves (1) witnesses *(martyres)* to the gospel (Augsburg, 1530); (2) protesting especially those added elements (often *adiaphora*) believed to be somehow necessary for the church's unity (Martin Luther King Jr.); (3) inviting the whole church to this confession, and often finding themselves joined by a wide ecumenical body of Christians in this stand (World Council of Churches on Apartheid); (4) needing to re-prioritize the authorities of God's law and promise for both church and state (Bonhoeffer); (5) appealing to and for the oppressed to join in this confessing movement (Philippine revolution of 1986); and (6) recognizing their own embarrassing, even mortifying, "ambiguous certitude" in making this confession (Seminex, 1974). The first five are examined in the first chapter, the sixth in the fourth chapter.

There were some unique challenges in editing these chapters. While it is clear that Bertram intended six emphases in his understanding of the concept of *status confessionis,* he only formally completed five of the chapters. The sixth chapter, which was never finally revised, was to be on "ambiguous certitude," with the Seminex experience as the principal historical case study. The selection of his essay published in *The Cresset* comes the closest to what he intended to say about "ambiguous certitude," most especially in the final paragraphs, including the addition of his brief commentary, "Seminex was about risk."

Another challenge was to address the grammatical tense of his essays. Some demonstrated historical distance from the subject matter; but others were written in the midst of shared experiences (this was the case especially in his chapters on apartheid, the Philippine revolution, and Seminex). I have attempted to provide some historical objectivity in these chapters, but not at the expense of the passion of Bertram's writing.

The most frustrating challenge was to provide the documentation to many of Bertram's citations, which he himself left undocumented. One of Bertram's oft-quoted phrases about "times for confessing" is that they are "like nailing Jell-o to the wall." By that colloquialism, Bob meant not only that the "local shower" *(Platzregen)* of the movement does not stay put very long. He meant also that such liberating, confessing movements do not always translate well into academic dictums of scholarship. Bob was a consummate scholar, and he had the evidence — of that I have no doubt. But I suspect that he, rightly, was more interested in establishing his argument than in marshalling his evidence, and thereby more deeply invested in each of the movements he studied. Several of the sources cited were written not for the purpose of a publication in books, but for sharing the confessing spirit (one thinks of Martin Luther King's "Letter from Birmingham Jail," Francisco Claver's unpublished papers, or even comments shared in the halls of Seminex by Eberhard Bethge on Bonhoeffer's life and work). As a result, many of the works that make up the theological sources of confessing movements are themselves indigenous.

Countless hours were spent in his personal library, which we are privileged to have inherited at Lutheran School of Theology in St. Louis. Occasionally, I would come upon a gold mine of insightful notations in Bob's impeccable penmanship left in the margins of his books and papers. These have helped provide many of the footnotes in these chapters. I am especially grateful for the work of Bonhoeffer scholar Charles E. Ford in finding many of the notations for Chapter Five. And it was a special honor to receive e-mail correspondence with regard to Chapter Six from Bishop Claver himself! In his own words to me, "I read through the chapter Bob Bertram wrote on the EDSA Revolution. He did a good job on it. Reading what he wrote, I recognized easily the sources of his quotes — things I had written." In later correspondence, Claver provided detailed references from his own essays and addresses. With the press toward publication, however, many of the notations are still missing, especially in the later chapters of this book. All that can be said is that this editor did his best to share as many notations as possible with the reader.

All in all, *A Time for Confessing* is monumental not only because Bertram was a leading authority on the subject, but because it demonstrates how deeply and personally he was connected with the evangelical, global, and ecumenical experiences that comprise these chapters. He placed himself at the feet of his fellow confessors to learn from their experiences, and also made them his own. As such he was truly a theologian-in-residence, enjoying the exile of fellow exiles, sharing their "joys and sorrows" (1 Cor. 12:26), always with cruciform passion and conviction.

The appended text of *Postmodernity's CRUX* is a much briefer work. It outlines a confessional theology of the cross for our postmodern era. It is a compilation of provocative theses, drawn from Bertram's own reflections on Second Corinthians, chapters 2-7, with four key theological foci: *C*riticism, *R*evelation, *U*niversality, and *X*ristening (Christening). Bertram continued to improve on it, and we have published here his latest (2000) edition.

I am grateful to some dear people — all especially dear to Bob — for their part in assisting in the publication of this work. First and foremost, my thanks to Thelda Bertram, Bob's spouse and partner for 56+ years. Thelda helped provide several earlier editions of Bob's notes and manuscripts that were kept on file in his home office and on his computer. These were invaluable resources for putting this final work together. Ed Schroeder, unquestionably Bob's best student and colleague, not only encouraged the project, but also added his own Foreword to it. Roy and Joan Cobb were instrumental in proofreading and assisting me in the editing of the manuscript of *A Time for Confessing*. Paul Rorem was a godsend; he not only encouraged this publication through Eerdmans, but has helped to edit further the entire tome. Andrew Hoogheem, who edited the manuscript for Eerdmans, offered encouragement and thoughtful engagement of the text. And finally, my profound thanks to the Crossings Community (including such dear ones as Cathy Lessmann, Steve Kuhl, Gary Simpson, and many, many others) who encouraged and supported this endeavor toward its final completion.

On March 13, 2003, Bob made the "final Crossing" of his baptism. He is dearly missed. Yet his work lives on not only in this work, but in all the "living letters" of those touched by his faithful preaching and teaching the gospel of Jesus the Christ. In the pages to follow, don't be surprised if you come to join those living letters.

MICHAEL HOY
The Ascension of our Lord, 2006

CHAPTER 1

Augsburg:
A Modern "Time for Confessing"

Introduction

Some of the most constructive moments in recent history have been those times, ironically, when Christians have had to disobey secular authority, including the church's own, in order to testify that for the one church of Jesus Christ his one gospel-and-sacraments is authority enough. Such moments of Christian disobedience, fateful times of last resort, are what the Formula of Concord called "a time for confessing," which at that "time" (1577) had already begun a half-century earlier with the "confessing" at Augsburg (1530). This Augsburg "time for confessing," from 1530 onwards, is one more reminder of how the church from its origin — for example, up against those authorities in its own native Judaism who opposed it — had to be, over and over, a confessing movement.

But Augsburg has also been epochal for subsequent history. Enough so, that it suggests a paradigm for such recent events as the *Kirchenkampf* in Nazi Germany, the Christian resistance against apartheid in South Africa, the resistance of Christian seminarians in South Korea, the civil rights movement in the United States, the "authority crisis" in today's Roman Catholicism, the current grassroots anti-bureaucracy in mainline denominations — for understanding these situations as themselves "times for confessing." That historic moment which took voice in the Augsburg Confession and which later came to further self-awareness in the Formula of Concord's Article X provides some clues — half a dozen, at least — as to what might constitute such confessional "times" also in our own more recent history.[1]

1. Confessing as *martyria*

The term "confession" in the context of Augsburg, as in dominant biblical contexts, connotes not just any declaration of one's faith — the sort of declaration, for instance, made by a candidate for baptism or in response to some friendly inquiry about "the reason of the hope that is in you." No, "a time for confessing" is more embattled than that. It is an adversary situation. In such a context confessing implies that the confessors are on trial for their faith before a superior critical tribunal from whose higher authority they must nevertheless dissent. The dominant metaphor is forensic: the confessors are defendants on a witness stand *(in statu confessionis)*, *martyres*, and their confession in that case is a martyrological act.

While the term "martyrdom" should not be taken here to connote, as it often does in popular usage, an exaggerated, self-pitying sense of persecution, neither should it lose the connotation of extreme — yes, ultimate — jeopardy. Emil Fackenheim, marveling at the defiant faith of the Holocaust martyrs, calls them "witnesses to God and man even if abandoned by God and man."[2] That, also, for Christian confessors, suggests what their ultimate jeopardy is: witnessing to a God who to all appearances is abandoning them, exactly because of the way they are obliged to witness to him.

That confessional risk has longstanding biblical precedent, all the way from Job's

> Behold he will slay me; I have no hope;
> yet I will defend my ways to his face. (13:15)

1. Hereafter, standard abbreviations from the Book of Concord will be used for citations: Augsburg Confession (AC), Apology of Augsburg Confession (Apol.), Small Catechism (SC), Large Catechism (LC), Smalcald Articles (SA), Treatise on the Power and Primacy of the Pope (TPPP), and Formula of Concord (FC).

2. Emil Fackenheim, *God's Presence in History: Jewish Affirmations and Philosophical Reflections* (New York: New York University Press, 1970), 97 (in Fackenheim's chapter on "The Commanding Voice of Auschwitz").

to Jesus' "cry of dereliction": "My God, my God, why have you forsaken me?" (Mark 15:34; Matt. 27:46; Ps. 22:1). At Augsburg, likewise, the confessors were not unaware of that same risk. As Melanchthon reminds his accusers, "Certainly we should not wish to put our own souls and consciences in grave peril before God by misusing his name or Word" (AC XXI, 1). The life-and-death dilemma which confessors face is that the God to whose authority they appeal to vindicate their witness is the same God who has installed their oppressors in positions of authority and who seems now to be vindicating that authority instead.

In face of that ultimate impasse, the only recourse of Christian confessors is the promise (and threat) of the Matthean Jesus: "So everyone who confesses me before human beings, I also will confess before my Father in heaven, but whoever denies me before human beings, I also will deny before my Father who is in heaven" (Matt. 10:32-33; FC X, 17). But those two options, and the fact that those are all there are, only underscore all the more how high the stakes are: either fidelity or apostasy, either divine acceptance or divine rejection. No wonder the situation is pictured as a case at court as if, behind and above the intimidating secular authorities of church and society, sat an unseen, still higher Authority who is waiting for the "witnesses'" testimony to be spoken — not into his ear secretly, as in the privacy of prayer, but publicly throughout his world, "before human beings."

It is only because of that final tribunal *coram Deo* that the "confessors" picture their ecclesiastical authorities in turn as likewise sitting in the forensic role of judges, the way a secular magistrate would. The ecclesiastical authorities, for their part, may well deny that that is what they are being, namely, judges, and may attribute such high-flown metaphors to the confessors' own self-dramatizing paranoia.

Of course, it need not be that in a confessional situation there literally are ecclesiastical trials, actual forensic proceedings with formal charges and evidence and judicial verdicts. Sometimes there are, but even then these are often so rigged as never to allow the gospel *martyria* a fair hearing. Just as often there are no trials at all, except perhaps through a controlled church press, for fear that the authorities' own pseudo-gospel might be cross-examined. That was a complaint already at Augsburg.

No, the metaphor of the courtroom is no more than a theological construct (and no less!), re-presenting the actual current situation according to the perceptions of faith. The church's "witness stand" is really only that concrete historical circumstance, whatever that may be, in which at the moment the gospel is being oppressed.

To call that situation by such a prestigious name, a *status confessionis,* a *martyria,* is to take what is to all appearances a ridiculous and petty ecclesiastical hassle and dignify it with the image of a cosmic tribunal — which in truth it is. Before this daunting tribunal it is really the whole church which is being arraigned. Not just the immediate confessors but the church everywhere is here and now being asked, in view of its secular authoritarianism, whether it does despair after all of the gospel's being "enough," whether it lusts for the gospel to be shored up by other, secular authorities.

With that as the question, the Court waits for a reply. The moment for the church to answer this interrogation, its "time for confessing," is agonizingly short and non-postponable. That is quite literally so for the immediate, historic "confessors." In that fleeting historical moment they have no choice but to speak for the church, to be its *satis*-sayers, and thus to do what otherwise they would never dream of doing, renounce their own authorities, and then only because these were replacing the one gospel-and-sacraments. Their confession, of course, includes taking the consequences, although — as Luther reminded — "never in silence." For their answer is too good to be silenced, in view of whose it finally is.

Considering the odds, we can understand why that sort of confessional confrontation is, if at all possible, to be avoided. That is why Christians regularly pray, "Do not put us to the test." "Save us from the time of trial." Jesus himself encouraged his followers to petition for such exemptions. Indeed, when faced with his own ordeal, he prayed that that bitter "cup" of being put to the ultimate test might be spared him as well.

But suppose the confrontation finally turns out to be unavoidable and the offensive testimony simply has to be given and the consequences taken. Then the confessors will have to rivet their attention upon that formidable Judge behind the judges and boldly affirm, as they did at Augsburg: "I will declare Thy testimonies before kings and shall not be put to shame" (AC, superscription; Ps. 119:46).

2. Confessing as Protesting Gospel-Plus

"Where there is too much," says a Jewish proverb, "something is missing." "More is less," went the credo of architect Mies van der Rohe. For the

Apostle Paul, to demand that believers in Christ also be circumcised is to negate Christ. Gospel-plus is gospel-minus, no gospel at all.

In "a time for confessing," it is the gospel which the authorities are adding to — presumably embellishing, reinforcing, safeguarding — and thereby diminishing, in fact subverting altogether. At Augsburg, where the Reformers were still appealing to their imperial and ecclesiastical superiors not to hereticize them or to count them out of the Roman Catholic Church, the basis of their appeal was this: so long as the gospel and sacraments of Christ are being communicated evangelically, the sole condition of church unity is being satisfied. "That is enough," *satis est* (AC VII, 2).

Conversely, the Augustana[3] continues, "it is not necessary for the true unity of the Christian church that ceremonies instituted by human beings should be observed uniformly in all places" (AC VII, 3; also XV). For in the last analysis such ceremonies are really only "adiaphora," as already the Apology called them (Apol. XV, 52; XXVII, 27, 58). But before long, crucially at the Leipzig Interim (1548), some of these very confessors — including Philip Melanchthon, the Augustana's and Apology's chief author — seemed to capitulate to imperial pressure and to Roman ceremonial impositions after all.

Ironically, these compromisers excused themselves by exploiting the Augustana's *satis est*. For, they argued, aren't even the oppressors' unpalatable practices mere non-essentials *(adiaphora)*? Then why not, for the sake of public peace, put up with them? Now suddenly some of the confessors were speaking as if "ceremonies instituted by human beings *should* be observed uniformly" after all.

It was this sort of manipulating the Augsburg Confession against its own intention, for the sake of an easy church unity without paying the price of protest, that the Formula of Concord eventually intervened to protest. On the one hand, the concordists freely acknowledged that "we can with a good conscience give in and yield to the weak in faith in . . . external matters of indifference" (FC X, 9). So far, the Formula is simply reiterating the stance at Augsburg. There, "in this very assembly," as Melanchthon reminded the opponents, "we have shown ample evidence of our willingness to observe adiaphora with others, even where this involved some disadvantage to us." For, he adds, "we believed that the greatest pub-

3. The Confessio Augustana (Augsburg Confession).

lic harmony, without offense to consciences, should be preferred to all other advantages" (Apol. XV, 52).

However, as the Formula of Concord came to see, it is quite another matter when practices which in themselves may be neutral or at least negotiable are instead insisted upon as essential, "necessary," even "necessary for righteousness and salvation," and are imposed "by force or chicanery." When that happens, it is time for Christians to refuse submission — "for the truth of the gospel" (FC X, 10-13). But in their calling now for such public disobedience, the concordists are still only carrying out the implications of the original confession at Augsburg, which likewise had repudiated any and all religious authority which presumed to demand more than the gospel: ". . . we have God's command not to be obedient in such cases" (AC XXVIII, 23).

The time for confessing arrives when adiaphora are imposed as a necessity, but not only adiaphora! Perhaps more often than not what is forced upon the church by its authorities was not an adiaphoron in the first place, was not something as neutral as that, even potentially, but was simply, intolerably evil.

For instance, there are institutional policies and practices "which are basically contrary to the Word of God" and, equally perverse, which are submitted to simply in order "to avoid persecution" or in order to "create the illusion" that the oppressor is not really oppressing the gospel. Such evils never were adiaphora to begin with and certainly dare not be disguised as such.

Moreover, any attempt by religious authorities to force such outright evils on the church must be met openly with Paul's strategy of withdrawal and disengagement: "Do not be mismated with unbelievers. . . . Come out from them and be separate from them . . ." (2 Cor. 6:14, 17; FC X, 6). The church is "not to be associated with and not to support impiety and unjust cruelty" (FC X, 23).

Accordingly, open church protest and boycott are required not only by tyrannical adiaphora. Indeed, it is misleading to suggest that the Formula of Concord's tenth article is primarily about adiaphora at all. Rather, it is about those times when adiaphora — "even adiaphora," *"auch in Mitteldingen"* (FC X, 3, 10) — are *not* adiaphora anymore!

True, when it is genuine adiaphora — practices which otherwise might be borne with, not practices which are downright iniquitous — which now are being made into necessities, at such times the concordists do not urge separating from the oppressors. But they do insist on dissenting from them, and always, of course, publicly and with word and action and in taking the consequences. So whether it is only adiaphora which are being inflicted or, worse yet, practices "which are basically contrary to the Word of God," in either case the churches must protest such fettering the gospel with conditions which do not at all enhance it, but on the contrary diminish and destroy it.

As for adiaphora, they are defined as those discretionary church practices which are "neither commanded nor forbidden by God," or "in the Word of God" (FC X, 2, 1). Offhand, that may give the misimpression that adiaphora are whatever is neither commanded nor forbidden *in Scripture,* so that if Scripture did command a particular practice, that practice would still be mandatory and not an adiaphoron at all.

But no, the Formula of Concord's term, "Word of God," should not in this case simply be equated with Scripture. For in Scripture God did explicitly command such practices as circumcision, the Sabbath, even women's head coverings. Yet all of these, no matter how biblical, the Formula, like the Augustana, freely regards as no longer binding but discretionary, or even as "the precepts of men" (FC X, 12, 13, 8; AC XXVIII, 54-56).

What God still does command, however, and what even in his New Covenant is never optional is what he has commanded through his "Word of God," through the historical Jesus Christ, namely, "the fresh teaching of the holy Good News" (FC X, 10). *That* "teaching and *all that pertains to it,* according to the Word of God," that teaching of the Good News *"in all its articulations,"* including "the right use of the sacraments," depends for its very *truth* — for how truly good its news is — on how truly it is spoken, yes, but also on how truly it is acted out in churchly praxis (FC X, 10, 31).

That is why Paul, who ordinarily could take or leave circumcision, made a point of acting out publicly his refusal to circumcise Titus, all for "the truth of the gospel." For "the false apostles . . . wanted to impose such things on consciences as necessary" (Gal. 2:4, 5; FC X, 11-13). When something so doctrinally neutral as an adiaphoron changes, as it often has, from being the gospel's servant to being the gospel's partner to being the gospel's rival to being the gospel's undoing, just when in that subtle shift does the reversal occur? Answer: when this adiaphoron assumes the importance of being "necessary."

But "necessary" for what? Why, "necessary for righteousness and salvation" (FC X, 12). Still, one wonders whether even the Judaizers in Galatia ever said in so many words that, besides faith in Christ, also circumcision was necessary for "salvation." That explicit they probably were not, or even that consciously implicit. Yet that — namely, that circumcision was a salvational prerequisite — was the net effect of their coercive praxis, at least as Paul exposed it.

Similarly, the confessors in the Augsburg tradition were not confining their protest to what ecclesiastical authorities merely said or did not say, but also to the consequences in praxis of what they did, and of what their victims suffered them to do. If what they exacted from the church was the operational equivalent of saying, "Submission to our brand of authority is 'necessary for righteousness,' necessary for being truly acceptably in the church, or else," then regardless of these authorities' reassuring rhetoric, the practice in question was being "forcibly imposed on the church as necessary and as though its omission were wrong and sinful" (FC X, 15). Then "the door has been opened to idolatry, and ultimately the commandments of human beings will be put . . . not only on a par with God's commandments but even above them" (FC X, 15). And what the concordists here mean by "God's commandments" is the one gospel-and-sacraments, which is all the authority Christ ever gave the church for its wholeness, that being "enough" — *satis*. Anything more than that, once it becomes "necessary" for the church to be church, is less than the gospel or, as Paul said, is "another gospel" altogether, and needs to be exposed as such.

3. Confessing as Ecumenical

One of the most notable features of confessing, as here defined, is its ecumenism, that is, its interest in churchly consensus as reunion. All the more notable, since that may be the one feature of confessing which is least evident. Surely the Augsburg confessional paradigm seems anything but church-uniting, particularly as the break with Rome and the empire widened, culminating in the Formula of Concord's "we reject and condemn" (FC X, 26-30). And there is no denying that the concordists were openly urging the rest of Christendom to take sides *against* the imperial and papal oppressors, at least to refuse them obedience. That scarcely seems ecumenical.

That being so, must we perhaps strike a compromise in favor of the Augustana and against the Formula by idealizing the former as an original ecumenical effort, at least in hope, but then conceding that its successors half a century later failed in their resolve: "we who are walking in [the Augsburgers'] footsteps intend by the grace of God to abide by this their confession" — at least failed their predecessors' ecumenism (FC X, 18)? No, such a concession would be premature, at least until more is said about the nature of confessional ecumenism, including its polemical edge.

Granted, the predecessors at Augsburg were still in a position to be considerably irenic. They could still assure the emperor that they were committed to recovering church unity at an earliest possible ecumenical council and would not weary in that resolve until "the matters in dissension are finally heard, amicably weighed, charitably settled, and brought to Christian concord in accordance with Your Imperial Majesty's summons" (AC, Preface, 23).

The question which this apparent contradiction between the Augustana and the Formula poses is not just whether the Augsburg Confession, in terms of FC X's later definition of "a time for confessing," ever really qualified as a *confessio* at all, given its irenicism. Nor is the question, on the other hand, whether the Formula of Concord's definition might not be too discordant for "confessional" concord. Those could be semantic quibbles.

The substantive question, and a more ecumenical one, is whether confessing movements of Christian dissent like the Augustana itself, especially in light of its outcome, can realistically have as their purpose the church's reunification. Aren't they rather, by the very logic of their dissent from authority, essentially divisive?

To the latter question the answer, I suggest, is No. Such confessional movements are not essentially divisive and, if they are, they are not authentic confessions. But such a negative minimum hardly insures the more ambitious positive claim that "times for confessing" are, also in their dissent, ecumenical moves toward reunification. In fact, it is here proposed that no real reunion is possible without them.

The truth is, even the Augsburg Confession, for all its undeniable commitment to "Christian concord" and all its pleading for "a general, free and Christian council" (AC, Preface, 21-23) was at the same time, from the outset, a most provocative critique — all our well-meaning efforts to mute its critique to the contrary notwithstanding.

Moreover, when the long-awaited council finally did materialize at Trent after so much intervening time for further polarization, that council could not humanly have been expected to grant the radical concessions for which the Augustana had petitioned. Indeed, it is a wonder that Trent — admittedly, by means of some strategic ambiguities — could concede what doctrinal reforms it did.

Furthermore, the Augustana soon came to be used in military-diplomatic trade-offs not at all to reunite but to quarantine those territorial "estates belonging to the Augsburg Confession" from the Roman Catholic territories and, among the former, to pit one partisan interpretation of the Augustana against another, almost always with political and economic investments as well.

Finally, therefore, after a half century of such disastrous civil and ecclesiastical disintegration, much of it associated with the Augsburg Confession, about the last thing we might expect the Formula of Concord to associate with the Augustana or with any "time for confessing" is that such times are preeminently occasions for ecumenism and evangelical consensus.

Still, notice in the following quotation, it is exactly the appeal for whole-church consensus which stands out in FC X's picture of "a time for confessing": "the entire community of God [*die ganze Gemeine Gottes*], yes, every individual Christian, and especially the ministers of the Word as the leaders of the community of God, are obligated to confess openly . . ." (FC X, 10).

To be sure, here ecumenical meant ecumenically polemical, a dimension of church unity which later ecumenism would sometimes lose the sense to grasp. When it is the freedom of the gospel which is being attacked, especially by the church's own authorities, then it is exactly in concerted opposition to that attack that "the entire community of God" finds its unity.

But not only must the church's fence-straddlers, in order to be one with the church, come down and identify with the confessors. The confessors themselves, first of all, must make their case to the rest of the church — not just to their immediate adversaries but to the whole encompassing cloud of witnesses — in order to vindicate their confession as the church's own rather than the complaint of some disgruntled sect.

The sectarian alternative to such ecumenical accountability, as the Augustana's nominal heirs, the Lutherans, have often tragically exhibited, is to take the confession which originally had been intended as the whole church's and withdraw it from the risks and disappointments of intrachurch exposure, and then, instead of suing for other Christians' corroboration, compensate by self-congratulation within the ghetto of a single denomination. Meanwhile the rest of the church is let off the hook, thus robbing Christian pluralism of its true mutuality.

The interest of Roman Catholic theologians like David Tracy in distinguishing that branch of theology which H. Richard Niebuhr once called "confessional" is all to the good, so long as such theology represents not only "the 'community of inquiry' of a particular church tradition," but also the public accountability which such a tradition has to the whole church (and beyond) and which Tracy does demand of "fundamental" theology.[4]

So if the Augsburg Confession may serve as a model of other, later "times for confessing," one of its modular features is its opening its books for public audit "both before God and among all nations, present and future" — "published and proclaimed in all of Christendom throughout the wide world" for just such highly vulnerable exposure (Apol. XIV, 5; FC, Preface). True, it would be a most disappointing irony if, as Elaine Pagels observes about the early Christian martyrs, the very appeal which such confessors make to other Christians throughout the world would then become the means by which "an increasingly stratified institutional hierarchy consolidated the Christian communities [into] . . . a network of groups with increasingly uniform doctrine, ritual, canon and political structure."[5]

The original purpose of "a time for confessing," as at Augsburg, is to prevent a split with authorities, especially church authorities, no matter how oppressive they are. But if what they persist in oppressing by means of their authority is the church's one gospel-and-sacraments, they then drive the confessors to invoke *that* authority against them.

Yet then more than ever the confessors, who for all the world now appear to stand against the church, must become ecumenists par excellence. For their dissent from their own authorities can now be defended only on the ground of that authority which the whole church has in common, and they must make that defense ecumenically — to "the whole of Christendom" (FC, Preface).

For such whole-church confirmation the confessors may have to wait for a long, long time. They may well have to wait, as Melanchthon antici-

---

4. Cf. David Tracy, *Blessed Rage for Order: The New Pluralism in Theology* (New York: Seabury Press, 1975), 15, n. 8.

5. Elaine Pagels, *The Gnostic Gospels* (New York: Random House, 1979), 100.

pated, until their "posterity" (Apol., Preface, 16). Wouldn't it be ironic if those who finally arose to confirm their confession would come from the "posterity" of their historic opponents — say, in an ecumenical council centuries later?

4. Confessing as Redefining Authority

"A time for confessing" or, as FC X repeatedly calls it, "a time of persecution" (2, 3, 28, 29), implies by the nature of the case opponents with superior power and authority — *"Gewalt," "Obrigkeit," "Herrschaft," "Regiment"* (20, 21). None of their superior authority would by itself be objectionable except that these "secular lords and princes" (*weltliche Herrn und Fürsten,* FC X, 19) insinuate their secular sort of authority into a realm of life where it simply is unauthorized. Notice, the objection is not only or even primarily that secular authority is violating its own divine mandate, as for instance when it perpetrates injustice, secular evil, in which case such civil authority directly contradicts itself.

True, such tyranny over its own realm is also involved, but there is a further, prior objection, a jurisdictional one. In "a time for confessing" secular authority has trespassed upon another whole dimension of authority than its own, namely the gospel's, where it is abjectly incompetent and ultimately damning.

To make matters worse, the "secular lords and princes" here referred to are not, as we might expect, some officious incumbents of civil government who have overreached themselves, but rather are leading clergy of the church, bishops and pope, who have abdicated their distinctively churchly brand of authority — the authority of the gospel and sacraments — in favor of some secular surrogate, yet still combining that with religious pretensions. They do not really "wish to be true bishops," Luther charged, and "are unwilling to preach or teach or baptize or administer communion or discharge any office or work in the church." On the contrary, "they expel, persecute and condemn those who have been called to do these things" (SA III, X, 2; FC X, 19).

Therefore, "we cannot suffer" this form of church leadership "to govern us as our head or lord" (SA II, IV, 14; FC X, 20). Ecclesiastical disobedience — considering the bishops' secular style of authority, even a kind of civil disobedience — is called for. "For deception, murder and the eternal destruction of body and soul are characteristic of" this sort of church government, which in truth is not *church* government at all but a usurping of secular power for messianic, soteriological claims (ibid.).

The purpose in disobeying such ecclesiastical tyranny is not only negative but also affirmative: when "the truth of the gospel" is being misrepresented and falsified by its very administrators — regardless of whether in their official doctrine, in any case by their exercise of authority — then surely the Lord must raise up someone else, as from "the very stones," to reassert that uniquely churchly authority, "the fresh teaching of the holy Good News," in "all that pertains to it" and "in all its articulations," including constructive Christian disobedience.

The point deserves repeating: the particular tyranny which is to be protested by churchly *confessio* is not just any and every abuse of secular authority, all of which abuses do indeed need to be exposed and resisted and corrected by the church as well as by anyone else.

Yet that need not always be a "case of confession," where, by contrast, dissent always is a uniquely churchly act, one in which the church engages for reasons all its own — namely, the gospel — and for which the church may just have to go it alone.

Usually, no doubt, the most flagrant way to abuse secular authority is to exploit it for enforcing injustice, explicit sin against one another, "unjust cruelty" (FC X, 23). But there is no reason why such violations of common humanity, especially at the hands of the authorities, should wait to be opposed by something so doctrinal as a Christian confession of faith.

On the other hand, while not every abuse of authority in the service of injustice may constitute a "time for confessing" — for churchly and civil opposition, yes, but not always for *confessional* protest — the reverse seems not to be the case. For it is doubtful whether in actual fact there ever could be "a time for confessing," "a time of persecution," which was not also simultaneously an occasion of social injustice and cruelty. So intimately does persecution of the gospel entail other forms of persecution as well, regardless of whether the reverse is true.

Recall how, according to Luther, the bishops' recourse to secular power had implicated them not only in the "eternal destruction of [people's] souls," but in the destruction of "bodies" as well, in "murder" and "deception" (FC X, 19). Such practices are hardly adiaphora, but an overt transgressing of what has been "either commanded or forbidden by God." There is all the more reason then, so as not to confuse the issues, to distinguish what in the midst of these other wrongs makes that additional tyranny against the gospel something special, *sui generis,* not necessarily more serious but also not just one more violation of the divine law.

It is evidently for that purpose — namely, to show that persecution of the gospel is not to be equated with persecution generally, or to be combated by the same authority — that the concordists wander into such an apparently hypothetical issue as adiaphora. After all, in "a time of persecution" aren't adiaphora purely academic?

I take the concordists to be arguing supposititiously, the way law students are taught to do, in order to disentangle what is truly at issue. As if they were saying, Suppose that in this "period of persecution" the authorities were not really inflicting injustices at all (though in fact they are) and were forcing nothing else upon the church except such practices as are "neither commanded nor forbidden by God," just value-neutral.

With that imaginary supposition the real question stands out: Would the church even then, even in face of such seemingly modest inconveniences — *"auch in Mitteldingen"* — still be constrained to disobey such impositions as a persecution of the gospel? Since the answer is still an emphatic Yes, this hypothetical questioning has served to show that when it is the gospel which is being persecuted, that is indeed something more than the failure of secular authority to do its own job. It is an effort to usurp another, a distinctly different whole range of evangelical authority beyond the secular — and "by force or chicanery" to displace it.

Although secular authority is frequently oppressive and in "times of persecution" oppresses even the gospel, we must not conclude from such abuses that secular authority is nothing more than a corrupt, flawed, imperfect version of Christian authority. Secular authority has more identity of its own than that.

Conversely, it is not that secular authority, if it were just cleaned up and could function the way it was meant to, could then govern people the way the gospel does. Ruling evangelically and ruling secularly differ from each other not merely by degree, say, the way the ideal differs from approximations to it. The authority of the gospel is more distinctive, more radically "new" than that.

In "a time for confessing" these two styles of governance are cruelly confused, and evidently one responsibility of a confessor is to recover their radical difference and to model a new way by which each might, in mutual respect, cooperate with the other. The Augsburg confessional movement employed several pairs of contrasting terms to describe "the distinction between Christ's kingdom and a political kingdom": the former is "spiritual" *(spirituale)*, the latter "civil" *(civile)*; the former produces a righteousness which is "from the heart" *(in corde)* and a life, or at least the beginnings of a life, which is "eternal" *(aeterna)*, whereas the righteousness of the secular realm is only "outward" *(foris, externa)* and temporary *(interim)* (Apol. XVI, XVIII). All these pairs of terms, though illuminating, are only second best for explaining the distinction and, as we know by hindsight, can also be misleading. For instance, to concentrate the *regnum Christi* within people's "hearts" may give the misimpression of privatism, as if Christ's kingdom had nothing to do with public life and instead abandoned all that to the worldlings.

Really, what the Augustana said was the exact opposite. It was reinstating secular society — politics, economy, peoplehood, ethnicity *(gentium, ethnicis)*, marriage and family — as the normative realm in which Christian participation is most Christ-pleasing, rather than in other worldly monastic or utopian communes (Apol. XVI, 2, 3). In fact, the advantage of Christians' *in corde* righteousness, precisely for their public influence in society, is that in their case — if indeed they are Christians — their social righteousness comes "from the heart" and infiltrates the public domain as genuine, spontaneous "love" *(caritas)* (ibid.).

Then their social righteousness is not, as with merely "external" righteousness, something which has to be extorted and cajoled from people by appeals to their self-interest or even against their wills by force, which are the uncertain means by which secular authority has to operate. That explains why this uncoerced, freely willed righteousness which Christ achieves in his followers, all of it quite public and political, is called "spiritual," as opposed to the alternative "righteousness of the flesh": it can be enacted only by "the operation of the holying *Spirit* in the reborn" — those who through dying and rising, God-fearing and God trusting, those whose terrified and gospelled consciences are beginning to be gifted with new, more-than-human selves (Apol. XVIII, 4-10).

And if the members of Christ's distinctive movement are political agents who personally are beginning to undergo a kind of cruciform deification, then that in turn explains why their style of righteousness and vitality are referred to as "eternal." The opposite regime, namely, the secular, as indispensable as that is for running the present old age *(saeculum)*, in the long run has no future and is only an "interim" arrangement.

However, none of these acknowledged inferiorities of the secular realm — its temporariness, its having to make do with sinners as they are, its having to make them righteous somehow in spite of themselves by exploiting (of all things) their very sinfulness — should discourage Christ's people from "using" *(uti)* that very realm as their Lord's preferred arena for practicing *caritas.* For in spite of the sin-conditioned limitations of these secular social systems, they are nevertheless not only "legitimate civil ordinances" *(legitimae ordinationes civiles),* but also "good creatures of God and divine ordinances" *(bonae creaturae Dei et ordinationes divinae)* (Apol. XVI, 1).

So, "secular" in this context is not the opposite of "sacred." God's old "worldly" *(weltlich)* way of governing people — namely, exploiting their very self-interests for the good of others — may not be Christ's new way. But in the interim it is still God's. Yet saying this, namely, that these temporary creational systems are the Creator's own, also relativizes their authority. For in those perverse circumstances when "commands of the civil authority cannot be obeyed without sin, we must obey God rather than men" (Acts 5:29; AC XVI, 7).

So the confessional "distinction between Christ's kingdom and a political kingdom" is really more radical than was implied by those previous contrasts — "heartfelt" versus "external," "eternal" versus "temporary," "spiritual" versus "civil" — all of which distinctions are only proximate and second-best. Ultimately the distinction is between two ways by which God in his governing of history deals "righteously." His old way, still very much in force, is to achieve righteousness *(iustitia)* through "the outward works of the law" *(legis)* (Apol. XVIII, 7).

God's "righteousness of the law," by contrast with the righteousness of his gospel, is essentially the righteousness, shall we say, of fairness: giving people what they have coming to them, both life and death. Even this old adage is still teeming with life: "all things visible and invisible," "me together with all that exists, body and soul, food and clothing, family and property" (SC II, 2). With so much life there must be ultimate authorization for it.

At the same time, life in this old age is always aging. Bodies die, whether persons' physiques or political bodies or even church bodies. With so much aging, that too must be authorized, and by the same ultimate authority. Between the rhythms of the Creator's life-giving and death-demanding there is a certain lawful, even rational rightness or, as we have called it, fairness.

In our response to the Creator's bounty — all of which comes to us "out of his pure, fatherly and divine goodness or mercy, without any merit or worthiness on our part" — we are expected simply "to thank, praise, serve and obey him" (ibid.). But seeing that we prefer not to receive this bounty as pure gift and not to respond in kind as grateful beneficiaries, but rather on the basis of entitlement, we are, in turn, taken at our word. Now the Creator's gifts, rather than liberate us for praise, obligate us as debtors *(schuldig)* (ibid.).

What originally was given graciously becomes instead something we take for granted as owed us, but then also something which the Creator demands must be reciprocated and repaid. Hence the prevailing "righteousness" of the old creation is retributive. Retribution may in extreme cases need to be enforced by courts or even by force. "Public redress through a judge is not forbidden but expressly commanded, and it is a work of God . . ." (Apol. XVI, 7). Ideally, though, retribution is more subtle than that, less obviously coercive, and quite rationally arrived at (Apol. XVIII, 4).

To say that the Creator's secular righteousness is fair is mostly a matter of faith, since in practice it works out that way only approximately, revealing how fragile and exploited the law of God is.

So then is God fair? Not obviously, not yet. But his day will come, his Day of Fairness. When it does, alas, no one — no person or institution — will be able to stand that much fairness (AC XVII).

That, finally, is the chief drawback in God's secular sort of righteousness: we yearn for it since none of us can live without it, but when it comes we cannot live with it either. Although the divine law in even its most refined and reasonable forms, let alone in its crasser coercive forms, cannot evince a righteousness by which sinners can survive divine criticism, it is that limitation of the law which secular tyrants conceal who arrogate to their law-like authority the claims of saviorhood.

Worse yet, if the Augsburg confessional experience is a precedent, such confusing of God's retributive authority with that of his gospel may be still more of a temptation for authorities in the church. They may weary of having to depend on the Good News' inherent winsomeness and may lust for more enforceable means of insuring conformity.

Either way, whether by soteriologizing secular authority or by legalizing the authority of the gospel, what happens, as FC X puts it, is "idolatry" (10, 14, 15, 16). One of God's creations, secular authority, has been substituted for what only God himself can do and has done, in Jesus his

Christ. Ironically, these authoritarians stand condemned as idolaters, by the law's own "first and greatest commandment."

The alternative "kingdom of Christ," governing solely by the authority of his one gospel-and-sacraments, is by contrast with God's retributive reign not all that fair. But it is considerably more conducive to life and salvation. Unfairly enough, at least to God, this authority of Christ does not give people what they have coming to them, divine criticism and death. That quite shockingly is borne by God instead. And what God has coming to him, love and life and service and praise, accrues rather to worldly believers. Call it, as the medievals and Luther did, the "Happy Exchange."

It is true that Christians — who are the only ones who believe this "foolishness," as Paul called it — really have no more authority for believing it than Jesus did. So "good" do they find this news that they are willing to believe as he did that his authority for it is God's own. They believe that by what Jesus did God has trumped his own other authority, his fairness toward the current *saeculum*, rendering it old and eventually obsolete. In the history of Jesus God's oncoming Day of Fairness has been scooped by a still more ultimate future, Jesus' own, and by quite another brand of fairness or "righteousness" — if that old word can still be used in this new context except as a Christian pun. It is fair the way the "forgiveness of sin" is fair (Apol. XVI, 6).

That is, Christ's new alternative to retribution and death is resurrection and life — "for those who are in Christ Jesus" — but through the wringer of crucifixion — also "for those who are in Christ Jesus." And the Spirit in which Jesus commends this alternative to us, being God's holying or healing Spirit, persuades always without coercion, "freely."

Because of the distinctively new authority of "the kingdom of Christ," "no one should assume lordship or authority over the church, nor burden the church with traditions, nor let anybody's authority count for more than the Word of God" (TPPP, 11; FC X, 21). When such authoritarianism does oppress the church, as in "a time for confessing," then confessors everywhere are to disobey.

Their ecclesiastical superiors, at the time of the Augustana, quoted back to the confessors the passage from Hebrews, "Obey your leaders" (13:17). The confessors, in turn, were then bound to reply: "This passage requires obedience to the *gospel;* it does not create an authority for bishops apart from the *gospel.* Bishops must not create traditions contrary to the *gospel,* nor interpret their traditions in a manner contrary to the *gospel.* When they do so, we are forbidden to obey them by the passage (Galatians 1:8), 'If anyone preaches another *gospel*, let him be accursed'" (Apol. XXVIII, 20).

The only authority which such risky testimony has — as with the "testimony given to the apostles so that we may believe them on the basis of another's Word rather than on the basis of their own" — is that "Christ requires them to teach in such a way that he might be heard, because he says, 'He who hears you hears me'" (ibid., 18, 19).

5. Confessing as Appealing for/to the Oppressed

As our second confessional criterion ("Confessing as Protesting Gospel-Plus") picked up FC X's concern for "the truth of the gospel," and as our fourth confessional criterion ("Confessing as Redefining Authority") picked up FC X's concern about "idolatry," so now our fifth confessional criterion picks up FC X's concern for "Christian liberty," *christliche Freiheit* (14, 15, 30).

The oppressed with whom the Augsburg confessional movement identified are those whom "Christ has set free," as Paul says, "for freedom," and who therefore should "not submit again to a yoke of slavery," to be oppressed all over again by "false brethren secretly brought in . . . to spy out our freedom which we have in Christ Jesus, that they might bring us into bondage" (Gal. 5:1; 2:4, 5; FC X, 11). Augustana's liberationist emphasis was centered around its plea for *sola fide,* that is, that what justifies sinners before God is entirely their faith in Christ independently of the good work their faith does.

What was then at stake, in other words, in the struggle between "slavery" and "freedom" was the question of people's ultimate worth: what value of their own, if any, entitles them to life rather than death? And what assurance have they of being so valued? Such questions had assumed particular poignancy in that "time for confessing" because the dominant system of secular-religious authority, as the confessors encountered it, was oppressive most of all in how it ascribed value, ultimate value, preferentially to some persons rather than others on the strength of their religious and moral performance.

As a consequence, the Augustana protests, "poor consciences were driven to rely on their own efforts, and all sorts of works were undertaken. Some were driven by their conscience into monasteries in the hope that there they might merit grace through monastic life. Others devised other works for the purpose of earning grace and making satisfaction for sins. Many of them discovered that they did not obtain peace by such means" (AC XX, 19-22).

This systematic demoralizing of people at the very base of their existence, hence their ultimate destruction, is met by Augustana's classic reply: ". . . we do not become good in God's sight by our works, but . . . it is only through faith in Christ that we obtain grace for Christ's sake" (AC XXVI, 5). With this radical re-valuing of sinners solely on the strength of their faith, which renders them valuable because of the One it trusts, the most basic disparity between oppressors and oppressed is effectively undercut: not just the disparity between powerful and powerless or between rich and poor or between one ethnic or sexual group and another, but the most insuperable inequality of all — the gap between the righteous and the ungodly, the good and the bad.

Notice, this universal leveling begins not by saying that everyone is equally inherently good or even potentially so but, on the contrary, that "all men are conceived and born in sin, . . . are full of evil lust and inclinations from their mothers' wombs and are unable by nature to have true fear of God and true faith in God," subjecting everyone alike, unexpectedly, to the divine judgment (AC II). In other words, the "slavery," the "bondage," extends every bit as much to the superior religious elite, those who administer and pace the whole system of people's value ascription and who in fact facilitate people's enslavement.

Such devastatingly critical egalitarianism is based not only on unconditional regard for the divine criticism but, more so, on the happy sufficiency of Christ for trumping that judgment. Otherwise, the confessors ask rhetorically, "what need is there for the grace of Christ?" (Apol. XX, 10). If it were not true that our common need is so abject and that we are all terminally sinful, then "Christ would have died in vain" (SA III, 1, 11).

By the same token, since Christ did not die in vain, those whom he reclaims now acquire a value of their own which resides not just in the divine mind, not just in God's favorable disposition toward them, not just in his valuing them from the distance of his transcendent mercy. Their new value is something which they themselves appropriate as responsive, acting subjects, at least incipiently, a righteousness which already they begin to embody in their own biographies. That personally possessed value is, as the Augustana calls it, the "righteousness of faith" (AC IV).

True, because our faith in Christ is still ever so meager and tenuous, it is essential that God "*regard* and *reckon* this faith as righteousness" (AC IV, 3). But that is not to say that what faith there is is not righteousness already. "Faith is truly righteousness because it . . . gives honor to God, gives him what is properly his . . . by accepting his promises" (Apol. IV, 308-9). The trouble is, our faith — righteousness, no doubt, so far as it goes — is still far too overwhelmed by our unfaith to qualify *us* as righteous. Instead, therefore, we are righteous "on account of someone else's righteousness, namely, Christ's, which is communicated to us through faith" (ibid., 305; cf. SA III, 13).

The significance of the *sola fide* for sinners' liberation from bondage is that, though admittedly they are being oppressed by their own fallenness and by the tyrannical value-ascription systems and legitimation structures of their world and church, still a "case of confession" arises not merely to intercede for them as oppressed objects, as helpless victims in whose behalf the confessors must intervene as third-party advocates. That could degenerate into a new and subtle form of patronizing.

The confessors' appeal is not merely an appeal *for* the oppressed but also *to* them, thereby taking them seriously as responsible agents. Their justification, their divine revaluing on account of Christ, is not some remote transaction conducted behind their backs, but on the contrary involves them quite directly as participating agents. That in fact is part and parcel of their being freed from their oppressive bondage, namely, that they are being drawn into responsible human subject-hood, no longer left to the mercy of other mediators, but now liberated by that one Mediator who treats them not as slaves but as friends.

The same dignity of the freed human subject is reiterated in the confessors' insistence that the sinners' faith in Christ is what gives ultimate value and significance to their "works" as well — "the whole person [*totus homo*], in respect both of his person and of his works" (SA XIII, 2) — seeing that their works likewise are done in the faith that these too delight God because of Christ. Besides, the confessors can report that "our theologians have explained the whole matter of political affairs so clearly that many good people involved in politics and in business have testified how they were helped after the theories of the monks had troubled them and put them in doubt whether the gospel permitted such public and private business" (Apol. XVI, 13).

The ways in which the newly liberated slaves now become participating agents in their own right are numerous. For instance, in order for them to benefit from the Mass it is now essential that they be personally present to receive and that they receive by their own faith. Their baptisms, though conferred upon them as outright gifts, are now reenacted by them personally in each day's penitential dying and rising with Christ. The forgiveness of sin is exercised not only upon them, but also by them, to one another, "through the mutual conversation and consolation of the brothers" and sisters (SA III, 4).

It is all this grand freedom from the former bondage which is once more being imperiled during "a period of persecution," when additional religious and moral criteria for human worth are reimposed over and above the quite sufficing resource provided by Christ in his one gospel-and-sacraments, which is to be had for the taking, freely and unconditionally as a gift to faith. "As soon as . . . human commandments are forcibly imposed on the church as necessary and as though their omission were wrong and sinful," it is high time to recall that "this concerns the article of Christian liberty . . . , an article which the Holy Spirit through the mouth of the holy apostle so seriously commanded the church to preserve" (FC X, 15).

CHAPTER 2

Confessio:
Self-Defense Becomes Subversive

As theological interest grows in the hermeneutics of confessing, in its martyrological sense, the confessions of the Reformation are frequently invoked as classic precedents. What follows is an effort to review one of those precedents, the confessional situation at Augsburg in 1530, specifically as that conditioned the confessors' forensic relation to authority.

One thing, surely, which matured the Reformers into confessors was their recognizing that, directly because of their reforms, it was they who were now on trial. The plaintiffs were now doubling as defendants, hence confessors, under suspicion of insurrection and heresy. What is more, they accepted that defensive role, sometimes grudgingly, sometimes ignorant of the new role's strategic potential, yet in full awareness that there was a role shift. What originally may have seemed to be nothing more than doing their job as priest or prince or professor, alerting the public to its hazards, increasingly boomeranged into what Luther called a "cause," that is, a *Sache* or *casus* as in a case at court.[1] But it was a case no longer for reform-

---

1. Really, as Luther came to see it, there were *two* causes, his side's and the opponents', each attempting to make its case against the other before God and history. Here *Sache* is not an inclusive, neutral term as, for instance, in "the matter" or "the subject" under discussion. These *Sachen* are disjunctive, adversarial to the point where the divine Judge is expected to rule for one and against the other. Martin Luther, *Werke*, Kritische Gesamtausgabe; "Weimarer Ausgabe" (Weimar: Boehlau, 1883-) (hereafter, *WA*), 30/3: 276, 277, 281, 289. *Luther's Works*, American ed. (St. Louis: Concordia; Philadelphia: Fortress, 1955-) (hereafter, *LW*), 47:12, 17, 27.

ers to prosecute so much as for them to defend with an "apology" as suspects. The table had been turned and it was they who for their pains now had to "render an accounting," an *Antwort,* to justify themselves.[2] Isn't that a mark of confessors, to be thrown back on their own defense?

That may have been galling enough, having to excuse their public improvements. What made the matter worse, yet all the more confessional, was that when these defendants did try to explain themselves as they were summoned to do, they were officially blocked. That made their compliance with the summons, that is, their effort at self-defense, soon look like non-compliance, which it also was. So they were saddled with that much more to be defensive about. In the process of their taking the authorities at their word and pressing for an airing of the issues, and then the authorities' attempts to silence them, what became increasingly apparent was the authorities' own theological and moral-political bankruptcy. This discrediting of authority backfired on the confessors, making them out as insubordinate and seditious. But more, it bereaved them of the very authorities whose credibility they needed, or thought they needed, to vindicate them.

It is this confessors' dilemma which calls for elaboration. On the one hand, their heady role as critics is soon burdened with the additional, reverse duty of suspects having to clear themselves for having committed reformation. That much already ought to allay any grand illusions about confessing as "prophetic" machismo, as if it answered to no one, least of all tyrants. On the other hand, the confessors' very "rendering of an account" becomes public disobedience once it is ruled out of order, and when they persist in being heard against the sovereign will, they undermine both its sovereignty and themselves who depend on it. That ought to dispel any sentimentality about confessors as "martyrs" in the sense of merely passive sufferers of repression. Confession, at least in the case before us, is answerability to one's critical superiors even when the answer has the ef-

---

2. *WA* 30/3:284; *LW* 47:21. As for the distinction between *confessio* and *apologia,* the former was not confined to the Augsburg Confession nor the latter to Melanchthon's Apology to the Augsburg Confession. Luther referred to the first draft of the Augustana both as *confessio* and *apologia,* though *confessio* seems to have become his preference, perhaps Melanchthon's as well. *LW* 49:297, n. 12. Gottfried Seebass, "'Apologia' und 'Confessio.' Ein Beitrag zum Selbstverständnis des Augsburgischen Bekenntnisses," in *Bekenntnis und Einheit der Kirche,* ed. Martin Brecht and Reinhard Schwarz (Stuttgart: Calwer, 1980), 9-21.

fect of over-asking the superiors, leaving both them and the confessors in question. Confessors must answer to their arraigning authorities, yet when they do that openly they contravene not only those authorities, but themselves as well. That tightening spiral from reformer to defendant to subversive, possibly inherent in Christian *martyria,* seems also to underlie the entire phenomenon of modern critical thinking.

At the Diet of Augsburg in 1530 the reformatory gospel, though still reformatory, bore the distinctly defensive form of a *confessio.* But that was not all. The confessors at Augsburg had to count it a favor that the emperor should so much as grant them a "hearing," and barely that, and then only to order them to plead guilty.[3] That demand they had to refuse, of course, yet their refusal only compounded their insubordination and in turn the defensiveness of their whole posture. Not only had they presented their confession originally under the vague onus of troublemakers. Their confession, the more they maintained it, rendered them all the more uncooperative. Simply as defendants they were now offending against imperial authority as they had long since done against ecclesiastical, the papacy and the bishops, who had tried to dissuade the emperor from allowing a hearing in the first place.

Consider a tract of the times, Luther's *Warning to His Dear German People* (1531).[4] In addition to being what its title suggests (the ethnicity of its appeal should not be underestimated), the treatise is a sustained self-defense of the Lutheran reforms. But more to our immediate purpose, the document makes vividly clear how the hopes the confessors had brought to Augsburg were now shattered by the imperial edict against them, how impossible it was for them to believe the emperor had not been manipulated and how, though they still hoped for some sign of clemency from him, they now had to face the prospect that he might soon be executing his edict by force. Their inch-by-inch acceptance of their role as defendants against those very authorities they had hoped would exonerate them, their recognizing that the effort to clear themselves only implicated them further, the fact that they did not rush to that role but often (and noisily) resented it, is instructive for understanding confessing.

---

3. For even such ambivalent treatment Luther, as of 1530-31, was still inclined to put the best construction on the intentions of Emperor Charles V. *WA* 30/3:291-96; *LW* 47: 30-33.

4. *WA* 30/3:276-320; *LW* 47:11-55.

I.

It is one thing to expose abuses and heresy (as we did at Uppsala in 1968 with "ethical heresy" and later at Dar es Salaam and Ottawa with the "heresy" of apartheid).[5] That much is the function of any serious reformers, all the more so if their critique enjoys clout and is enforceable. But isn't it something else when these reformers in turn are reduced to the same forensic status as their culprits, or instead of their culprits, and are no longer in the superior position of putting the questions but are on the witness stand to free themselves and their gospel of the charge, of all things, of heresy? It is then that they incur the "martyrdom" of confessors, bearing the prejudicial burden of exonerating themselves of insubordination to the Word and will of God. And what if, as the confessors heard at Augsburg, those who circulated rumors of heresy against them and now might carry out sentence militarily, were conceding in private that the confessors' gospel was right but, because it was insubordinate and destabilizing, had to be exterminated as wrong?[6] Understandably, such cynicism made it harder for the confessors to take their role as suppliants for the faith seriously, let alone to expect practical advantage from that.

Might there not also be a deeper, a theological humiliation implied in reformers' having to justify themselves "before God and all the world"?[7] Especially so when, as with the Lutherans, the very heart of their reformatory claim was that they had been justified entirely by the divine mercy in Christ and so were liberated from all compulsions internally or externally, psychically or politically, to justify themselves. And wasn't it that which was most embarrassing of all, that it was *themselves* they were now obliged to defend, not the gospel as such or Christ in lofty abstraction but their own past conduct of this gospel, down to the most personal details and

---

5. *Uppsala Report* (Geneva: World Council of Churches, 1968), 53, 337; *In Christ — A New Community: The Proceedings of the Sixth Assembly of the Lutheran World Federation, Dar-es-Salaam, Tanzania, June 13-25, 1977* (Geneva: LWF, 1977), 179-80, 210-14; *Documents from the Twenty-First General Council of the World Alliance of Reformed Churches, Ottawa, Canada, August 17-21, 1982,* in *Reformed Press Service* 206 (September 1982): 4-17. Articles reporting similar actions against apartheid as "heresy" by Reformed, Presbyterians, Methodists, and Anglicans in southern Africa appear in *Ecunews* 10 (December 1982): 5-13, 18-19.

6. *WA* 30/3:283-91; *LW* 47:20-30.

7. *WA* 30/3:278, 279, 299; *LW* 47:13, 15, 34.

offhand quotations? Wouldn't that force them to change the subject back to their own dubious rightness, away from righteousness in Christ, surely away from any altruistic, other-directed concerns of national and ecclesial reform? Might that be why it was so demeaning for the Lutheran reformers to lower themselves to the status of confessors/defendants, seeing how that contradicted their "chief article" on justification by faith?

But then, did it really contradict? Could it be that, exactly because sinners are justified in Christ, they are then first free to suffer the disgrace, as Christ did, of justifying themselves confessionally, *für Gott und aller welt?*[8] It is conceivable that their success depended only proximately on how rightly they had performed or even on how right their doctrine of Christ was but ultimately on whether their defense of all that could achieve something more: keeping that doctrine of theirs from being silenced and instead in public circulation. For they believed that without that gospel's public continuance, even if in the odious form of confessors' self-defense, there would simply be no community resource left wherewith wrong people, including themselves, could be rendered right. So the odium had to be borne for the public good — "good," *coram Deo.*[9]

This much is clear: for Luther the odium of the defendant is of the essence of confessorhood. It seemed to him to diminish his credibility as a confessor that, because he was a wanted man, he had been disallowed by his colleagues and protectors from coming to the imperial diet at Augsburg. It would have been better, he thought, had he been there with them to share their humiliation. (We know what it does to our own credibility when we have to "confess" against apartheid from the safe distance of our Coburgs in the U.S.A. or against ecclesiastical hierarchy from behind our diplomatic immunity in academe or in some separate denominational jurisdiction, where the risk of humiliation is minimal.) True, Luther too had had to confess in self-defense on earlier occasions and so knew about the confessor's need of humility at first hand. (Humility, notably in his case, is not to be confused with modesty.) But it was still a bitter pill for

---

8. Not only does Luther coordinate the Augsburgers' confessing of Christ with Christ's confessing of them (*WA*, Briefe [Br] 12:119; *LW* 49:365), also he ventures that in their confessing of Christ the latter's very lordship is at stake: "If [Christ] loses this title ["King of kings and Lord of lords"] now at Augsburg then he has also lost it in heaven and on earth." *WA*, Br 5:459; *LW* 49:370.

9. *WA* 30/3:308-11, 316-20; *LW* 47:41-44, 51-54.

him "when our people were threatened and challenged, defied, jeered and mocked at the diet by the papists," even though socially these confessors were "princes, lords, and godly and honorable people." As good confessors, nevertheless, "they humbled themselves most abjectly and let themselves simply be trampled underfoot."[10]

The reformer Münzer and his followers, so Luther complained, had declined that sort of humiliation. "They refused to submit their teaching to a hearing as our people now have done at Augsburg."[11] To be sure, the opposite fault occurs in Melanchthon, Luther's close colleague and the immediate author of the Augsburg Confession. He comes off not much better than Münzer. Instead of returning home from Augsburg he stayed behind with the papal critics to negotiate and renegotiate — as Luther feared, to compromise away — the *confessio*.[12] The latter rebuked him in the stern language of Psalm 118 for lusting to be thought of as a "builder" and shirking the stigma of a "destroyer."[13] Fairly or not, Luther pictured Münzer as a reformer who evaded the odium of confessional "apology," and Melanchthon as a reformer who evaded such an apology's seditiousness.

Perhaps these are converse sides of the same coin. The same two aversions, avoiding accountability and avoiding culpability, may still inhibit confessing in our day, or theology generally, from being as critical as it ought to be. It is hard enough to be critical in the reformatory, prophetic sense of asserting criticism, but evidently harder still to submit to criticism, for which Luther thought Münzer incapable.[14] Hardest of all, if Melanchthon is a clue, is suffering the criticism to the breaking point, the opponents' own and very nearly the confessors' as well.

At the moment it is the former of the two aversions we are considering. Reformers, as confessors, are humbled to the rank of defendants. The cardinal virtue we are accustomed to associate with confessors is courage.

10. *WA* 30/3:278; *LW* 47:14.
11. *WA* 30/3:278; *LW* 47:14.
12. *WA,* Br 5:416-17; *LW* 49:340-41.
13. *WA,* Br 5:436; *LW* 49:344.
14. Alvin Gouldner describes how the modern culture of critical discourse "always moves on to auto-critique, *and* to the critique of *that* auto-critique." "The culture of critical discourse must put its hands around its own throat, and see how long it can squeeze." *The Future of Intellectuals and the Rise of the New Class* (New York: Seabury, 1979), 60. In a confessional situation, moreover, the hands to which one bares one's throat are not only one's own hands, and so not only auto-critique.

Luther did that, too, calling it "boldness and cheerfulness."[15] But the proof of confessional courage lay in its humility. "We appeared voluntarily at Augsburg," Luther says of his colleagues there, "and offered humbly [*mit aller demut*] and eagerly to render an account." Not only that, "we plead, implore, and clamor for a chance to do this" and, in the process, "suffer every indignity, mockery, contempt and danger." At bottom, as we shall see, what is most needed is faith. But the faith for confessing, apparently, eventuates as humility. Luther marveled at his heroes in Augsburg: "Such a confession, . . . such humility, . . . such patience."[16]

So prepared were the confessors to be further humiliated, should that be the price of their gaining a hearing, that already at Augsburg they were appealing beyond that diet to another possible forum, "a general, free and Christian council" of the church.[17] Such a council Pope Clement VII was reluctant to convoke. Eventually, though, his successor, Paul III, relented and was about to call the conciliarists' bluff. Or so it seemed. Then it was confessors like Luther's own Elector John Frederick who reneged, suspecting a trap. Luther and his colleagues, too, hoped for little from such a council, yet they urged their prince to accept the papal invitation even so. Trap or no trap, martyrdom was still an opportunity to give an account of their faith.[18]

"Not surprisingly," says Mark Edwards, "they lost the argument with their prince. And they acquired the task of justifying this [political] decision and discrediting the papal council."[19] There, as Luther fully expected, his papal judges would have little intention of granting a hearing but only of condemning. Yet not even that final ignominy prevented him from going to the eventual council, not "by horse and wagon but by paper and ink," and posthumously.[20] For that unpromising occasion he had written (and had done so at the request of the same Elector John Frederick) what came to be called the Smalcald Articles, so that "those who live after me

15. *WA* 30/3:286, 287, 289; *LW* 47:23, 25, 26.

16. *WA* 30/3:278; *LW* 47:14.

17. Preface to the Augsburg Confession, *Die Bekenntnisschriften der evangelisch-lutherischen Kirche*, 6th ed. (Göttingen: Vandenhoeck & Ruprecht, 1967) (hereafter, *BS*), 48; *The Book of Concord* (Philadelphia: Fortress, 1959) (hereafter, *BC*), 27.

18. *WA*, Br 8:35-38; *LW* 50:157-65.

19. Mark U. Edwards, Jr., *Luther's Last Battles: Politics and Polemics, 1531-46* (Ithaca: Cornell, 1983), 69.

20. Cited in Edwards, *Luther's Last Battles*, 81.

may have my testimony and confession."[21] For Luther as for the psalmist, what is it that needs most to be trusted when "I will speak of thy testimonies before kings"? Answer: that I, all appearances to the contrary, "shall not be put to shame."[22]

II.

So much for confessors' humiliation, that is, in having to defend their reforms. How about the other pole of the dilemma, the disobedience in their doing so? Are confessors simply victims? Or are they, *qua* defendants, offenders? Having to defend oneself as a "destroyer" obviously entails suffering, perhaps largely undeserved, yet not as undeserved as one may think. What I have in mind is not the confessors' ordinary sinfulness. That goes without saying. Beyond that the confessors were, as confessors, disobeying constituted authority, in fact undermining it. Moreover, they were coming to sense that. What was disobedient was not only the disruptiveness of their initial programmatic reforms but even their falling back "humbly" to defend themselves by such apparently passive means as their "apology." For as defendants, too, they were still invoking the same offensive gospel, yet now necessarily against their superiors since their accusers *were* their superiors and, alas, one of the last conspicuous links to the confessors' own legitimacy.

There seems to be something about the *confessio* the defendants were pleading which itself constituted an act of resistance — unarmed resistance at first, but not inevitably so. The very substance of what they were confessing, or whom, seems to have implicated them in disobedience both ecclesiastical and civil. When Luther reminded Melanchthon that they, like the Cornerstone whom the builders rejected, were necessarily perceived as destroyers, he conceded the ironic justice of it all: "and this is just" *(merito)*.[23] If that is true, then what we have been saying about confessional humiliation is all the more understandable. Confessors are regularly faulted for being far readier to confess their faith than their sin.[24] But is their reluc-

---

21. Preface to the Smalcald Articles, *BS* 409; *BC* 289.

22. *WA*, Br 5:442; *LW* 49:354.

23. *WA*, Br 5:436; *LW* 49:344.

24. On how "telling the truth means not to discuss one's sins with the devil," see William Jay Peck, "The Role of the 'Enemy' in Bonhoeffer's Life and Thought," in *A*

tance really that hard to understand? If in confessing their faith, that is, defending it, they already create the impression of obstruction and anarchy, why should they want to exacerbate that image by concentrating further attention upon their sin?

Now it might be objected that the confessors were not really being disobedient, but only seemed to be so in the eyes of their detractors. For if we are committed to understand confessing optimally from the vantage of the confessors themselves, as we are,[25] then must we not allow that they at least did not acknowledge themselves to be seditious? Even though Luther's *Warning* explicitly urges his dear Germans to "refuse obedience" to pope and emperor, does he not justify their disobedience on the grounds of a higher obedience both in civil law (the imperial right of resistance) and in Scripture (Acts 5:29, "We must obey God rather than human beings")?[26] Granted. But contrariwise, does not his whole juridical self-justification beg the question at issue, that his gospel could prove its case if only given a fair hearing? Luther is right, "Even God did not condemn Adam until he first gave him a chance to reply."[27] But whether the confessors' reply could have

---

Bonhoeffer Legacy, ed. J. Klassen (Grand Rapids: Eerdmans, 1981), 345-61; Gerhard Sauter, "Vergib uns unsere Schuld . . . : eine theologische Besinnung auf das Stuttgarter Schuldbekenntnis," in *Wie Christen ihre Schuld bekennen: Die Stuttgarter Erklaerung 1945,* ed. Gerhard Besier and Gerhard Sauter (Göttingen: Vandenhoeck & Ruprecht, 1985), 63-128; "Commentaries" (on the Stuttgart Declaration) by Hans Asmussen and Martin Niemöller, in *Im Zeichen der Schuld: 40 Jahre Stuttgarter Schuldbekenntnis,* ed. Martin Greschat (Neukirchen-Vluyn: Neukirchener Verlag, 1985), 47-72.

25. The argument for defining a situation by what it means for its immediate agents on the ground that that alone provides adequate access to their behavior is classically summarized in W. I. Thomas's maxim (called by Robert Merton the "Thomas Theorem"), "If men define situations as real, they are real in their consequences." W. I. Thomas and D. S. Thomas, *The Child in America* (New York: Knopf, 1928), 572; *Social Behavior and Personality: Contributions of W. I. Thomas to Theory and Social Research,* ed. Edmund Volkart (New York: Social Sciences Research Council, 1951), 80ff. The implications of Thomas's thesis for the systematic methodology to which I am indebted are elaborated in Jürgen Habermas, *Zur Logik der Sozialwissenschaften* (Frankfurt: Suhrkamp, 1970), 125-285. Thus a case may be made for understanding the confessors in terms of their own intentions rather than behavioristically. Of course that does not obviate the further challenge to adjudicate theologically between one group of agents, the confessors, and another group, their opponents. That exactly is the confessional task.

26. WA 30/3:282-84, 299, 317, 319-20; LW 47:19-21, 35, 52, 54.

27. WA 30/3:284; LW 47:21. It is equally clear that Luther had no illusions about es-

profited from further chances any better than Adam's did is highly questionable. Not untenable altogether, admittedly, but questionable indeed. Furthermore, while Luther may have been able to absolve his fellow-confessors legally of the maximum charge of insurrection, not even he claimed that their resisting would not be illegal in some sense.[28]

The one thing which seemed most to cast suspicion upon the confessors' self-defense, possibly also in their own eyes, was the obvious fact that they were failing. If theirs was not a losing cause, why was it looking like one? Their base of support was shrinking, their publications read more and more like preaching to the choir, the kind of support they had to resort to grew in violence and shrillness, many who still identified with the movement seemed scarcely to grasp what it was all about.[29] Why were they faring like outlaws if that was not what they were? Never mind that a similar fate was afflicting their opponents. What was at stake after all was the confessors' *gospel,* and should they not have reason to expect its vindication imminently?

The confessors predated the kind of later idealism which dismisses historical consequences as irrelevant to one's personal rightness. On that score the Reformers might have felt closer to a later pragmatism. Verification was still somehow consequentialist, and vindication was by ordeal. Much less was theirs the kind of irrationalist "theology of the cross" which construes suffering as open *proof* of their rightness. By that token they would surely have been overshadowed by the tragic Münzer. The concern of these confessors was how they were actually being treated, not by their opponents or by history, but by history's God. Given that concern, so incriminating was the current discouraging course of affairs that Luther, in his *Warning,* suggested two alternatives about God, one of which was that there appears to be no God at all, the other of which was at least as sobering.[30] Both interpretations were propounded to account for the damaging evidence against the confessors. Either way, though the confessors *believed* they were not seditious, the evidence for that, which they still counted on adducing, was not compellingly at hand. Not yet. Not even for themselves.

---

caping condemnation in any case, with or without a fair hearing. *WA,* Br 5:259; *LW* 49: 278.

28. *WA* 30/3:282-83; *LW* 47: 19-20.

29. Edwards, *Luther's Last Battles,* 6-37.

30. *WA* 30/3:277-78, 279; *LW* 47: 13, 15.

Nowadays that feature of the Lutheran confessors (not only the Reformed but also the Lutheran), who merely as defendants behaved disobediently, is sometimes overlooked by their Lutheran admirers. Well-meaningly, the confessors are contrasted, say, with today's "European political theology."[31] They are commended not for "taking a firm stand *against* evil on the basis of faith," but rather for "*suffering* evil for their act" of confessing, and suffering it in one of two ways, "martyrdom or flight."[32] That description captures an important half-truth but little more. *Martyria* always involves suffering evil, of course, if only the ignominy of having to play the culprit, let alone what Luther called *blut und marter*.[33] That is why the Formula of Concord spoke of a "time for confessing" interchangeably with "times of persecution."[34]

But persecution was subsequent, not prior. Whatever suffering befell the confessors, they themselves had occasioned by what they first of all *refused* to suffer, the subversion of the gospel in high places. At that most radical level they were, as we might say today, out-and-out refuseniks. True, they did not refuse what they faulted Münzer for refusing, "to submit their teaching to a hearing." To that they acceded. But that is hardly "flight" and, though it is "martyrdom," it is that only in a sense — a very activist sense — which begs to be explained. In fact, it was by their "submitting"

---

31. Paul Hinlicky, "The Debate over *Status Confessionis*," *Lutheran Forum* 18, no. 4 (1984): 24.

32. Hinlicky, "Debate over *Status Confessionis*," emphasis added. If I understand him, Hinlicky does see that what confessors do is a "refusal to cooperate, with the persecutors." What he does not concede, evidently, is that that is precisely a refusal to "suffer evil" at the hands of authorities, or that the confessors' refusal is precisely "taking firm stands against evil" in high places, possibly also politically and even militarily. Such forms of refusal are admittedly inferior and ambiguous as confessions. The prior question, I believe, remains: *what* evil, what authoritative evil is it that confessing does indeed withstand and by means of what opposing alternative? Hinlicky followed up the above article with a generous but still preliminary clarification. *Lutheran Forum* 19, no. 2 (1985): 11. A related question, whether martyrdom has to be "passive" and may not also be quite "active," was addressed by Karl Rahner, "Dimensions of Martyrdom: A Plea for the Broadening of a Classical Concept," in *Martyrdom Today*, ed. Johannes-Baptist Metz and Edward Schillebeeckx, *Concilium* 163 (New York: Seabury, 1983), 9-11.

33. On the other hand, there is a long tradition according to which confessors are those heroic witnesses to the faith who, by contrast with martyrs, do not suffer death for the faith. For the present discussion that distinction is not essential.

34. Formula of Concord, Solid Declaration, *BS* 1054; *BC* 610-11.

that they were doing their refusing. Directly by the act of submitting their teaching the confessors were nonetheless teaching, probably more publicly than ever and now in conscious defiance of ecclesiastical policy and, soon after, of imperial policy as well.

What the confessors' latter-day Lutheran admirers may overlook is not that what was there being defended was the gospel — that is lavishly recognized — but that its defense in face of antagonistic authority was already a refusal to suffer evil in its most authoritative form, and was thus open resistance and at least de facto disobedience. Whatever suffering the confessors were willing to endure was only consequent, rooted in this prior refusal to suffer. In refusing that, and in refusing to cease refusing, they were both ecclesiastically and civilly disobedient. For that much disobedience, at the very least, they were as they knew obliged to explain themselves. As they also knew, though perhaps only vaguely, their society's most basic institutional forms of authority would have to be replaced, perhaps by nothing less than the eschaton, before their own disobedience could be publicly justified.[35]

As for the confessors' defensive use of force, that too (like suffering) was only a secondary issue, not a primary one. The prior question was, is what is being defended or confessed — that is, the confessors' own reformatory gospel — truly the gospel of God? If it is, and assuming that armed resistance is at all lawful, there may be conscientious differences between confessors over whether force may be employed. That much Luther was persuaded to concede, and he did that publicly as the imperial forces seemed to be threatening invasion in order to enforce the post-Augsburg edict against the confessors' lands.[36] The one alternative, however, which no confessor dared opt for, was to acquiesce in the invasion, even peaceably. The whole point of Luther's *Warning to His Dear German People*, who were liable to military conscription by the papal-imperial invaders, was that on no condition dared they comply — on pain of damnation as traitors to Christ.[37]

---

35. That sentiment was heightened by the confessors' growing conviction that the papacy had become the apocalyptic Counter-Christ and that the emperor as well might become his enforcer, thus casting both those historic institutions hopelessly on the side of the *status quo ante* while God, by contrast, was surely moving history toward something new, probably final. *WA* 30/3:306, 319; *LW* 47:40-41, 53-54.

36. *WA* 30/3:282-84; *LW* 47:18-21.

37. *WA* 30/3:291, 299-300, 320; *LW* 47:30, 35, 54.

But even non-military, passive cooperation with "the enemies of the gospel" was quite as damnable. Later, after Luther's death, Lutherans at Magdeburg (whom Melanchthon dubbed "Gnesio-Lutherans") repudiated the Melanchthonians ("Philippists") in Wittenberg for capitulating to the imperial occupational force on the pretext that the concessions they were making were doctrinally harmless adiaphora. Of those two camps it was the militant Magdeburgers who more faithfully reflected the confessional intention of Augsburg.[38]

Thereby they set the stage for subsequent theories of armed resistance in Calvinism.[39] Still later the Formula of Concord insisted that persecution of the gospel demands frontal resistance from all who confess it and, significantly, did not specify that such resistance has to be unarmed.[40] That issue is not prejudged if only because that issue, grave as it is, is not the gravest. What is, is *what* is being defended, or *who* — not *how*. In Luther's *Warning*, if anything was adiaphoral it was whether the confessors' resistance may be armed. But that they should resist at all costs and in no way cooperate was anything but an adiaphoron. That was as nonnegotiable as anything a later age might call orthopraxy.

Was that not disobedience? If it was, which is highly possible, that was required, notice, by the very defense of the gospel. But then, by definition, should that not have excused the "disobedience" and reconstrued it as a higher obedience? Only if it was already established, which it was not,

---

38. Oliver Olson, "Theology of Revolution: Magdeburg, 1550-1551," *Sixteenth Century Journal*, no. 1 (April 1972): 56-79; "Matthias Flacius Illyricus, 1520-1575," in *Shapers of Religious Traditions in Germany, Switzerland, and Poland, 1560-1600*, ed. Jill Raitt (New Haven: Yale University Press, 1981), 1-17. Robert Kolb, "The Flacian Rejection of the Concordia: Prophetic Style and Action in the German Late Reformation," *Archiv für Reformationsgeschichte* 73 (1982): 196-217.

39. Karl Holl, *The Cultural Significance of the Reformation* (New York: Meridian, 1959), Chapter 2. Brian Gerrish, *The Old Protestantism and the New* (Chicago: University of Chicago Press, 1982), 25, 44. Cynthia Grant Shoenberger, "The Development of the Lutheran Theory of Resistance, 1523-1530," *The Sixteenth Century Journal* 8, no. 1 (April 1977): 61-76; "Luther and the Justifiability of Resistance to Legitimate Authority," *Journal of the History of Ideas* 40, no. 1 (1979): 3-20; Quentin Skinner, *The Foundations of Modern Political Thought*, vol. 2 (Cambridge: Cambridge University Press, 1978), 206-7; John W. deGruchy, "Bonhoeffer, Calvinism and Civil Disobedience," in *Bonhoeffer and South Africa* (Grand Rapids: Eerdmans, 1984), 103-5; Formula of Concord, Article X, *BS* 1053-63; *BC* 610-16.

40. Formula of Concord, Article X, *BS* 1053-63; *BC* 610-16.

that the gospel the confessors were defending really was the gospel. Still, *can* that be established? Must that not simply be believed? But if so, why did the confessors insist on having their *confessio* adjudicated "before God and all the world," and evidently always both?[41] At the same time, it is true, the very judicatories on whom the confessors had depended were being unmasked by the confessors. Would that not leave both judges and defendants without public credence? It would seem so, unless by exhausting the existing authorities, the defendants wittingly or unwittingly might have been paving the way for some new, transcending tribunal ("God and the world?") to finally give the confessors their favorable hearing.

The question is bound to arise, if Luther in his *Warning* was so ready to mount an all-out defense against "the enemies of the gospel," why does he in that same treatise still commend martyrdom ("to suffer the madness even of tyrants") over armed self-defense?[42] Right; that question is crucial for any further understanding of confessing, particularly as an eschatological event — that is, as final showdown. So the question dare not be kept waiting long (though it cannot be addressed in the present chapter).

Meanwhile we ought not suppose that, by counseling martyrdom over recourse to force, Luther was for a moment relaxing the confessors' vocation as resistors. Quite the contrary. Martyrdom *is*, if need be, the defendants' extremist Christian form of ecclesiastical-civil disobedience — refusal! — against the powers that be, if only because that has the effect of dethroning them from their advantage of power as judges and reducing them to the level of defendants like the confessors themselves. Not to mention that martyrdom has a way of disclosing who the adversaries' own real Judge is and, conversely, who the confessors' co-Defendant is. For now it is

41. The confessors were certain enough that their *confessio* had proved its case at Augsburg on the publicly testable — might we say, "scientific"? — grounds of "Scripture and sound reasons" and, what is more, that some of the leading opponents there had admitted as much. Yet in spite of this theological vindication, if it was that, their opponents on the level of *practice* were still acting (and not unsuccessfully) as though nothing had been proved at all, and seemed to be doing so against their own better knowledge. It is significant that this perplexing course of events against the confessors implied, also for themselves, public evidentiary force, nearly incriminating force, which simply cried out for theological explanation. For them their case could not yet be regarded as publicly and conclusively decided. *WA* 30/3:280, 283-84, 287-88, 294-96, 299-301, 314-16, 319-20; *LW* 47:16, 20-21, 24-26, 32, 35-36, 49-51, 54-55.

42. *WA* 30/3:278; *LW* 47:13.

enough to note that to be confessors meant to be humbled to the rank of defendants and that even that, self-defense, further implicated the defendants in de facto disobedience and in forfeiting the historic institutional supports for their own plausibility.

III.

"They refused to submit their teaching to a hearing," Luther complained against Münzer and his supporters, as if by their unaccountability they disqualified themselves as confessors. A similar complaint is heard against some theologians of our day, for example, Karl Barth. He too has been faulted for abjuring Christian theology's accountability to the world, for insisting — positivistically, as Bonhoeffer complained[43] — on the privileged immunity, the arbitrary givenness of Christian revelation or, in Bartley's words, for his "retreat to commitment."[44] Ironically, however, almost no one has dared suggest that such unaccountability to the authorities of the age diminishes the *confessing* character of Barthian theology. Yet must that not follow if to be a confessor is to stand as defendant answerable to one's critics?

To cast doubt on a theology's martyrological integrity, even if only in this limited respect, does seem preposterous in the case of Barth, who everywhere is recognized as preeminent among the Barmen confessors. Even Heinrich Scholz, who perhaps most trenchantly of all Barth's friends exposed his lack of scientific accountability, himself assumed that a theology so "exempt from all earthly questioning" still is, if nothing else, "a personal confession of faith in the most decided sense."[45] Personal, yes. But (for the reasons given) a confession? Scholz's dubious intimation that a confession can still be "exempt from all earthly questioning" even Wolfhart Pannen-

---

43. Dietrich Bonhoeffer, *Letters and Papers from Prison*, enlarged ed., ed. Eberhard Bethge (New York: Macmillan, 1972), 280, 286, 329.

44. William Bartley, *The Retreat to Commitment*, rev. ed. (LaSalle, Ill.: Open Court, 1962), 64.

45. "Wie ist eine evangelische Theologie als Wissenschraft moeglich?" *Zwischen den Zeiten* 9 (1931): 48; reprinted in Gerhard Sauter, ed., *Theologie als Wissenschaft* (Munich: Christian Kaiser, 1971), 221-64. The quotation from Scholz in English, above, is from Wolfhart Pannenberg, *Theology and the Philosophy of Science* (Philadelphia: Westminster, 1976), 271.

berg permits to go unchallenged, all the while agreeing that Barth's claim to "be accountable to everyone" defies meaning.[46]

But if confessing entails answerability to the relevant principalities and powers, it also entails, as we suggested, something else. Confessors, exactly by insisting upon a hearing from those who judge them, risk in the process discrediting the judges' credibility, including any credibility they might still have had for accrediting the confessors. Authority, as Richard Sennett (heeding Hegel) has reminded us, means "precisely someone who will use his strength to care for others" and, except in paternalistic authority, to so care for others as to make them stronger.[47] Confessors implicitly affirm that fact when they appeal to their authorities for adjudication. Yet as their very appeal proceeds to disclose the authorities' incompetence, they seem to be sawing off the branch onto which they had crawled. Of course, not only they are then rid of the branch. So is the whole tree.

Whatever normative tribunals a given theology faces — society, academy, church, to take David Tracy's threesome — that theology would then be martyrologically credible only if it takes its tribunals so seriously that it is prepared to exhaust them, if necessary to bankrupt them, to price itself out of their market.[48] By that demanding criterion, however, many a theology today which faults a Barth for his unaccountability (*merito*, I believe) would soon find that its own vaunted accountability, ecclesial or scientific or political, is too abjectly dependent upon the authorities to test their limits, and if need be to retire them in hopes of something new and better.

---

46. Pannenberg, *Theology and the Philosophy of Science*, 271-72.

47. Sennett, *Authority* (New York: Vintage, 1981), 82.

48. *The Analogical Imagination: Christian Theology and the Culture of Pluralism* (New York: Crossroad, 1981). Tracy, too, tends to use the term "confessional" in a sense which ignores how publicly accountable an original historical *confessio* might have been. Yet it is Tracy, I acknowledge gratefully, who issues the challenge which the present chapter endeavors to heighten: ". . . The need for a 'confessional' position which incorporates methods for truly public discourse seems especially pertinent. . . ." *Blessed Rage for Order* (New York: Seabury, 1975), 250.

CHAPTER 3

Black Churches in the Civil Rights Movement as a Confessing Movement: *Confessio* as Disencumbering the Gospel

"The gospel of freedom," Martin Luther King Jr., called it, making a point. His point was that the one feature of the gospel which is most compromised by American racism is the gospel's freedom. It was no accident that on this occasion, April of 1963, King was writing his gospel of freedom from prison, against jailhouse rules, smuggling it out in surreptitious bits and pieces. Moreover, this now-celebrated "Letter from Birmingham Jail" is written in the subdued form of a self-defense, a posture which had to be humiliating for a reformer who knew he was right and his accusers wrong. "Seldom," he explains from the outset, "do I pause to answer criticism of my work and ideas. . . . But. . . ."

It was this posture that Martin Luther had admired in the confessors at Augsburg and had missed in Thomas Münzer (also in himself), the confessors' courageous "humility" *(humilitas)*, not now as initiators of reform or as prophetic critics, but as lowly culprits on trial for having committed reformation. King was now in the martyrological posture of a respondent deigning to explain himself in what he hoped would be "patient and reasonable terms." He was a defendant, and in that sense, a *martyr,* a *confessor.* Yet what he was confessing to, of all things, was a "gospel of freedom." This freedom, whose superiority consists in the power to bear a cross, was for prisoner King a shadow of things to come.

Quickly, a few disclaimers are in order. In concentrating on "Letter from Birmingham Jail," as this chapter does, there are no illusions about that document, either about its efficacy or about its authorship. The letter probably had little to do with the effectiveness of the Birmingham demonstrations of 1963, ambiguous as those effects were. Even after it was finally published, it was not an immediate sensation, despite the fact that its occasion was somewhat staged and it went through several editings. Neither need we romanticize King, as more and more we are being cautioned not to do. A whole chorus of friends and family, from Julian Bond in *Eyes on the Prize* to Andrew Young and Ella Baker and Hosea Williams and Diane Nash and his own sister and daughter, make the point, "The movement made Martin rather than Martin making the movement."[1]

We are being made to remember even King's adultery, whether by Eleanor Holmes Norton and Alice Walker, who extenuate it, or by other writers who call it "sexual bigotry." None of that, including what so tormented King himself, his recurring fearfulness and depression, do I mean to ignore. My intention is rather to examine "Letter from Birmingham Jail" as a public witness to the Christian gospel under fire, a form of martyrological *confessio,* which so far as I know is always made by known sinners. Moreover, "Letter" is here construed not only in context of King's larger movement, but also, since that movement likewise did not make itself, in context of a God to whom the movement and King both felt acutely indebted. In other words, this reconstruction of "Letter" as *confessio* will be riskily theological and in that modest respect like the original.

I. The Encumbrance of Adiaphora

In order for the gospel to remain free it dare not be bound, least of all by geographical boundaries. It was partly for having overstepped such boundaries — a state line, a city limit — that King, from Georgia, was being faulted for outside interference in Birmingham. Eight Alabama clergymen, all of them white moderates who previously had been sympathetic with King's cause, had just published a statement in the *Birmingham News* condemning his demonstrations (without naming him) for exacerbating "our local problems." In self-defense, King's "Letter" explains that the gospel must respond to "the Macedonian call" wherever it originates, just as

1. The original reference is credited to Ella Baker. Cf. Julian Bond, *Eyes on the Prize: America's Civil Rights Years (1954-1965),* PBS video (originally aired January-February 1987).

the itinerant apostle Paul's "gospel of Jesus Christ" had to. Geographical boundaries, though they do deserve respect, may not hamper "the gospel of freedom."

King's invoking Paul as apostolic precedent calls to mind one of the classical characteristics of all confessional moments — and that will be the point of this chapter. Such a moment, such "a time for confessing" as the Formula of Concord called it, has arrived when an oppressive establishment has exalted some favorite feature of its culture to salvational significance, insinuating it into the gospel itself as a condition of human worth, thus nullifying the unconditional grace of God in Christ. For Paul such a subversive accretion to the gospel had appeared in Galatia with the reimposition of circumcision for Gentile converts. He felt constrained to risk his very ministry by standing up to the circumcision party and, of course, for doing so he became answerable. Thus he acceded to the role of confessor, as he said, "for the truth of the gospel" (Gal. 2:5); that is, for the gospel's unencumbered integrity not only in words but in praxis. Gospel-plus, in that case gospel plus circumcision, actually amounted to gospel-minus. More was less. Unless the Good News thus encumbered was disencumbered it would be a false gospel, "another gospel" as Paul charged, and in truth not the Good News of "freedom" at all. Such encumbering of the gospel is a tripwire for triggering "a time for confessing."

The Pauline precedent at Galatia influenced the confessing movement of the Reformation, a movement in turn which King and his associates in the Southern Christian Leadership Conference occasionally invoked as precedent for themselves. The Reformation phrase we just quoted, "a time for confessing," appeared in the Formula of Concord, Article X, a document which centuries later inspired Dietrich Bonhoeffer in his underground seminary at Finkenwalde. Such "a time for confessing" has come, said the concordists of 1580, whenever "human commandments are forcibly imposed on the church as necessary and as though their omission were wrong and sinful" (FC/SD X, 15). The "human commandments," which at that time were in danger of being "forcibly imposed" following the Leipzig Interim with Rome, were largely prescriptions concerning church ceremony. That is, they were practices which in themselves were not all that objectionable and which under other, uncoerced circumstances might have been borne with, especially out of deference to those less liberated members of the community who were "weak in faith." As such, as morally and religiously tolerable, those practices were called adiaphora.

But adiaphora promptly forfeited all adiaphoral, neutral status once they acquired obligatory force alongside the gospel, imperiling the freedom of Christian conscience, or faith. Once that occurred, the Christian community was no longer free to honor such impositions, but on the contrary asserted its freedom by withstanding them as idolatrous. Applicable once more in such "a time for confessing" was Paul's earlier admonition to the Galatians, "For freedom Christ has set us free; stand fast therefore and do not submit again to a yoke of slavery" (Gal. 5:1; FC/SD X, 11). There is continuity, I am suggesting, between those earlier Christian "times for confessing" and the recent witness of black Christians in places like Alabama's jails, particularly on this single confessional point: such otherwise neutral adiaphora as Birmingham's city limits and its local autonomy, by themselves respectable, may require to be trespassed if they serve to silence "the gospel of freedom." At risk of imprisonment they require breaching, or even martyrdom, that being the shape of this extraordinary "freedom."

Spatial boundaries were not the only restrictions King's critics imposed on the gospel of freedom. They sought also to restrict its time, that is, to some future time: later perhaps but not now. Why, they were asking, could not the demonstrations have waited? The present was too soon, "untimely." "Some have asked," King observes, "'Why didn't you give the new city administration time to act?'" He quotes a letter he had received from "a white brother in Texas": "All Christians know that the colored people will receive equal rights eventually, but it is possible that you are in too great a religious hurry. . . . The teachings of Christ take time to come to earth." In face of such "a tragic misconception of time," "a mythical concept of time," it is obviously hard for King, the defendant, to restrain his exasperation and abide by his earlier pledge of "patient and reasonable terms." But he tries. "Actually," he explains, "time itself is neutral." He could as well have called it an adiaphoron. Time "can be used either destructively or constructively."

Yet what King is likewise compelled to say, as a confessor he is, is that whereas time may be "neutral" in "itself," in historic fact it is not neutral or adiaphoral. Certainly not now it isn't, in this "time for confessing." What makes white moderates' notion of time so "strangely irrational" is that they seem to suppose "that there is something in the very flow of time that will inevitably cure all ill." They forget the hard truth "that the people of ill will have used time more effectively than have the people of good will." "Frankly," says King, "I have yet to engage in a direct-action campaign that

was 'well-timed' in the view of those who [themselves] have not suffered
. . . segregation." Their favorite word "'Wait' has almost always meant
'Never.'" The white moderate "who constantly advises the Negro to wait
for 'a more convenient season'" is really a paternalist who "believes he can
set the timetable for another man's freedom." Notice, this is the discourse
of confessorhood. When some factor which might otherwise be neutral, in
this case the factor of timing, is exploited by the authorities to neutralize
the gospel, confessors must expose that illusory neutrality, opposing it in
decidedly non-neutral, unconditional terms.

That puts a strain, of course, on King's "patient and reasonable
terms." It is the strain between being a defendant trying reasonably to justify his offense and yet justifying it by a "timetable" which only he and his
fellow defendants, not their accusers, are able to grasp. "A time for confessing" demands of its confessors such an absolute judgment about that historic moment, repudiating every moderating effort to relativize it, that
they are doomed to appear perilously cocksure, especially in the eyes of
traditionally gradualist liberals. That is why King's "Letter" can sustain the
posture of the defendant, the patiently answerable confessor, through only
the first half of the document. By the second half he has reverted to the ag-
gressive role of the plaintiff. Yet it is noteworthy that also that part of the
letter he still designates, mock-apologetically, as a "confession." As if he is
still confessing some failing of his own, the failing however now being his
"disappointment" with his clergy critics.

But that, too, is the burden of the confessor, to have to announce
with embarrassing certitude amidst the relativities of history and the tem-
porizing of the moderates that, whatever appearances to the contrary,
"now is the time." The language again is Pauline (2 Cor. 6:2), and for good
measure King cites it twice in close succession, "Now is the time." Paul's
word *kairos* King has learned from Tillich, on whom he had written his
doctoral dissertation. As with Paul (and Paul Tillich), there is no slightest
suggestion on King's part that this decisive, non-negotiable *kairos* — what
Walter Benjamin had called *Jetztzeit,* "Now-time" — was a timetable humanly devised.[2] On the contrary, "the American Negro . . . [along] with his

---

2. Martin Luther King Jr., "Letter from Birmingham Jail," in *Why We Can't Wait*
(New York: New American Library, 1963, 1964), 86, 79. Cf. Walter Benjamin, *Selected Writ-*
ings, vol. 4, trans. Edmund Jephcott et al., ed. Howard Eiland anad Michael W. Jennings
(Cambridge, Mass.: Harvard University Press, 2003), 395.

black brothers of Africa and his brown and yellow brothers of Asia, South America and the Caribbean," "has been caught up by the *Zeitgeist*."[3] (In just the three years before, 1960-1962, sixteen African and Caribbean countries had won independence.)

"Something within the American Negro has reminded him of his birthright of freedom, and something without has reminded him that it can be gained." King's reference to *Zeitgeist* recalls Luther's similar metaphor of the gospel as *Platzregen*: because the gospel like a local shower never tarries with one country for long, it has to be heeded while there is still time. So while the gospel's timetable is by no means ours to set, it is only "through the tireless efforts of men willing to be [as also Paul and Luther had called them] co-workers with God" that the "time for confessing" that gospel comes true.

My contention has been that the "civil rights movement" among black churches exemplifies a particular theological characteristic of also another kind of movement, a confessing movement. Witness King's "Letter." Namely, when some relatively tolerable restriction like geographical boundaries or chronological postponement is so magnified as to muffle the Christian gospel, then the relative has by definition been absolutized and "the gospel of freedom," which alone deserves such ultimacy, must oppose these otherwise neutral adiaphora unconditionally. True, for King's clergy critics in Birmingham in 1963, spatial and temporal objections were probably the least of their concerns. They raised other, more substantive objections as well. But the pattern in King's response was always the same. At first he grants their objection in principle, then refutes it with a yes-but. In other words, the critics' critique was valid only provisionally, until it subverted "the gospel of freedom."

For example, as King hears his accusers, "You express a great deal of anxiety over our willingness to break laws," and he concedes that "this is certainly a legitimate concern."[4] That is equivalent to admitting that their concern might be allowable, an adiaphoron. But then in the sequel that runs on for two full pages, painstaking almost to the point of pedantry, King elaborates the difference between laws which are just and laws which are unjust, the latter requiring to be disobeyed. Or, a little later, he lists another of the critics' seemingly reasonable grievances. "In your statement

3. "Letter," 87.
4. "Letter," 82.

you assert that our actions, even though peaceful, must be condemned because they precipitate violence." And again King takes pains to justify why that grievance too had to be overridden. Similarly, he and his fellow demonstrators have been branded as "extremists," and once more almost tediously he explains that there is extremism and there is extremism, the defensible kind being represented by Paul's "I bear in my body the marks of the Lord Jesus" or by Martin Luther's "Here I stand, I cannot do otherwise, so help me God," or by the crucified Jesus Christ, "an extremist for love."[5]

II. The Encumbrance of Anti-Gospel

Yet when all is said and done, these high-sounding protestations from the opposition, no matter how adiaphoral they might have been ordinarily, are in fact merely ideological smokescreens for an underlying sinister plot which is not adiaphoral and, this is the point, never has been. What is this real but hidden enemy? Initially we might call it by such civil rights epithets as "segregation" or the withholding of "basic constitutional rights" or inequality "made legal," although that seriously under-diagnoses the threat. If that were the extent of it, the problem might be met by restoring the civil rights of black citizens legislatively and through the courts, as a means to such legal redress, by recourse to civil disobedience. To be sure, the remedy dare not be less than juridical though it most assuredly must be more. Nevertheless, even that much of a diagnosis, just at the level of civil law, already exposes that the current threat to the gospel is more invidious by far than one of adiaphora turned absolute. The very fact that adiaphora are being perverted to bridle something so redemptive as the gospel's freedom is itself a symptom of something graver which is perverse inherently. Legalized segregation, for instance, even if that were all that is at work, never was adiaphoral or neutral whether in the abstract or any other way.

Come to think of it, that is the same warning that was sounded by the Reformation document cited earlier, the Formula of Concord. Before it says anything about adiaphora turned bad, it begins by warning against practices which are really not and never have been adiaphora at all, although the authorities may pass them off as such. No, there simply are practices like

---

5. "Letter," 88.

this which are "forbidden by God, . . . basically contrary to the Word of God, even though they go under the name and guise of . . . adiaphora and are given a different color from their true one" (FC/SD X, 5). Isn't it noteworthy that this Article X of the Formula of Concord, which recent revisionist historians cite as a clue to early modern theories of revolution, might also anticipate modern theories of ideology criticism? In any event, this confessors' warning against apparently harmless practices which, for all their endorsement by the establishment, are inherently, and not just circumstantially, wrong, does find an echo in M. L. King's warning.

King too is saying that, beneath the adiaphora, beneath even the segregationist violations of civil law, which already are evil enough and in no sense morally neutral, there lurks a deeper malignancy which only metastasizes under the moderates' ideological appeals to "law and order." Call that spiritual disease by its full name, "prejudice" or "racism" or in King's (and Tillich's) preferred biblical idiom, "man's tragic separation, his awful estrangement, his terrible sinfulness" — in a word, "injustice."[6] Confessors may at first seem only to be blowing the whistle on adiaphora which happens to have been exaggerated into coercion and thus accidentally into fetters on the gospel. But confessors, once having probed that far, cannot stop there. The whole logic of their witness, their *martyria,* impels them to expose what more it is that provokes reasonable human beings in the first place so to manipulate adiaphora as to throttle their own liberating gospel. What is afoot is not just the hardening of honest differences of opinion into dogmatisms, but more basically a hostile, anti-freedom dogma, what Paul called "another gospel" and King called "injustice."

Are those two terms equivalent, King's term "injustice" and Paul's term, "another gospel"? Isn't King's term essentially ethical and Paul's term, shall we say, soteriological? Does King mean by "injustice," as Paul does by "another gospel," such an antithetical, inimical way of salvation, really a way of damnation, that the Christian gospel cannot even coexist with it? I suggest that that *is* what King means by "injustice"; at least sometimes he does. For Paul, granted, it is the genius of the gospel that it can absorb something so alien as "unrighteousness." But "another gospel"? Granted, it is precisely the "unrighteous" and the "ungodly" whom the gospel of Christ specializes in justifying. But what it evidently cannot justify or salvage is an opposing "gospel" like that of the Galatian circum-

6. "Letter," 82-83. For King's reference to "injustice," see especially pp. 77, 85, 94.

cisionists. Those two gospels, the one ultimately liberating and the other ultimately enslaving, are mutually and utterly exclusive.

My impression is that what King identifies as racist "injustice" has likewise worsened into that damnable and damning condition. Not only is it atrociously immoral, also it is or threatens to be a way of ultimate perdition. As such it is unforgivable in the sense that it simply cannot be lived with, even by King's gospel of nonviolent, suffering *agape*. So destructive is that "injustice" of faith and of "souls." It must altogether be displaced by "the gospel of freedom," one or the other, in a fight to the finish. This "injustice" not only is not an adiaphoron and not only immoral, but is also a dooming soteriology, for which American pluralism, and even the pluralism of Christian forgiveness, has no room.

If that seems to exaggerate King's meaning of "injustice," that he compounds its ethical meaning with a soteriological one, "social issues" with spiritual ones, then a reminder is in order because that was exactly what white moderate churchmen were accusing him of doing. Perceptively so. King recalls, "in the midst of a mighty struggle to rid our nation of racial and economic injustice, I have heard many ministers say: 'Those are social issues, with which the gospel has no real concern.'"[7] This is one charge against him, unlike all the others, for which King makes no apologies, even provisionally. Not only does he not deny the criticism, he runs with it and turns it back upon his accusers. This time he does not complain that his critics have misunderstood his movement. On this point they have understood well enough. What they have misunderstood, he claims, is the biblical gospel for which he and his colleagues must now suffer as witnesses. The separating of "social issues" from the "real concern" of the gospel betrays in these white churchmen "a strange unbiblical distinction between body and soul, between the sacred and the secular."[8]

Consider how the violation of people's "bodies" can in the same process violate their "souls" as well, how their so-called secular environment can influence their "sacred" self-identity either toward "despair" or toward "faith" so as to make or break them as persons. When "injustice" becomes that ultimately consequential it has acquired the soteriological proportions of "another gospel." For that "the gospel has no real concern"? The real antitheses in the current struggle between "injustice" and justice, or

7. "Letter," 90.
8. "Letter," 90

better, between "injustice" and "freedom," is "a degenerating sense of 'nobodiness'" versus "a sense of 'somebodiness,'" "the abyss of despair" versus "faith."[9] The latter, "faith," is soteriologically essential to "freedom," for King as it was for Paul. But that freedom of faith can be eroded by the alien message, the violent "plausibility structures" of economic and social degradation as devastatingly as by any preached gospel. Paul thought that even vegetarian Christians who ate meat against their own tender consciences because they were shamed into that by those who were stronger and freer in faith, were being made to sin. "He who has doubts is condemned, if he eats, because he does not act from faith; for whatever does not proceed from faith is sin" (Rom. 14:23).

How much more damaging, by comparison, must be that "degenerating sense of 'nobodiness'" for which King blames racial injustice.

> When you have seen hate-filled policemen curse, kick and even kill your black brothers and sisters; when you see the vast majority of your twenty million Negro brothers smothering in an airtight cage of poverty in the midst of an affluent society; when you suddenly find . . . your speech stammering as you seek to explain to your six-year-old daughter why . . . Funtown is closed to colored children, and see ominous clouds of inferiority beginning to form in her little mental sky, and . . . an unconscious bitterness toward white people,[10]

then surely it is understandable why three and a half centuries of such treatment could leave America's blacks "drained of self-respect and a sense of 'somebodiness,'" in short, of faith.[11] How in face of that overwhelming message to the contrary, King might have asked, could a people still be confident that they were righteous and worthy and pleasing to God? How, short of a miracle?

Is King saying that when people lose all confidence in their worth they have lost not only confidence, but worth? He says they are "plunged into the abyss of despair," a metaphor which is dominant in the spirituality of Calvin. For Calvin, however, the "abyss" was not only subjective; it was also trans-subjective, ontic. Was it that for King, too? Does racial injustice

---

9. "Letter," 82.
10. "Letter," 81.
11. "Letter," 86.

not only *do* injustice to those it violates? Might it also erode their own righteousness? That would be the ultimate violence. True, King insists on "the dignity and worth of human personality" as a given, and he charges that segregation gives the segregated a "sense of inferiority" which he labels "false."[12] Does he mean then that segregation does not really render its victims inferior, but only mistaken? Still, that kind of mistakenness is already a dreadful form of "inferiority." My guess is, at this point any distinction between subjective and objective would strike King as academic. With Luther he might shrug; for in the end, what real difference is there between feeling doomed and being doomed?

> When your first name becomes 'nigger', and your middle name becomes 'boy' (however old you are) and your last name becomes 'John', and your wife and mother are never given the respected title 'Mrs.'; when you are harried by day and haunted by night by the fact that you are a Negro, . . . never quite knowing what to expect next . . . ,[13]

what more needs to be said than that segregation, as "another gospel," effectually "distorts the soul and damages the personality"?

More than that, this "degenerating sense of 'nobodiness'" is not confined to the victims' souls. As one might expect from a confession like King's, which abhors the "un-Biblical distinction between body and soul, between the sacred and the secular," where "self-respect and a sense of 'somebodiness'" are "drained" away, the dispirited victims may act that out socially by becoming complacent and adjusting to segregation, or by actually profiting from it and exploiting their segregated fellows, or by yielding to "bitterness and hatred" and like "black nationalist groups" coming "perilously close to advocating violence." King stops short of saying what Luther said against Erasmus, that those who do not trust that they please God, thereby do not please God, for God wants us to trust we are God-pleasing. But then Luther was writing that against the oppressors, not the oppressed, whereas King in describing the despairing is describing the oppressed. Why should he make their despair worse than it is!

King writes more scathingly, as confessionally he must, when addressing the oppressors, in this case his critics, that white moderate clergy

---

12. "Letter," 85.
13. "Letter," 81.

of Birmingham. He laments "the South's beautiful churches with their lofty spires pointing heavenward." "Over and over," he recalls, "I have found myself asking: 'What kind of people worship here? Who is their God?'" King might have answered his question the way W. E. B. DuBois did, namely, that the god of the white segregationist was a different god altogether, that is to say, a false god.[14] That is no more blunt than Paul's curse against "another gospel." King's question, "Who is their God?" is just as searching for being left unanswered. If segregation gives the segregated a false sense of inferiority, to the segregator it gives "a false sense of superiority." And with that blasphemous soteriology comes "the judgment of God . . . upon the church as never before." It is not an otherworldly judgment, but one which is quite as earthy and public as segregation has been. The church under judgment "will lose its authenticity, forfeit the loyalty of millions [especially of "young people"], and be dismissed as an irrelevant social club with no meaning for the twentieth century."[15]

III. Encumbrance as Cross

As a proper *confessio,* King's "Letter from Birmingham Jail" defends his "gospel of freedom" not only against seemingly reasonable complaints, but also against the demonic force behind those shows of reasonableness, racism's counter-gospel. That soul-violating soteriology and not just its legalistic mandating of adiaphora is what encumbers the gospel. However, for confessors to expose the encumbrance is not yet to remove it. For them, the defendants, to turn the tables and criticize their critics — as King would say, to bring them to "crisis," the New Testament word for judgment *(krisis)* — is only the gospel's first step and by itself not a liberating step, not liberating for the encumbered and still less for their encumberers.

Especially so, when the formers' critique of the latter comes not in the mild form of a prisoner's epistle, but as massive, organized "nonviolent direct action . . . to foster such a tension that the community . . . is forced [sic!] to confront the issue."[16] That by itself is still "law" as Paul called it,

---

14. "Letter," 91. Cf. James H. Cone, *The Spirituals and the Blues* (San Francisco: Harper & Row, 1972), 12-13.

15. "Letter," 92.

16. "Letter," 79.

and serves only to anger the accused, exacerbating their sin and hardening them in it. King knew that "injustice must be exposed, with all the tension its exposure creates, to the light of human conscience and . . . national opinion before it can be cured."[17] He also knew that that is not yet the cure for either side.

The cure requires that the onus of inferiority be lifted from its victims. They are a confessor's first concern. But by whom will their burden be borne? By whom else except those whose superior force and violence are inflicting it? Yet the afflicters, who are anything but superior, are themselves unfree to assume the onerous weight of guilt. That is why they have shifted it to others. Still, they must be made to take it back, preferably in a way that will not crush them in turn. But in any case, take it back they must. If they cannot, then someone must help them, regardless of whether they have any right to be helped, if only to relieve their victims. As we know, the solution called "the gospel of freedom" proposes that the victims themselves shoulder the load — as King says, "bear the cross." They are to bear it not because they are forced to — that has been the case far too long — but only if they are free to; and not because the onus rightly is theirs but to return it to those violators whose fault it is, yet return it in a form that is bearable.

What makes the guilty truth bearable by the oppressors, if anything does, is that those whom they violate return that burden to them forgivingly. But return it they do. The oppressors, those presumptive superiors, are made to recognize that it is they who are diseased. (With King the medical metaphor is a favorite.) And it is their victims, the presumed inferiors who actually have suffered from the oppressors' disease, who now enable the real patients to assume responsibility, yet in a way that is mercifully not terminal. If there are deaths to be died, and there are, they will be died instead by the victims. Though they do not deserve that, they are so free to suffer even death as not to be overcome by it.

Their "way," as it is called, is not "submission," not "accepting domination," not "non-resistance." "Non-resistance merely reinforces the myth that one race is inherently inferior to another," which is exactly what the forgivers resist and refute. But then neither is their resistance retaliatory — not only not violent but also, which I think is something more, not even condemnatory. In that mortifying crush between resistance and non-

17. "Letter," 85.

retribution, a crush bearable only by the few who are free, lies the "remedy for injustice" at its roots. For that sacrificial cross-bearing is what "challenges the myth of inferiority." "Even the most reluctant are forced to recognize that no . . . people could choose and successfully pursue a course involving such extensive sacrifice, bravery and skill," and still be inferior. That is because the course they have chosen is "the more excellent way of love and nonviolent protest."[18]

It does not take much imagination to see that the rationale for this cruciform disencumbering of the gospel, freeing it from the anti-gospel of racial inferiority by the way of the cross, is Christological. Nor is it necessary, it seems to me, to defend that Christological attribution by pitting Jesus against Gandhi. The debt that Martin Luther King Jr. owed to Gandhi's *satyagraha* need not be minimized. Maybe the debt is not as extensive as, for example, John Ansbro claims, who notes that a sermon King heard on that subject "was so inspirational that he read several books on Gandhi." On the other hand, Gandhi's influence may not have been as slight as Taylor Branch suggests (who favors the "prime influence" of Reinhold Niebuhr) noting that, of the books on Gandhi which King bought, "he never bothered to name or describe any of them." It may even be, as Lerone Bennett Jr. claims, that as a black youngster in the South and the son of a forceful father, "Long before King heard of Gandhi or India, he had mastered the technique of resisting by apparent submission." Perhaps. But for our purpose the Christological premise of King's public *confessio* can be considered apart from, as another author has called them, "the minutiae of King's life."

In King's public testimony, Gandhism is assimilated to Christianity, not vice versa, the way means are assimilated to ends, or method to goal. This, despite the fact that in their Indian origins *satyagraha* (truth telling) and *ahimsa* (nonviolence) were themselves goal as well as means. Nevertheless, as King explained the Montgomery Boycott in *Stride Toward Freedom*,[19] Christ had furnished the spirit and Gandhi the method. It is possible to fake the method without Christ, a temptation which increasingly plagued King's own movement. Even Bull Connor's police in Birmingham, like Chief of Police Pritchett in Albany, could imitate a version of nonvio-

18. "Letter," 87.

19. Martin Luther King Jr., *Stride Toward Freedom: The Montgomery Story* (New York: Harper and Brothers, 1958).

lence for the diametrically opposite end, "to preserve the evil system of segregation," and in the process hoodwink Birmingham's white moderate clergy. Regardless, freedom is sure to come to America's blacks through nonviolence or violence, with or without benefit of clergy and the Christian church, simply because God wills it. But any freedom gained that way, without the church, will be a divine judgment upon the church. That Word of judgment, notice, King derived not from Gandhism but from biblical Christianity and its Christ.

On the affirmative side, it is the very *linkage* between a "method" which is non-retaliatory and the "goal" of God's freeing forgiveness in Christ to which King's movement was committed uncompromisingly. At least at that time and place it was, if in fact that was "a time for confessing." To academic theology, which as King complained always prefers to contemplate both sides of an issue, it may seem arbitrary to tie "the gospel of freedom" to one particular praxis, an extra-Christian praxis at that. Indeed, isn't that re-encumbering the gospel, the very sin against which confessors inveigh?

So it must have seemed also in Galatia when Paul insisted upon the Gentile practice of non-circumcision as a non-negotiable and did so in the name of Christ "for freedom," or when the Formula of Concord insisted that at that historic moment non-cooperation was exclusively what Christian freedom entailed. Similarly, King, not one given to understatement, could tell *Christian Century*, "It is ironic, yet inescapably true that the greatest Christian of the modern world [namely, Gandhi] was a man who never embraced Christianity."[20] Or somewhat more modestly, "Christ showed us the way and Gandhi showed us it could work." When it worked, King said, it was a "witness" (in Greek *martyria*) which "preserved the true meaning of the gospel in these troubled times." That is, "in these troubled times" of institutionalized violence the Gandhian method worked, as Paul put it, "for the truth of the gospel."

If the church is itself in league with the anti-gospel of violence and racial injustice and thus will incur judgment, how could King and his Southern Christian Leadership Conference continue to cast their lot with that church? The truth is, they did. They did not indulge the luxury of keeping their motor running for a quick escape from the church's impend-

20. Cf. Martin Luther King Jr., "Pilgrimage to Nonviolence," *Christian Century* 77 (April 13, 1960): 139-41.

ing doom. Not that that wasn't a temptation, to retreat into "the inner spiritual church, the church within the church." Instead, as King's "Letter" says of the whole church, "I see the church as the body of Christ, . . . blemished and scarred [though] that body" is. "Yes, I love the church." What befalls the church may be, from the lofty vantage of a prophet, "the judgment of God," but from the lowly vantage of a fellow-sinner who stays to share that fate in the same one Body as one of the "we," judgment is modulated into mere "disappointment" and "tears of love."

Stanley Levison and Bayard Rustin, King's close associates who taught him much about Gandhian nonviolence, had proposed calling the new organization "Southern Leadership Conference," but King insisted on identifying it with the churches as "Southern Christian Leadership Conference." I gather the reason was more than strategic. Confessionally, wasn't it Christological? "Letter" explains how "the way of nonviolence became an integral part of our struggle," namely, "through the influence of the Negro church." But the Negro church, too, is part of the same body of Christ. If the church with all its scars and blemishes is Christ's body, then presumably that is where he with his members, the victims, transacts the exchange with the oppressors, also his members. There the violated disarm the violent with Christ's forgiveness and free them too to share the cross. King refers to that communion as the "Brotherhood," including in it himself together with the Birmingham clergy who oppose him.

That the encumbrance King's movement was called to bear was identified by him with the cross of Christ, is a matter of public record. David Garrow's monumental study of King and the S.C.L.C., entitled *Bearing the Cross,* has now documented that identification more publicly still.[21] King was not ashamed of, though he also did not flaunt, his experience in the kitchen of his Montgomery parsonage on that January night in 1956. He was then, as he would more and more frequently be, in the abyss of despair. It was then that "I heard the voice of Jesus saying still to fight on. He promised never to leave me, never to leave me alone. No never alone. No never alone. He promised never to leave me, never to leave me alone."[22]

21. David Garrow, *Bearing the Cross: Martin Luther King, Jr., and the Southern Christian Leadership Conference* (New York: William Morrow and Company, 1986).

22. Garrow, *Bearing the Cross,* 58. Cf. also King's sermon "Unfulfilled Dreams" in *A Knock at Midnight: Inspiration from the Great Sermons of Reverend Martin Luther King, Jr.,* ed. Clayborne Carson and Peter Holloran (New York: IPM/Warner, 1998).

Because of the obvious privacy of this experience, it might seem to hold little significance as a public *confessio,* at least for those in the "magisterial" traditions of the church. True, Garrow might have added to his account, as one writer has since reminded him, that the promise which King was hearing from Christ privately was really quite public and widely familiar, "a nearly exact quotation from the old hymn, 'Never Alone.'" That does have the effect of realigning the experience with "the public proclamation of the Word."

But if there is one circumstance especially which renders King's personal identification with Christ, or Christ's with him, pertinent as public *martyria,* it is King's death. That was ever so public, and the sort for which people everywhere sought a meaning. Within the movement, surely, there was never any secret about the meaning. "When I took up the cross," King reminded his staff in 1967, "I recognized its meaning." And what was that? "The cross is something that you bear, and ultimately that you die on." One year later that was openly demonstrated.

As for demonstrations, I understand that in Baptist theology the term is sometimes used for what other churches call sacraments. Baptism, for instance, is a "demonstration." In Birmingham in 1963 when King wrote his "Letter" from jail, the demonstration which had gotten him and his colleagues arrested, carried its own sacramental symbolism, distinctly Christological, more in fact than the planners had bargained for. King later recalled the preparations for that demonstration. "We decided that Good Friday, because of its symbolic significance, would be the day that Ralph Abernathy and I would present our bodies as personal witnesses in this crusade." But as Good Friday arrived, plans for the demonstration were on the verge of collapse, bail money was gone, the leaders "were overwhelmed by a feeling of hopelessness."

Still, the demonstration had to go on, as a sheer "faith act." King landed in jail, in fact in solitary confinement. "Having no contact of any kind, I was besieged with worry. How was the movement faring?" "You will never know the meaning of utter darkness until you have lain in such a dungeon. . . . There was more to the blackness than a phenomenon conjured up by a worried mind. Whatever the cause, the fact remained that I could not see the light." King had not reckoned with such a literal reenactment of Black Friday, or the *descensus ad infernum.*

But then came Easter, and Easter Monday, and with that came word from the outside, "Harry Belafonte has been able to raise fifty thousand dollars for bail bonds."[23] The movement was intact. Reminiscent of his "kitchen experience," King suddenly realized, "I had never been truly in solitary confinement; God's companionship does not stop at the door of a jail cell." And evidently not even at the cross, if Good Friday is followed by Easter. For King and his colleagues the Good Friday-Easter connection was crucial to the Birmingham "demonstration." Yet they were not only the agents of that demonstration, but also its recipients. King had reminded an audience in Chicago a few months earlier, "The cross we bear precedes the crown we wear."[24] "The gospel of freedom's" encumbrance, even the encumbrance of the cross, is not the last word; freedom is, considering Who the disencumberer is.

23. The words spoken to King by his attorney Clarence Jones on Easter Monday after King's weekend in the Birmingham jail. Cf. Clayborne Carson, ed., *The Autobiography of Martin Luther King, Jr.* (New York: IPM/Warner, 2001), Chapter 18, "Letter from Birmingham Jail."

24. At the Religion and Race in Chicago Conference in 1963.

CHAPTER 4

"Confession" against Apartheid: When Faith Is Ethos

I. Confessing: Faith as Ethos

The policy in Southern Africa which forced separate development of the races (apartheid), particularly since that is being powered by a coalition of religious as well as secular authorities, evoked from Christians — blacks and Coloreds but also some whites — a mounting counter-witness *(confessio)* to the effect that apartheid is not only an ethical issue but a "confessional" one as well, an ecclesial case of "heresy."[1]

If apartheid is already discredited utterly by reason of its injustice, its sinfulness, its violation of the divine law, what is gained by adding that it is also a "heretical" violation of the Christian "gospel," a *casus confessionis* — except perhaps to turn up the volume of ethical protest by recourse to church Latin? If that is all, isn't the eventual effect quite the opposite, obscuring apartheid's sheer moral scandal, also its martyrdoms? The challenge is to define "confessing" meta-ethically and yet not sub-ethically.

There were those confessors in Southern Africa — that is, South Africa and Namibia (South-West Africa) — who were Lutheran and Reformed whose Reformation heritage might dispose them to "confessional" terminology, but there were also others — Anglicans, Methodists, Roman Catholics — who without those terms nevertheless were acting

---

1. Desmond D. Tutu, *The Divine Intention* (Braamfontein: SACC Publication, 1982), 3.

out the operational, martyrological equivalent of confessing. That suggests that Christian confessing depends not only on definition but also on a peculiar sort of action — meta-ethical, yes, but enfleshed in a distinctive ethos, *praxis* as well as *theoria.*

Paul Ricoeur's "hermeneutics of testimony" speaks of "the profound unity between testimony about facts and events, and the testimony about meaning and truth."[2] The unity of facts-and-meaning in "testimony" corresponds to what we are describing as a unity of faith-and-ethos in *confessio.* But then "confessional" theology probably should not mean — as I take H. Richard Niebuhr and David Tracy to mean by it — a merely private, in-group theology of a particular faith-community, inaccessible to public scrutiny. Not if confessing has at least one foot in public fact and ethos.

Designating a distinctive faith-ethos as *confessio* has its precedents, for instance, in the Confessing Church under Nazism and, before that, in the "confessions" of the Reformation and, as those confessors in turn remembered, in the earliest crises of the New Testament communities. Out of the tradition of the Confessio Augustana came the technical term, "a time for confessing" *(tempus confessionis),* for identifying just such kairological moments, fateful times of last resort. "Times for confessing," we might generalize, are those special, embattled occasions when Christians have had to disobey secular authority, including the church's own, in order to testify that for the integrity of the church the gospel of Christ is authority enough.

Under this general definition of *confessio* we might specify half a dozen sub-features. Notice, while each of these six characteristics presents a definitional, logical component of what confession *means,* it simultaneously implies something actionable, consequential — what confessing *does.* And what it does is integral to what it means.

First, confessing, in the present sense, is not just any declaration of one's faith. It is *martyria,* in an adversary situation, implying that the confessors — indeed, the whole church — are at that moment on a witness stand *(in statu confessionis)* before a superior critical tribunal, to all appearances divinely ordained, from whose authority the witnesses must nevertheless dissent — as Fackenheim says of the Holocaust martyrs, for

---

2. Paul Ricoeur, "The Hermeneutics of Testimony," in *Essays on Biblical Interpretation* (Philadelphia: Fortress Press, 1980), pp. 119-54.

God against God.[3] No wonder Christians pray (on rather high recommendation), "Save us from the time of trial," the ultimate jeopardy being not only the loss of one's reputation or of one's life, but also blasphemy.

Second, in such a "time for confessing" what the *martyres* seem most to be protesting against is that the authorities (civil and/or ecclesiastical) have added this or that condition to the gospel — for instance, circumcision or, in Southern Africa, apartheid. They do so perhaps with the well-meaning intention of thus "putting some teeth" in the gospel, or of reinforcing it, or even of safeguarding it, but with the disastrous result that, by this gratuitous addition, the gospel is subverted. Confessing is protesting against gospel-plus.

Third, the "time for confessing" is also ecumenical in nature, inviting the whole church to join on the witness stand. With this feature, too, what faith confesses begins to come true in practice. In the act of confessing that Christians are one, apartheid to the contrary notwithstanding, their oneness thereby proceeds to materialize. This will be the primary focus in the second part of this chapter.

Fourth, to confess, as we are using that term, means also to oppose authority, or rather a confusion of authorities: "secular" with "spiritual," and vice versa. The confessional objection to secular authority is not that it operates by appeal to self-interest (a necessity in this "old aeon," *saeculum*), or that it is not God's (it is), or even that it perpetuates moral evil like apartheid (one need not be Christian to see that); but rather that, in "times for confessing," secular authority displaces the authority of Christ, who effects goodness and human worth by quite scandalously non-secular means, his own unjust martyrdom, freely given for the undeserving. When the church loses that, its sole distinguishing authority, it will have to fall back upon (possibly uncredentialed) confessors who intervene and seize the microphone from the church's established, unevangelical authorities.

Fifth, this confessional protest has a strongly liberationist ring to it, hence an ethical ring, though the intention is as much soteriological as ethical. Since secular-religious authority is a legitimation and plausibility structure on which people depend for their worth, it can rival the gospel as a value-ascriptive authority and then, as with apartheid, becomes the enslavement which must be opposed by the freedom of the gospel. Con-

3. Emil Fackenheim, *God's Presence in History: Jewish Affirmations and Philosophical Reflections* (New York: Jason Aronson, 1997).

fessing means appealing for and to the oppressed, the disvalued, for their social emancipation, yes, but finally for their very salvation.

Sixth, that sort of confession is characterized, we might say, by an ambiguous certitude. Not the least of its ambiguities are the confessors themselves, who seem acutely aware that they too do not have clean hands and that even their protest is compromised morally by their own mixed motives. All of which, however, only intensifies the ironic certainty that their witness must have been authorized then by One who casts his lot with sinners — a test which, by contrast, the elitist authority of apartheid fails.

To summarize, confessing means a) an ultimate-risk *martyria;* b) protesting against encumbrances upon the gospel; c) uniting the church in an ecumenical movement; d) recombining secular and spiritual authority; e) liberating the disvalued; and f) ambiguous certitude.

Again, while all of these features belong to a Christian "time for confessing," we will especially turn our focus to the Christian confessing against apartheid on the feature of confessing as ecumenical, as church-uniting.

II. Confessing as Ecumenical

The ecumenism of the confessors in Southern Africa consists first of all not in the consensus they had won from international ecumenical organizations like the World Council of Churches, Lutheran World Federation, and World Alliance of Reformed Churches; and not even in the inter-denominational cooperatives they had formed with one another locally and regionally, like the Christian Institute, the South African Council of Churches, or the Council of Churches of Namibia.

Prior to those extramural associations, logically prior and most often chronologically prior, are the efforts the confessors made at union with those in their own denominational fellowships from whom they are most immediately divided by apartheid — their white fellow-Reformed, for instance. Usually it has been only when those intra-denominational attempts at union have failed that recourse has been taken to wider ecumenical fellowships for outside help.

Whatever outside assistance there is has had as its announced objective not to substitute external ecumenism for internal (though that has been charged), but rather to encourage locals to gather in face-to-face, as "Word-and-sacraments" congregations irrespective of race, but still respective of common doctrinal and liturgical and denominational traditions — for instance, Namibian white Lutherans with Namibian black Lutherans.

That is the whole ecumenical point of confessing. Apartheid betrays how "another gospel" divides Christians: namely, it divides them from one another only by dividing them all from a third reality, from their joint hearing of the gospel of Christ and their joint reception of his sacraments.

The task is to counter this apartness at the point of origin — the apartness, once more, not only of whites from blacks and Coloreds, but of all of them, on one hand, from the single, unifying message of Christ, on the other. When those in the fellowship who have been authorized to speak this message of unity refuse, being themselves the separators, all that is left is for it to be spoken by the separated, the confessors, but directly to the separators. Thus the mutual speaking and hearing of the gospel of unity is reinstated across the divide.

There is a risk. The gospel of unity which the confessors call over to their separators comes across as a gospel of stern prophetic reproof, which it also is. If that reproof, even though it comes from within the same family, is heard by pro-apartheid Christians through their alien filter of "another gospel," then all they can hear is rebellion and schism. And it is the confessors they blame as separatistic and not ecumenical at all.

Nor did it escape the notice of pro-apartheid Christians that the confessors more and more have turned for support — moral and financial support and especially the support of world-Christian opinion — to ecumenical agencies outside the immediate denominational connections. This is construed as evidence of the confessors' playing to the grandstand, as insincerity, and as exacerbating local disunities.

Add to that also that the international ecumenical organizations came under the suspicion of self-aggrandizement by involving themselves in local and regional church disputes, especially morally popular ones like apartheid. They incurred the criticism from their member churches, themselves vehemently anti-apartheid, that those umbrella organizations, which were intended to be only voluntary associations of churches, had begun to arrogate to themselves the prerogatives of "super-churches."

Back home in Africa, those white advocates of apartheid who endeavored to turn the tables on the confessors and made them out instead to be the real instigators of division, claimed to find the most incriminating evidence for their accusation in another, more recent development. These whites, for their persistent practice of apartheid, were made the targets of disciplinary action by several monitoring ecumenical organizations. The World Alliance of Reformed Churches suspended them from membership, as did others; and the Lutheran World Federation threatened as much.

These church-like sanctions and warnings from Geneva and Ottawa and other ecumenical centers all came, of course, in response to appeals from aggrieved African sisters and brothers, the confessors. What further need, the apartheid churches are saying, have they of witnesses: at bottom, it really is and all along has been the confessors who are the separatists. In fact, some of the newly outcast white churches have exulted that the exclusion they now suffer serves only to drive them closer to one another, as if to signal where the real Christian solidarity, the solidarity of martyrdom, is thriving in Africa.

In view of this apparent reversal of roles — the confessors now as divisive, the separatists as unifying — the claim that Christian *confessio* is ecumenical begins to lose credence, or at least evidence. However, though it is true that the confessors' efforts to overcome apartheid in their firsthand denominational communities provoked a pseudo-ecumenical backlash on the part of white Christian separatists, even that disappointing reaction can work to dramatize the *confessio's* inherent ecumenism.

To accomplish that there is no need to romanticize the confessors. Their white critics' charges — about the confessors' grandstanding, their ulterior wishes for violence and vengeance, the ecumenical movement's exploiting its advocacy role to feather its own nest — none of that need be denied out of hand, as the confessors sometimes are the first to admit. (Their *confessio* includes confession also in another sense, of their own guilt.)

However, there is in their white opponents' allegations an at least implicit and more serious charge. And that is that the confessors, in their theological denunciation of apartheid, are presuming to speak for the whole church of Christ, by implication for Christ himself, and that that presumption is arrogant and unfounded, seeing that the confessors obviously do not speak for most white Christians of Southern Africa.

Oddly, it is that very disavowal by pro-apartheid Christians, disavowing that the confessors speak for the one church since they do not speak for them, which all the more incites other Christians of the world to come down off the bleachers and to be numbered with the confessors. The ecclesiastical claims of apartheid, the more they contest the confessors' ecumenism, become the more self-refuting in fact by virtue of the contrary evidence they provoke from an expanding circle of Christian witnesses.

And the fact that ecumenical agencies and councils, in order to join the confessors' witness, resort to stretching the letter of the law in their own constitutions, while that may be legally inexcusable, may also say something else: confessing, while usually it exhausts every possibility to be law-abiding, cannot forever be bound by what is legal, perhaps not even when the legalities seem to have been divinely ordained.

Yet even though the confessors' testimony does attract a host of fellow-witnesses, that merely human consensus, no matter how wide-spread, is still not proof that they speak for the one Body of Christ, unless they can show that they speak for the Body's Head. That mark of unity may be harder to manifest. On the other hand, it isn't as though their Christ is inaccessible altogether. He is not a wax nose to be twisted into just any shape. He did say this and not that, and he had a history. After all, the testimony, as Ricoeur reminds us, is "to an incarnate person."[4]

The claim to speak for the church's Lord, hence for his church, is not one from which African confessors retreated. Invoking Christ as their source, of course through his biblical reflection in apostles and evangelists, is the most usual theological mode of the confessors' testimony against apartheid. True, that is the approach also of their opponents, who if anything were more biblicistic, and Christologically more cautious. Yet mightn't that subtle difference be telltale?

Regardless of whether it is telltale, the confessors' christic identification is not limited to exegetical arguments from the Christ of Scripture but appears also in other, more demonstrative forms. Consider, for instance, their Christlike refusal to be parted from their enemies, whether or not sincerely, just syntactically. I mean, when the white persecutors are the grammatical objects of the *confessio*, they are not only that, objects in the third-person — else *confessio* would degenerate into gossip — but sooner or later they are addressed directly as dialogical subjects. Or when the *confessio* bristles with prophetic indignation, or even when it suspends the white separatists from the fellowship, in the last analysis it does even that,

4. Ricoeur, "Hermeneutics of Testimony."

and does it explicitly, so that the adversary might be regained. That does smack of ecumenism.

That such Christlike witness can be unifying is best evidenced, no doubt, when those white separatists who once were afar off draw near and become *martyres* themselves, like C. F. Beyers Naudé or Frikkie Conradie or numberless unsung white Christians.[5] But what of those white hold-outs, and their name is legion, who zealously insisted on remaining apart and always will, refuting the *confessio's* power to unify? Not quite. Also they, especially they, appear in the testimony of one black bishop of Soweto who mourns them, his persecutors, in view of the almost certain bloodbath which he feared awaited them. In the end, trapped in their apartheid churches, they too will learn martyrdom — yet no longer from Christ, but by then from a very different agent of God — some violent, unsparing "Cyrus." With those impenitent whites as well, this black confessor identifies.

---

5. Cf. *The Trial of Beyers Naudé: Christian Witness and the Rule of Law,* ed. International Commission of Jurists, Geneva (London: Search Press, 1975).

CHAPTER 5

Bonhoeffer's "Battle(s) for Christendom": His "Responsible Interpretation" of Barmen

It is a "time for confessing," the Formula of Concord calls it, whenever the church is in danger of abdicating its unique authority to an overreaching secular authority. The secular pretender may be the state or the people as a whole or the secular power of the ecclesiastical institution itself or, most likely, all of these together. Against these usurpers the church's confessors must testify, even when the state is immensely popular as under Hitler, even when the people are a defeated and voiceless nationality as the Germans were then, even when the church's own leadership sides with this yearning ethnic folk and their revolutionary government. Against these encroaching secular powers the confessing church must testify, not in order to nullify secular authority, but in order rather to restore the church to its own distinctive priorities, where the authority of Christ's gospel is supreme and where secular authority, even if that also is Christ's, is strictly subordinate.

In our time the confessional statement most noted for its re-prioritizing of authorities is the Barmen Declaration of 1934. And by now one of the most visible witnesses for the Declaration is Dietrich Bonhoeffer. That seems at first an unlikely role for him. For he did not attend the synod which issued the Declaration. In fact he seems not to have been invited. Also, he more and more identified with only one wing of the Barmen movement, the so-called "Dahlemites," and even with them, more and more as their critic. Yet for all his increasing exclusiveness (and excludedness), Bonhoeffer does provide what the Barmen Declaration explicitly acknowledged it still needed, a "responsible interpretation" of it. Indeed, his version of a *verantwortliche Interpretation* addresses Barmen's single most contested issue, the re-prioritizing of churchly and civil authorities.

Bonhoeffer's interpretation, by his life no less than by his writings, did have the effect of dramatizing the Barmen Declaration's exclusiveness — shall we say, its "Law"? The Declaration's opening thesis announces, "Jesus Christ . . . is the one Word of God which we have to hear, . . . trust and obey in life and in death," such that any other "source of [church] proclamation . . . besides this one Word of God," "we reject . . . as false doctrine."[1] Bonhoeffer became notorious for his rejecting not only "doctrine," but the doctrine's adherents — church people. If one of the chief features of God's "secular" authority is the power to pronounce judgment, critically, and if need be excludingly, then Bonhoeffer exemplifies how the church, not only the state, employs this authority, too.

Still, in Bonhoeffer's Lutheran tradition God's exclusivist Word, the "Law," is meant to be only "penultimate," not "ultimate." Law is that critical authority by which God governs the "old" secular order, where people are to expect fairness, what is their due, but merely that. I say "merely," for fairness cuts both ways. Ultimately, no sinner can stand that much fairness. By contrast, God's ultimate authority is the "gospel," God's cruciform mercy in Christ through the church, which is not exclusive but indiscriminately inclusive. It is with this gospel inclusivity that Bonhoeffer construed Barmen's second thesis, that "Jesus Christ is the assurance of the forgiveness of all our sins, so . . . also God's mighty claim upon our whole life,"[2] embracing even the most secular of secular authorities: compromisers, oath-breakers, deceivers, professional killers. Indeed, Bonhoeffer became one with them, guilt and all — guilt, notice, before God — yet all the while as an agent in Christ's atoning. And for whom? For the severely excluded, the German people. The church of Christ alone has authority for such scandalous, atoning inclusivity.

Thus, those who are excluded from the church and from God are not the sinners, as such, but rather those who persist in imposing God's secular, legal authority as ultimate, thereby rendering both kinds of authority, both secular and churchly, impossible. Bonhoeffer attacked this inverting

1. Cf. Klaus Scholder, *The Churches and the Third Reich,* vol. 2, *The Year of Disillusionment: 1934, Barmen and Rome* (Philadelphia: Fortress Press, 1988), 149.

2. Scholder, *Churches and the Third Reich,* 2:151.

of authorities, this ecclesiastical majoring in minors, not only in the "German Christians" but also in current Lutheran distortions of Luther's theology of "two kingdoms" and, more and more, in what he branded as "Enthusiasm" and "ecclesiastical theocracy" in his own Confessing Church, and classically in American Protestantism. For Bonhoeffer there is between God's two authorities an undeniable two-ness, which theocrats suppress, as well as an essential inseparability — a "polemical unity," but only through shared suffering. Bonhoeffer's "responsible interpretation" of Barmen was his effort, intentionally, to recapture for his times Luther's theology of "two kingdoms." But more on Bonhoeffer later. First, a look at the beginnings in Barmen.

I. From Barmen to Dahlem: A Narrowing

The "Theological Declaration on the Present Situation of the German Evangelical Church [DEK]" was a protest by an ad hoc group within DEK. Calling itself a "Confessional Synod," the group protested the takeover of DEK by that church body's powerful new majority, the revolutionary, pro-Nazi "German Christians." This impromptu synod was reacting against the new "German Christian" church leaders, at least in part, because of their National Socialist ideology of Germanic race and space, "blood and soil." That was at the time the popular new program for ethnic-national liberation.

Yet at least as offensive as the "German Christians'" "false doctrine" was their attempt to nationalize DEK, a voluntary federation of church bodies, into a single Reich church. This national church was to be controlled by the state under a Reich bishop appointed by Hitler. That forcible assimilation *(Gleichschaltung)* under the national government threatened DEK's traditionally autonomous territorial churches and church confessions (Lutheran, Reformed, and United), not to mention the Roman Catholic Church.

The mixture of motives behind the Barmen Declaration, motives of doctrine but also of governance, was so complex and volatile that the confessors themselves could not agree on what their Declaration entailed practically. Eventually they so differed from one another on the issue of governance, specifically on how the church's governance relates to the state's, that that difference itself assumed the force of doctrinal division among them. That their common foe, the "German Christians," were *mis-*prioritizing their authorities, the secular over the spiritual, the confessors were well enough agreed. That the most immediate threat therefore was to the authority of the *churches,* on that point too the confessors were united — united, notice, not against the National Socialist state as such, but against the state's lackeys in the church, the "German Christians." In fact the confessors seemed agreed even on this, that the "German Christians'" politicizing of the church's authority, the gospel of Christ, thereby violated DEK's own constitution. And since that constitution had been incorporated under civil law, the "German Christians" were thus at odds with the civil government itself.

However, beyond the Barmen confessors' common front against the inner-church threat of the "German Christians" there was far less consensus, indeed there was deepening disagreement, on a practical alternative for relating ecclesial authority to civil. The split between the confessors became increasingly public in the months following Barmen as they had to contend less and less with the inept "German Christians" and more and more directly with a hostile state. Remember, that state enjoyed broad support among the people *(Volk)* and in the people's churches *(Volkskirchen).* Already at the time of Barmen, Bonhoeffer, writing from his self-imposed "exile" in a London pastorate, ventured a prediction. He foresaw that the church conflict *(Kirchenkampf)* which was then festering, a largely internal church-political conflict, would turn out in the long run to have been merely a "preliminary skirmish" *(Vorgeplänkel)* compared to the "second," really decisive "battle for Christendom" *(Kampf um das Christentum)* which still lay ahead.

Just how preliminary Barmen was, how insufficient for the main battle ahead, how internally undecided on the key issue of spiritual and secular authority, becomes apparent only by hindsight. The text of the Declaration, taken by itself, looks ever so confessionally solid and forthright, especially in its singular witness to Christ. Its six theses, each with a scriptural lead-in and with a corresponding antithesis, are lean and to the point, as is the important preamble. And doesn't that preamble stress that "as members of Lutheran, Reformed and United churches we may and must speak with one voice in this matter"? Isn't it also true, as all popular histories of Barmen record, that in the end the synod's almost 140 delegates from all over Protestant Germany adopted the final revision of the Declaration unanimously?

Given this highly publicized unanimity, Barmen's advocates have long seemed reluctant to acknowledge the stormy inter-confessional differences which churned just beneath its surface. And given that defensiveness, the recent historical revisionism which is now setting the record straight must sound to traditional interpreters like sour grapes, like a hermeneutics of suspicion bent on exposing family secrets. This reactionary *non sequitur*, that dissent is inadmissible except as schism, is a fallacy which Bonhoeffer himself tried to correct, unsuccessfully.

Does it really detract from the Barmen Declaration that Karl Barth's boast, that he had drafted it virtually alone with no help from the Lutherans on the drafting committee, now turns out to be a gross oversimplification of Barmen's prehistory? If even the late Klaus Scholder, one of the most eminent of *Kirchenkampf* historians, could have been swayed by Barth's claim, isn't it a tribute to Scholder's students that they rescued his posthumous publication from that error, thanks to the latest documentary discoveries by Carsten Nicolaisen? The same discoveries reveal that Barth himself, at the last moment before the final draft went before the synod for its vote, consented to rewrite Thesis Five, on church and state, to include the crucial point insisted upon by the Bavarian Lutherans.[3]

Their point was, just as a totalitarian state must be condemned for arrogating to itself the function of a church, so must any church be condemned which takes to itself the function of a state. That broad indictment could apply not only to the "German Christians," but also to any Barmenites who might hope to coerce Lutherans into a new kind of Union church. (The majority of delegates at Barmen were from the Evangelical Church of the Old Prussian Union, one of the largest Protestant bodies in the world, a corporate giant with a history of state-enforced "Union" between Lutherans and Reformed.) The antithesis which the non-Union Bavarians insisted on adding to Thesis Five could apply also to those Barmenites (and Barthians) whom Bonhoeffer would later reproach as "ecclesiastical theocrats." In any case it surely does no harm to learn that Hans Asmussen, himself one of the Declaration's drafters and the one appointed to explain the text to the assembly, included this acknowledgement in his closing remarks, "In no small way are we indebted to the perseverance of our Bavarian brothers, who did not relent until this new formulation was put forward." Here the minutes record "spirited applause."

3. Cf. Scholder, *Churches and the Third Reich*, 2:152.

In fact, the record shows "applause" even for a Bavarian Lutheran whom Asmussen had not intended to commend, Werner Elert.[4] Not only was Elert not present at the synod, he soon became one of its sharpest critics, for a while even favoring a third front against both the "German Christians" and the "Unionists." Politically, he hoped for a church that could identify with the ethnic-political liberation of the people. He has been likened to a liberation theologian, a title which is anachronistic if apt. Theologically, his major complaint against the Barmen Declaration was not against its fifth thesis but against Thesis One — Barth's favorite — and Thesis Two: against the first because it restricts revelation to Christ and denies to the world any revealed law; against the second because it then compensates by reducing Christ to a new lawgiver.

As for the Declaration's Thesis Five, Elert was amused by how it now contradicts Thesis One: it seems to admit after all, though grudgingly, that beyond "Jesus Christ as the one Word of God," the secular political order is also from God. Elert's critique hardly endeared him to the Confessing Movement. Scholder calls him "prickly," the selfsame adjective that has been applied to Bonhoeffer. But it is significant that Asmussen's quoting of Elert before the Barmen assembly, obviously pejoratively, could nevertheless earn Elert a hand.

On the other hand, maybe the applause was meant to be *against* Elert. In any case, the evidence continues to show how unresolved were the synod's differences, particularly on the prickly issue of secular and spiritual authority. True, in the end the confessors did vote for the Declaration "with one voice." Even that, however, they did with a portentous proviso: that the Declaration be transmitted to the three different confessional bodies "for the purpose of providing responsible interpretations from their *respective confessional traditions*." Bonhoeffer's confessional tradition was Lutheran, but he was a Lutheran in the Church of the Old Prussian Union. That dual role would impair his credibility in both communions.

The proviso calling for separate "interpretations" does portend an infra-Barmen conflict. But that conflict was not only inter-confessional, Reformed versus Lutheran versus Union. No, the ensuing divisions within the "Confessing Church" *(Bekennende Kirche)*, as the confessional movement came to be called, stemmed also from another difference. The member churches represented at Barmen were each suffering quite different

4. Cf. Scholder, *Churches and the Third Reich,* 2:162.

fates back home at the hands of the "German Christians." The latters' take-over had succeeded in some territorial churches, for instance, those of the Old Prussian Union, more than in others, for instance, Bavaria and Württemberg, whose established Lutheran churches were successfully frustrating the "German Christian" takeover and so were still more or less "intact."

The "destroyed" churches, by contrast with the "intact" ones, were having to create emergency administrations and funding and networks of their own in defiance of their new "German Christian," state-supported overlords. Suddenly cut off from the traditional church-tax *(Kirchen-steuer)* for pastors' salaries, publication, and theological education, and hard pressed by antagonistic civil governments, these "destroyed" churches more and more believed that their hard-won independence entitled them alone to be the "Confessing *Church*." By contrast their fellow-confessors in the "intact" churches were scorned for being more "privileged" because still "legal" (though barely) in their home territories. These "intact" churches were therefore thought to be ecclesially inferior and at best a "confessing *movement*" or *"front"* or, worse yet, not even a "confess*ing*," but merely a "confess*ional*" front.

The intactness of the "intact" churches irked not only their fellow confessors in the "destroyed" churches but also, of course, the frustrated "German Christians" in those "intact" territories, like Bavaria and Württemberg. There the *confessing* churches were still the legally *estab-lished* churches, not yet forced underground as "free" churches to main-tain their confessional status. But there also, with covert support from Hitler, the "German Christians" were intensifying their efforts to "de-stroy" these confessing churches as well by forcing them into the one Reich church, so far unsuccessfully. For instance, one September evening after the Barmen synod, the "German Christians" of Bavaria chose Nuremberg, a hotbed of Nazi partisanship, for a mass demonstration in the city's Adolf Hitler Platz. They were calling for the removal of the Lu-theran bishop of Bavaria, Hans Meiser, whom they denounced as a leader of the confessing movement.

On that same evening in Nuremberg, church people loyal to Bishop Meiser, having been denied a permit for a counter-demonstration, crowded instead into their churches — three churches full. Right outside were the "German Christians" and their crowds, fortified by the uni-formed *Sturmabteilung* (Nazi storm troopers). Inside the three churches each congregation awaited its turn for the bishop to arrive and preach. An eyewitness recounts the following:

> From around 6:30 p.m. until 11:30 p.m. people sat and stood in the Lorenzkirche — the old hymns of faith resounded throughout the nave and rang out so loudly that the doors had to be shut by the police. . . . Nuremberg has experienced a church revival. Christ is our Lord. He is confessed on the streets, in the houses around, in bakers' and butchers' shops. We stand firmly together.[5]

The bishop's supporters included Party members as well as non-Party members, unaware as yet of the contradiction. But the Party leadership was getting the message: if people had to choose, they "would not hesitate to turn their backs on the Party."

The German Christians and their Reich church administration tightened the screws. Next they tried firing Bishop Meiser and, failing that, they brought in the political police to put him under house arrest and a ban of silence. He responded with a public declaration, "We summon our pastors and communities to offer no obedience to this church government." The state president of Bavaria, who was descended upon by his own Party members warning him that ninety-five percent of the farmers from their region supported Meiser, concluded that they "are not afraid of any force and would prefer to have themselves branded as martyrs." "All this," says Scholder, "was without doubt one of the . . . most remarkable protest demonstrations ever experienced in the Third Reich."[6] At about the same time in the neighboring state of Württemberg, a similar attempt was made to depose the Lutheran bishop there, Theophil Wurm, for his leadership in the confessing movement. As in Bavaria, the Württemberger bishop and his pastors and congregations prevailed "intact," but again by recourse to what amounted to civil disobedience.

Quickly a second confessional synod convened, a sequel to Barmen, this time in the Berlin suburb of Dahlem. With Bishops Meiser and Wurm under house arrest at the time, it was reasonable for the delegates to assume that *all* the confessing churches, even the "intact" ones in Bavaria and Württemberg, had now finally been "destroyed." That mistaken assumption,

---

5. Scholder, *Churches and the Third Reich*, 2:251.
6. Scholder, *Churches and the Third Reich*, 2:263.

for events soon disproved it, was all that the so-called "radical" minority at the Dahlem synod needed to get their way. For at that juncture it did seem that at any moment the Hitler government would officially incorporate the Reich church into the Reich government, and all territorial churches with it, including the heretofore "intact" ones. Little did anyone guess that within days the Bavarian and Württemberger populace would prevail after all, that their two bishops would be released and even invited for a meeting with the Führer, and that the "German Christians" would be discredited along with their Reich bishop and any prospect of a Reich church.

But meanwhile at Dahlem the synod delegates (those who stayed) voted, far from unanimously, that the Confessing Church was announcing an "emergency" church law, in effect a counter-takeover of DEK, substituting the confessors' governance for that of the "German Christians." All cooperation with the latter was forthwith to be severed. One incredulous delegate asked how such a confessors' takeover could make sense, since in his entire home territory of Thuringia all the churches together "have only a thousand members in the Confessing Community." Pastor Martin Niemöller, on the other hand, insisted that there not even be joint Scripture study with the "German Christians." In the end it was voices like Niemöller's, from the United Church, and Barth's, from the Reformed, which prevailed at Dahlem. And it was into hands like theirs, in the new Council of Brethren and its inner Council of Six that the Dahlem synod now entrusted the leadership of the Confessing Church. But it did so without strong consensus.

By November 1934, hardly two weeks after Dahlem, the synod's fragile consensus began to come apart openly, specifically over the synod's sharp separation from "German Christians" and from the Reich church. In opposition to this exclusivist claim that Dahlem and its Council of Brethren must monopolize the leadership of DEK, other veterans of Dahlem now created instead the "First Provisional Church Government of DEK." This temporary, pluralist approach to governance met the regulations of the Reich church, yet also represented those upstart Lutheran churches like Bavaria and Württemberg, which meanwhile had prevailed "intact." Indeed, the idea of the Provisional Church Government was officially negotiated with the state by none other than the president of the Council of Six and was supported by a majority of the Council of Brethren despite Niemöller's and Barth's (temporary) resignations. Bonhoeffer sided emphatically with Niemöller, who was the Bonhoeffer family's unofficial pastor in Berlin, and with Barth, to whose theological influence Bonhoeffer owed much. One wonders whether Bonhoeffer, who again had not been present at Dahlem, knew how divided the opinion at that synod had actually been.

But weren't Niemöller and Barth right? Didn't this new compromise, the First Provisional Church Government, violate Section III of Dahlem's Message, "that in matters of the church's . . . teaching and order, the church" was "called to judge and decide alone, regardless of the state's right of supervision"? No doubt. On the other hand, the same Dahlem Message, Section IV, did defer to the Reich government asking it to recognize the church's right to self-determination. It was clear that the church wanted recognition by the secular authorities. Should the church want that? If the state acceded to the Message's demands, fine. But if not, then what? How important is it for the church to have legal title, if only for its independence? Yet must it win its independence at the cost of becoming exclusive and sectarian, no longer a church of the people? But if a church of the people, also of the people's political aspirations? How inconclusive Barmen had been on these questions, for all of its apparent "unanimity," Dahlem was now exposing by its glaring lack of unanimity.

II. The Authority to Exclude, But Whom All?

Enter Bonhoeffer, specifically Bonhoeffer the "Dahlemite," the "radical," the "legalist," the "sectarian" — in a word, the exclusivist. For eventually all these epithets were applied to him, and all in connection with his interpretation of Barmen — and Dahlem. That is what made him a "Dahlemite": he insisted on interpreting Barmen strictly *in light of Dahlem.* No one could honestly make Barmen's confession of faith, so Bonhoeffer claimed, unless they complied with Dahlem's prescriptions for church governance. And the one church governance which was binding was Dahlem's Council of Brethren, not the post-Dahlem First Provisional Church Government, which Bonhoeffer condemned as a betrayal and a capitulation to state interference. Even though he had attended neither synod at Barmen or Dahlem, nor was his absence widely lamented, he esteemed Barmen's Declaration and, as its organizational follow-through, Dahlem's Message as inviolable. Together they were for him definitive of the authentic Confessing Church and, at its boundaries, of who could and could not be saved.

Maybe Bonhoeffer would have acknowledged, as recent critics of Dahlem have, that "the narrow principles of Dahlem . . . were accepted fully within the Confessing Church only by a small minority." Certainly Bonhoeffer counted himself in that minority. But just as certainly he would not have conceded a criticism like Scholder's. Though Scholder could admire the resolutions which Dahlem passed, he objected to how they were legalistically universalized. "It was wrong to turn these resolutions, born out of an emergency situation, into a law for all churches and communities [even the Bavarian and Württemberger Lutherans] without distinction, [as] the basis on which it was decided whether or not they belonged to the Confessing Church." For only a few days later, Scholder observed, the resolutions would have been stated differently, the Lutheran bishops of southern Germany would have been able to cooperate, and Dahlem "would have been understood everywhere as the synod of the whole Confessing Church and not just . . . of its radical wing." Bonhoeffer belonged to that "radical wing."

Why did he? Why, on what confessional grounds, could he defend such exclusion of even his fellow-confessors? It wasn't only that they were perpetrating injustice. Who wasn't? And since when is the church to be restricted only to the just? The breaking point, so I am suggesting, came when injustices which in mercy might have been borne with, in hopes of correcting them, hardened instead into *de facto* church policy, when the evangelical patience of the Christian community came to be extorted by law, enforceable law, in fact civil law. Whether in fact that happened, or to what extent it did, is open to historical inquiry. It is the confessional issue at stake which I wish to pursue here. To do that, we follow Bonhoeffer to Finkenwalde in Pomerania, where he learned new ways of being Lutheran, some of which would endear him to almost no one.

It was less than a year after Barmen when Bonhoeffer returned to northern Germany from his London exile to become director of a seminary at Finkenwalde on the Baltic coast. This was one of five underground seminaries newly opened by the Confessing Church of the Old Prussian Union. They were the work of the new Brotherhood Councils of Dahlem, opposition-seminaries to the established Old Prussian Union faculties now controlled by "German Christians."[7]

There was of course no need of such "illegal" seminaries in the Lu-

---

7. Cf. Scholder, *Churches and the Third Reich*, 2:169.

theran "intact" churches, where the confessing movement still controlled official theological education, however precariously. This created additional friction between "intact" and "destroyed" churches, all still within the same larger confessing movement. The seminaries of the "destroyed" churches disdained the "intact" ones as "privileged" and not really "church." The "intact" faculties accused the "destroyed" of "Pharisaism" and "legalism." That made life more miserable for both camps. Also it obscured to each of them the sacrifices and bravery of the other, though both of them were resisting a common enemy of the gospel.

Fortunately Bonhoeffer's seminary at Finkenwalde has been spared much of that undeserved obscurity. Thanks to the reporting by its most eloquent spokesperson, Eberhard Bethge, Bonhoeffer's student and best friend and biographer, we know of the awesome Christian heroism of the Finkenwalde community. Not only that, it was wondrous for its accomplishments in pastoral formation under very straitened conditions and all within the two and a half short years before it was closed by the Gestapo. The record of Finkenwalde is part of Bonhoeffer's "responsible interpretation" of Barmen. It may even be that Finkenwalde could not have made the Barmen witness it did, especially on the re-prioritizing of authorities, had it not been for Bonhoeffer's alleged "legalism," objectionable though that also may have been.

Bonhoeffer's work at Finkenwalde was not made easier by the fact that it was located in Pomerania, not easier but perhaps more theologically responsible. Pomerania was a church province of the Old Prussian Union which, in protest against the "German Christian" takeover there, had duly mounted its own "Dahlemite" counter-church government through a provincial Council of Brethren. However, the Pomeranian confessors still prided themselves on their Lutheranism. For Lutheran Bonhoeffer, who did the same, that by itself would have been no problem. The trouble was, these Pomeranian fellow-confessors of his felt a close affinity with the Lutherans in the "intact" church of Bavaria, specifically with Bavarian Lutheran theologians on the faculty at Erlangen like Althaus and Elert. As Bethge reports, these "two theologians' criticism that the Barmen theses had erred in following Barth's rejection of 'original revelation' in creation and history had met with a large measure of agreement here." Consequently, it was hard to enforce the measures legislated by Barmen and Dahlem. The result for Bonhoeffer was that in that Lutheran context he was made to appear "isolated and radical."

At the same time, when it came to the question of who was being more Lutheran, Bonhoeffer was not about to take a backseat, even at the point where his Lutheran critics thought him most "radical." For him it was anything but a matter of indifference whether his position did justice to Luther's Reformation and the Lutheran Confessions. On the contrary, he consistently invoked that tradition in his own support against "the so-called Lutherans." Aggressively he accepted the same confessional accountabilities as did those Lutherans who so differed from him on church-political issues. But were he and they really all that different theologically?

The Lutheranism of the Finkenwalde Bonhoeffer extended not only to his Christology and his theology of the Lord's Supper, where his Lutheranism is sometimes acknowledged by his followers today, though not always enthusiastically. But more and more his Lutheranism surfaced also on those very issues which most sharply divided Lutherans from Barthians: law and gospel, two kingdoms, secular and spiritual authorities. At Finkenwalde Bonhoeffer was being distanced both from Lutherans and, more and more, from Barthians as well. Because of his Lutheranism? Not altogether for that reason, certainly. But that hypothesis — the Lutheran reason for his alleged "legalism" and "sectarianism" — does bear investigating.

Bethge reports that at Finkenwalde "study was centered almost wholly on the confessional writings," which "at that time aroused . . . passionate interest," and that "with each term more and more time was allocated to these classes than to any other subject."[8] One of the confessional themes that aroused such interest was the theme of adiaphora. In the Lutheran confessional writings the classical discussion of adiaphora appears in the Formula of Concord of 1577, specifically its tenth article. More on this later. For now let it be noted that it was first at Finkenwalde that the Formula of Concord became virtually a "discovery" for Bonhoeffer, also for his ordinands. In his later courses at Finkenwalde it was to become a "predominant theme." "He loved the *Formula Concordiae*."[9] His personal copy abounds in underlinings and marginal notes.

8. Eberhard Bethge, *Dietrich Bonhoeffer: Man of Vision, Man of Courage* (New York: Harper and Row, 1970), 366; Eberhard Bethge, *Dietrich Bonhoeffer: A Biography* (Minneapolis: Fortress Press, 2000), 447. These are two editions of a biography on Bonhoeffer, hereafter designated *DB I* and *DB II*, respectively.

9. Bethge, *DB I*, 368; Bethge, *DB II*, 449; cf. 88. Noted also in Robert Bertram, "'Scripture and Tradition' in the Lutheran Confessions," *Pro Ecclesia* 10, no. 2 (Spring

One passage in Formula of Concord, Article X, must have struck Bonhoeffer as especially compatible. He emphasizes it with double markings. "To dissent from the consensus of so many nations and to be called schismatics is a serious matter. But divine authority commands us all not to be associated with and not to support impiety and unjust cruelty."[10] "To dissent" to the point of being called "schismatic" was an agony Bonhoeffer was learning firsthand, and he was finding confessional warrant for the experience in the Lutheran declaration on adiaphora.

What earned him such reproaches as "schismatic" and "legalist" was an article he published in the summer of 1936 on the subject of "church fellowship." The article included this offending sentence of his, "Whoever knowingly separates himself from the Confessing Church in Germany separates himself from salvation." That scandalous quotation, Bethge reports, "spread like wildfire throughout the German churches." In the retelling, it was soon caricatured into "Those without a Red Card [membership card in the Confessing Church] won't go to heaven." Within months Bonhoeffer was, as he said, "the most reviled man of our persuasion."

What had occasioned Bonhoeffer's provocative article, first presented as lectures to his Finkenwalde students, was the worsening situation right within his own Confessing Church. This church was dwindling not only in financial support and in numbers and in pastorates for its "illegal" ordinands, but also in its spiritual resolve to remain separate. The more credible alternative, even for some members of the Councils of Brethren, yes, even for ordinands from Finkenwalde, was to reconsider their former exclusiveness and to join forces instead with the so-called Church Committees. These committees were now the latest attempt to salvage the leadership of DEK by accommodating both the concerns of the National Church and also the concerns of the confessing movement. Enviably, the "intact" churches of Bavaria, Württemberg, Baden, and Hanover managed to stay clear of these Committees. The "destroyed" churches in the Old Prussian Union, like Pomerania, did not. Regardless, for Bonhoeffer it was the quite separate, dwindling Confessing Church which remained the only

---

2001): 179-94. Also verbally shared with Robert Bertram and Edward Schroeder during Bethge's visit to Seminex in the late 1970s. Cf. "Some Reverie Brought on by Renate Bethge's Bonhoeffer Book," Thursday Theology #322, August 12, 2004; available online at www.crossings.org/thursday/Thur081204.htm.

10. FC X, 23.

true church of Christ in Germany, from which members "separated" (his word) only on pain of their damnation.

One need not be naïve to grant that Bonhoeffer, regardless of whether he was right, was also misunderstood. Also there may be reason to believe that he was misinformed, for example, about how united (rather, disunited) the decision at Dahlem had actually been. Hence, he may have been wrong about its authority as a binding council of the church united by the Holy Spirit. Moreover, he may have been mistaken about how "privileged" the "intact" churches really were, thus underestimating their confessorhood. In other words, he may have had his facts wrong about the exact scope of the "Confessing Church," and in that factual respect may himself have "separated" from the authentic confessing church those who had not separated themselves. That may or may not make him "schismatic." It still need not follow, however, that his exclusionary statement, "Whoever knowingly separates himself from 'the Confessing Church' in Germany separates himself from salvation," was false or "legalistic" in its confessional intention. On the contrary, it was Bonhoeffer's intention thereby to *combat* legalism, and in so many words.

Those who misunderstood Bonhoeffer's intention legalistically included not only his detractors but his defenders, whom he tried to disabuse or, when that failed, had to disclaim. These sympathizers with Bonhoeffer, right within the Confessing Church, even within the Finkenwalde community, imported their own legalistic preconceptions into his intention, though they did so well-meaningly. Bethge reports that the Finkenwalde seminarians were at first hard-pressed to defend their teacher's controversial article and themselves had to learn that in that article his foremost accent had in fact been a "*denial* of the whole legalistic view [of the] church," namely, the view "that the Church was to set her own boundaries and determine their extent."

Bonhoeffer's point had been quite the opposite. The church, he argued, was now having boundaries set *for* her, "drawn against her from outside," for instance, when seminarians were pressured by "outsiders" to withdraw from the Finkenwalde community. Once that happened, must not these outsiders' self-imposed boundaries be recognized as the real boundaries they then become, for those outsiders? Then the self-imposed boundaries become barriers not to membership in some human organization, but to the body of Christ, barriers to Christ himself? That is the way Scholder, too, read Bonhoeffer's intention: he "began from the gospel call to salvation which did not itself set limits, but came up against limits." Yet Scholder also saw that Bonhoeffer's colleagues in the Confessing Church did not always read matters the same way: "the claim of the Confessing Church to be the sole church of Jesus Christ hardened into a confessional orthodoxy which inevitably put [an end] to any evangelical freedom."[11] *That* sort of exclusiveness, as Bonhoeffer himself would later say, is the direct antithesis of evangelical freedom. It is the "timid impulse to draw narrow limits."[12] Bonhoeffer, probably not altogether without fault of his own, incurred the charge of "legalism" by his very efforts to the contrary, to guard the church against legalism and for freedom.

Terms like legalism and freedom, premised as they are upon more basic terms like law and gospel, return us to the Formula of Concord, which had become a preoccupation of Bonhoeffer's at Finkenwalde. The Formula's tenth article, as we noted, purportedly deals with the subject of adiaphora, judging from the title. But only purportedly, for in fact the article deals with those circumstances when adiaphora are *not* adiaphora any longer. Ordinarily, in the church there are always adiaphora, those controversial practices and teachings about which the members of the community differ and, if God's Word is not being compromised, should be free to differ. The practices in question might even be offensive to some members, but if these members are "the strong," as Paul calls them, they ought to use their strength to bear with the failings of "the weak" rather than flaunt their freedom and thereby pressure "the weak" to conform against their own convictions.

However, and this is the point of Article X, there are limits to such adiaphoral freedom. There are times when the weak ones exploit this freedom as a subterfuge for forcing their "weak" ways upon the community, thus blackmailing the strong and in fact perverting Christian freedom into bondage. That is exactly what Bonhoeffer saw happening in the congregations where a strong pro-German spirit prevailed, by itself understandable, but where the pastor was pressured to leave because he was "non-Aryan." Even that, so Bonhoeffer told his seminarians, *might* be a conceivable

11. Cf. Scholder, *Churches and the Third Reich*, 2:156-57.

12. Dietrich Bonhoeffer, *Ethics* (New York: Macmillan, 1955), 58. These notations are from the paperback Collier Books edition. It should be noted that the pagination will vary in other editions, including especially the earliest hardbound editions which follow closely Bonhoeffer's 1940 sketching of an outline for his *Ethics*.

course of action, however regrettable. But it dare not be allowed if the gospel's freedom was being breached. Presumably a similar breach occurred when Finkenwaldians, who were vulnerable to begin with, were being subjected to superior pressure from "the weak," namely the Church Committees. Especially was that happening when the Church Committees, which might have been tolerable in theory, seemed more and more to be harboring the very state which, as Bonhoeffer foresaw, was Antichrist itself, the determined enemy of Christendom.

When such a time comes, says Formula of Concord X, that is a "time for confessing." For then the freedom of the gospel has been twisted into its opposite: legalistic coercion and the enslavement of consciences, the very torment which Bonhoeffer was witnessing in his seminarians and, beyond them, in Christian Germany generally.

Following the cue of the Formula, Bonhoeffer scribbles in the margin, "The DCs' [German Christians'] policy on the Jews is false doctrine" — not merely sin, a violation of God's law, but heresy against the gospel. Another marginal note reads: "By its incursion into adiaphora what is being inserted is a legalistic [*gesetzliches*] understanding" — that is, of the gospel.

At such "times," says the Formula, "we should not yield to adversaries even in matters of indifference, nor should we tolerate" them. That is the language not of gospel inclusivity but of judgment, which the church's authority also obliges it to pronounce. This exclusionary authority is not unique to the church but, even though it contrasts with the gospel, it is essential to the church. "It is written, 'For freedom Christ has set us free; stand fast therefore, and do not submit again to a yoke of slavery' (Gal. 5:1)." Paul's very metaphor of the rebelling slave is drawn from civil law, but in the service of that very different authority, the gospel of freedom.

Employing Luther's two-kingdoms terminology, Bonhoeffer summarizes the exclusionary thrust of his article on church fellowship: the church "will be doing alien work [law] in order to carry out more efficiently its proper task [gospel]." But "the Law," "alien" as it may be to the gospel, is not "legalism," which is a distortion *both* of law and of gospel. Granted, an Erlanger Lutheran like Elert might not at all have agreed with how Bonhoeffer *applied* this reprioritizing of authorities in the situation at hand. Still, with the reprioritizing itself he could — or should — scarcely have agreed more, particularly in view of its source in that "Gnesio-Lutheran" symbol, Formula of Concord X.

But Bonhoeffer's article, which reflects this reprioritizing of churchly authorities, the authority of gospel as "proper" over the authority of law as "alien," was after all an article on *church* fellowship, merely intra-ecclesial reprioritizing. What does that have to do with the church's external relation to the state? Does it follow from the reprioritizing of gospel over law that the church takes priority over the state? We come to that next. But first, a reminder is in order. As late as 1942 Bonhoeffer, by then a member of a political plot against Hitler, was asked by members of another plot, "The Freiburg Group," to project a plan for the Protestant church of Germany should it survive the war. Even at that late date, when church life in Germany was nearing its nadir and the state's hostility to Christianity was by then undisguised, Bonhoeffer wrote, "It is possible to settle the relations between state and church only if the *Kirchenkampf* is settled." However true it may have been that the struggle *within* the church to reprioritize its own authorities was merely a *Vorgeplänkel* compared to its coming great conflict with the Nazi state, for Bonhoeffer the "preliminary skirmish" still came first.

III. The Authority to Include: Polemically, Atoningly

Surely there is more to Bonhoeffer's "responsible interpretation" of Barmen than his exclusivist disclaimer, "Whoever knowingly separates himself from the Confessing Church in Germany separates himself from salvation."[13] We may still put the best construction on his statement, reminding ourselves that the separatists are those who set limits to the church from outside and so, from that "alien" distance, receive merely the church's law, not its gospel. We may remind ourselves also that for Bonhoeffer to equate the Christian church in Germany with "the Confessing Church" only reflects what for him was always axiomatic. God's Word for the church is "concrete," historically situated, not abstract or vague. Even so, doesn't Bonhoeffer's interpretation of Barmen somewhere provide a church-world relation which is not just exclusive but also inclusive? Indeed it does.

In fact, for Bonhoeffer Christ's claim upon the world is inclusive, "total" *(ganz)* exactly because it is "exclusive" *(ausschliesslich)*. In support of this dialectical claim of Christ, Bonhoeffer refers autobiographically to

13. Bethge, *DB I,* 430; *DB II,* 520.

"one of our most astonishing experiences during the years when everything Christian was sorely oppressed."[14] So formative must this "experience" have been — Bonhoeffer calls it "an experience of our days," "an actual concrete experience," a "living experience" — that the reader is reminded of Luther's *Turmerlebnis*. True, the experience did confirm Jesus' words of "Law," that "Whoever is not with me is against me" (Matt. 12:30).[15] That much is exclusive. But the same experience soon confirmed the amazing contrary as well, "Whoever is not against us is for us" (Mark 9:40). That is inclusive in the extreme, and the church has Jesus' authorization for that.

The experience began with the "confessing congregations" and with their "exclusive demand for a clear profession of allegiance to Christ." The exclusiveness of their demand, as we saw, was directed not just against the "anti-Christian forces" of Nazism, which actually had had the effect of bringing the confessing congregations together in the first place. No, "the greatest of all the dangers which threatened the Church with *inner* disintegration . . . lay in the neutrality of large numbers of *Christians*."[16] Alas, "the exclusive demand for a clear profession of allegiance to Christ caused the band of confessing Christians to become ever smaller." The excluders — or shall we say, those who pronounced judgment on the self-excluders? — had become the excluded.

However, "precisely through [the church's] concentration on the essential," on Christ alone, so Bonhoeffer recalls, "there gathered around her [those] people who came from very far away, and people to whom she could not refuse her fellowship and her protection." Who were these new outsiders? "Injured justice, oppressed truth, vilified humanity and violated freedom all sought for [the church], or rather for her Master, Jesus Christ."[17] Bonhoeffer seems to have had in mind Germans like those he joined in the conspiracy, those humanists whom his Jewish-Christian brother-in-law, Gerhard Leibholz, called "the other Germany," "the upholders of the European and Western tradition in Germany." The church, as Bonhoeffer marvels, "now had the living experience of that other saying of Jesus: 'Whoever is not against us is for us.'"[18]

14. Bonhoeffer, *Ethics*, 55.
15. Bonhoeffer, *Ethics*, 57-58.
16. Bonhoeffer, *Ethics*, 58.
17. Bonhoeffer, *Ethics*, 58.
18. Bonhoeffer, *Ethics*, 58.

They are "for us," Bonhoeffer explains, because "Jesus gives his support to those who suffer for the sake of a just cause, even if this cause is not precisely the confession of His name." That is, "He takes them under His protection, He accepts responsibility for them, and He lays claim to them," all to the surprise of those people themselves. Thus "it happens that in the hour of suffering and responsibility, perhaps for the first time in his life and in a way which is strange and surprising to him . . . , such a person appeals to Christ and professes himself a Christian because at this moment . . . he becomes aware that he belongs to Christ." Again Bonhoeffer assures his reader, this "is not an abstract deduction but . . . an experience which we ourselves have undergone, . . . in which the power of Jesus Christ became manifest in fields of life where it had previously remained unknown."[19]

Bonhoeffer's theological explanation of this experience, I am suggesting, is part of his "responsible interpretation" of Barmen, specifically on the issue of *reprioritizing the authorities*. First, consider those cultural values in European humanism which at the time were so under attack from the prevailing nihilism and bestiality: "reason, culture, humanity, tolerance and self-determination, . . . concepts which until very recently had served as battle slogans against the Church, against Christianity, against Jesus Christ Himself."[20] Historically, where had those values come from? From Christianity. Their "origin [*Ursprung*] is Jesus Christ." But in the intervening centuries of widespread defection from Christ, the "good" Europeans had "fallen away from their origin."[21]

Only as they are now made to suffer for their humane causes at the hands of Antichrist do these persecuted, "homeless"[22] humanists rediscover their own *Ursprung* in Christ, who himself suffers for his claims of exclusiveness. What these secular martyrs discover is that the values for which they are persecuted are ultimately unsustainable without their basis in Christ. "It is not Christ who must justify Himself before the world by the acknowledgement of the values of justice, truth and freedom, but it is these values which have come to need justification, and their justification can only be Jesus Christ."[23]

19. Bonhoeffer, *Ethics*, 60.
20. Bonhoeffer, *Ethics*, 55.
21. Bonhoeffer, *Ethics*, 56.
22. Bonhoeffer, *Ethics*, 56.
23. Bonhoeffer, *Ethics*, 59.

Is Bonhoeffer suggesting, contrary to Barmen's first thesis, that there is after all in worldly history another "kingdom" or rule of God — say, the "wrath" of God — alongside God's gracious rule in Christ? If the answer is yes, it can only be a very nuanced yes. For, notice, even though the cultural values of a secularized Christendom might somehow persist for a while without their humanist practitioners acknowledging their source in Christ, *he* still graciously acknowledges *them* — in the inclusive claim which the church makes in his behalf. So his grace alone does seem to prevail. However, sooner or later Christ in turn must *be* acknowledged if those values are to be "protected" and "justified." They cannot indefinitely survive apart from Christ. And when those values perish for lack of nourishment from their root, possibly forever, isn't that also a judgment of God, perhaps even a judgment of Christ, but certainly not a judgment of Christ's grace? Does Bonhoeffer bring that qualification to Barmen's Thesis One?

What does seem to be the case is that "one of [Bonhoeffer's] most astonishing experiences" brought home to him that there is also something *besides* Christ, even *contrary* to Christ, which nevertheless reveals the *need* of Christ, namely, the tyrant's persecution of good causes and values? Wasn't Nazism's very terrorizing of the humane tradition "sufficient to awaken the consciousness of a kind of alliance and comradeship between the defenders of these endangered values and the Christians"? "The children of the Church, who had become independent and gone their own ways, now in the hour of danger returned to their mother."[24]

That there should be a "mother" was of course essential, but so was the humanists' "hour of danger," their "hour of suffering and responsibility." Without this "hour" they may well not have returned home. There does seem to be a necessary affinity and fit between "the Christ who is persecuted and suffers"[25] and the good people's own "concrete suffering of injustice."[26] The need of Christ is driven home, unwittingly of course, by something other than Christ, indeed by "Antichrist." So then is that one, namely, the one whom Bonhoeffer calls Antichrist, the one who conducts the contrary reign to Christ's reign of grace in the world? That dualistic explanation might have the advantage of exempting God from the onus. Still,

---

24. Bonhoeffer, *Ethics*, 56.
25. Bonhoeffer, *Ethics*, 59.
26. Bonhoeffer, *Ethics*, 58.

Bonhoeffer unflinchingly traces the current affliction he and his people are suffering to the retributive "wrath of God," which is not grace. Indeed, the "grace," says Bonhoeffer, lies in being able to recognize, as few of his contemporaries could, the "wrath of God" for what it is.

Accordingly, it is not just the reign of human perversity, or even of Antichrist, but finally of divine "wrath" which God's grace in Christ must supersede. In fact, the surest proof that, for Bonhoeffer, the Antichrist is not the final antithesis but "the wrath of God," is where Bonhoeffer recognizes that the divine wrath is pitted also against Antichrist. And God opposes Antichrist, in this case the Nazi tyranny, not only by means of the church, but also by the coercive, exclusive "power of the state." Notice, the Nazi regime no longer qualifies as "the state" but as its enemy. "The power of the state," which has now passed to other hands, finds itself in a strange alliance with the church of Christ against a common foe, though the two allies, state and church, fight with markedly different, even antithetical weapons.

In 2 Thessalonians who is it, besides the church, who opposes Antichrist? It is as the apostle calls him "the restrainer" (2 Thess. 2:7), whom Bonhoeffer identifies with "the force of order, equipped with great physical strength." "'The restrainer' is the power of the state to establish and maintain order."[27] In Bonhoeffer's current circumstance "the restrainer" appears in the persons of those anti-Hitler co-conspirators like his brother Klaus, his brother-in-law Dohnanyi, Admiral Canaris, General Oster and others, military officers and politicians, secret agents and lawyers, executives and intellectuals who are using their power to plot tyrannicide.

"'The restrainer,' the force of order, sees in the Church an ally, and will . . . seek a place at her side."[28] The two, church and "restrainer," "are entirely different in nature [*verschieden in ihrem Wesen*], yet in the face of imminent chaos they are in close alliance." The church's unique task is that of the proclaimer, "preaching the risen Jesus Christ," "the saving act of God, which intervenes from . . . *beyond* whatever is historically attainable." By contrast, "the 'restrainer' is the force which takes effect *within* history through God's governance of the world, and which sets due limits to evil." Yet the proclaimer and the "restrainer" are "both alike objects of the ha-

27. Bonhoeffer, *Ethics*, 108.
28. Bonhoeffer, *Ethics*, 109.

tred of the forces of destruction, which see in them [both] their deadliest enemies."[29]

Notice the incongruity. The "restrainers" — admirals and generals and political conspirators — are by vocation and commitment all people of power, "equipped with great physical strength," "the power of the state to establish and maintain order." Yet in this "hour of suffering and responsibility" they find themselves to be instead the weak, the persecuted, the suffering. In their "hour of danger" they, the weakened strong, see the proclaimer-church likewise suffering — for instance, suffering exclusion for its exclusiveness. Yet they also see that its "suffering presents an infinitely greater danger to the spirit of destruction than does any political power which may still remain." Above all "through her message of the living Lord Jesus Christ the Church makes it clear that she is not concerned merely for the maintenance and preservation of the past."[30] The "miracle" entrusted to her is "a raising of the dead."[31] With that, "even the forces of order she compels to listen and turn back."[32] They, "after long straying from the path, are once more finding their way back to their fountain-head."[33]

The church in turn dare "not reject those who come to her and seek to place themselves at her side." "While still preserving the essential distinction [*wohl gewahrter Unterscheidung*] between herself and these forces," at the same time "she unreservedly allies herself with them [*in aufrichtiger Bundesgenossenschaft*]."[34] How the church is to do that, we shall soon see. But in passing, let us note that in this long section in his *Ethics* Bonhoeffer is quite explicitly trying to recoup Luther's "doctrine of the two kingdoms," which in the centuries after the Reformation had degenerated into a false "emancipation and sanctification of the world and of the natural."[35] For Luther, as for Bonhoeffer, "there are two kingdoms which, so long as the world continues, must neither be mixed together nor yet be torn asunder. There is the kingdom of the preached word of God, and there is the kingdom of the sword." "But the Lord of both kingdoms is

---

29. Bonhoeffer, *Ethics*, 108.
30. Bonhoeffer, *Ethics*, 109.
31. Bonhoeffer, *Ethics*, 108.
32. Bonhoeffer, *Ethics*, 109.
33. Bonhoeffer, *Ethics*, 109.
34. Bonhoeffer, *Ethics*, 109.
35. Bonhoeffer, *Ethics*, 96.

the God who is made manifest in Jesus Christ."[36] How to retrieve *that* "doctrine of the two kingdoms" for a suffering church ministering to suffering "restrainers" on its doorstep?

In answering that question, we should emphasize what in Bonhoeffer studies is often de-emphasized, that the weak and the suffering for whom Bonhoeffer found himself called always included, perhaps especially, this "Germany" as a Christian *Volk,* this reunion of the church and "the promising Godless,"[37] this *Christentum.* "I have loved this people," he exclaimed. Of all the "voiceless" ones in whose behalf he spoke — the Jews, the victims of euthanasia, the "illegal" Finkenwaldians — no oppressed group seems so fully to have engaged his confessor's energies as did his fellow-countrymen, and surely not because of their innocence.

In this special sense, Bonhoeffer was as outspokenly pro-German as those in the confessing movement who, church-politically, seemed to be his opposites — for example, Elert, who long before had written his own *Kampf um das Christentum.* Bonhoeffer opposed "internationalism" for the same reason he opposed its cause, "nationalism," since both were alike "revolutionary" enemies of the *corpus christianum.*[38] It may be that Bonhoeffer's agonizing for his own people is under-emphasized in the histories about him lest he might appear insufficiently different on that score from the "German Christians." That would be the gravest of errors. His theological cause was diametrically opposed to theirs. For him, "the question really is: Germanism or Christianity."[39] His passion, as it was Elert's, was not for a German Christianity, but for a Christian Germany. Without Christ the *Ursprung,* at least for Bonhoeffer, Germany could not truly be a people.

During his first stay in the United States, in 1930, Bonhoeffer told a New York congregation, "We [Christians] are no longer Americans or Germans, we are one large congregation of brethren,"[40] but soon added, "Now I stand before you not only as a Christian, but also as a German, who rejoices with his people and who suffers when he sees his people suffer-

36. Bonhoeffer, *Ethics,* 95.

37. Bonhoeffer, *Ethics,* 104.

38. Bonhoeffer, *Ethics,* 101.

39. Bethge, *DB I,* 232; *DB II,* 302. This was in a letter to his grandmother while working with Sasse on the Bethel Confession.

40. Dietrich Bonhoeffer, *No Rusty Swords: Letters, Lectures and Notes, 1928-1936,* ed. Edwin H. Robertson and John Bowden (London: William Collins Sons & Co., 1970), 73.

ing. . . ."[41] And their suffering, their mass deaths and impoverishment and starvation and epidemics as a result of World War I, but still evident in 1930, Bonhoeffer vividly recounts to his American hearers. He has the boldness to add, no one "who knows well the history of the origin of the war believes that Germany bears the sole guilt of the war — a sentence which we were compelled to sign in the Treaty of Versailles."[42]

Less than a decade after that sermon Bonhoeffer was back in New York, but this time for barely a month. Germany was now going back to war. On second thought, Bonhoeffer cancels his plans for an American stay and promptly returns, as he explained to Reinhold Niebuhr, because "I must live through this difficult period of our national history with the Christian people of Germany." "Christians in Germany will face the terrible alternative of either willing the defeat of their nation in order that Christian civilization may survive, or willing the victory of their nation and thereby destroying our civilization. I know which of these alternatives I must choose."[43] There, in that choice of his, we have Bonhoeffer's rationale for the conspiracy: to give evidence to the Allies that there is in fact an "other Germany," which the victors dare not again destroy by demanding unconditional surrender. Leave aside that the conspiracy failed.

Bonhoeffer's role in the conspiracy concretizes how he saw the church entering into *aufrichtigen Bundesgenossenschaft* with the state, specifically with the "restrainer," that "power of the state to establish and maintain order." His own conspiratorial role in this church-state alliance was not as a public representative of the church, but nonetheless as one of its servantlike, "arcane" disciples.[44] Yet as I see it, that very feature of arcane, servantlike discipleship is exactly the most significant feature of Bonhoeffer's "responsible interpretation" of Barmen. That is, in the end it is a "nonreligious interpretation," particularly so with reference to Barmen's prickliest issue, the reprioritizing of spiritual and secular authorities. And Bonhoeffer's non-religious interpretation is, as Bethge would add, "more an ethical than a hermeneutical category and also a direct call to penitence directed to the Church and its present form."[45] "Non-

41. Bonhoeffer, *No Rusty Swords*, 74.
42. Bonhoeffer, *No Rusty Swords*, 75.
43. Bethge, *DB I*, 559; *DB II*, 655.
44. Bethge, *DB I*, 784; *DB II*, 880.
45. Bethge, *DB I*, 783; *DB II*, 880.

religious" and "arcane" entail repentance, and repentance is emphatically servantlike.

What is arcane or hidden about the disciples' "discipline" as they practice it concretely amongst their homesick humanists is precisely the "non-religious" exterior of that discipline. Amongst themselves, by contrast, when they gather in the explicit name of their Lord to hear his gospel and receive his sacraments, or in private intra-believer conversation or correspondence, there the cultus and prayers and hymnody and theological discourse are still openly exercised. But in the believers' secular associations their *disciplina* is kept secret or, if we may put it so, is restrained. Their self-restraint on religiousness, not to mention religiosity, is not altogether different from the restraint placed upon civil evil and disorder by the "restrainer." For it is part of the very promise of our age that it is "godless," not only by its own apostasy, but by God's intentional acquiescence thereto, so as to make of the age an age of grown-up responsibility, no longer baby-sat by the tutelary supports of religion and pietism.

However, arcane as the believers' discipline is in their associations with "the promising godless," they do very much exercise that arcanum right in those most worldly contexts, though now hiddenly. And what is this well-kept secret of their inner-worldly discipleship? It is their world-affirming solidarity with the other worldlings, especially in the latters' sufferings and most especially in their suffering together from sin. Theirs is a solidarity of the penitents. Four and a half years after Bonhoeffer's return from America, he finds himself in Tegel prison on trial for his crimes, justly so, and writes of this to his friend Bethge. "I haven't for a moment regretted coming back in 1939 — nor any of the *consequences*, either. . . . And I regard my being kept here . . . as being involved in Germany's fate, as I was resolved to be." But the arcanum, the secret of one's penitential co-involvement with fellow-sinners, is the doing of that "in faith." "All we can do," Bonhoeffer confides to Bethge, "is to live in assurance and faith — you out there with the soldiers, and I in my cell."[46]

Bonhoeffer's collusion with the "restrainers" implicated him in the most grievous sins. That he was mortally guilty, as he himself recognized, we minimize or heroize only by not taking his penitence seriously. He and his fellow conspirators were "good" people only relatively to the "wicked,"

---

46. Dietrich Bonhoeffer, *Letters and Papers from Prison* (New York: Macmillan, 1953), 174-75. Letter of 22 December 1943.

whose sin is not "suffering" sin, but not because the conspirators and their acts did not need Christ's "justification." That was their most abject need. For all of them, deceit, connivance, forgery, feigning loyalty to the Führer, misleading their fellow Christians, endangering the lives of others, conspiring to kill were not lapses of weakness but deliberate policy. Worse yet, with all this came their often overwhelming temptations to cynicism and despair. However, the culpability of those few conspirators only writes large what is everyday truth for the church in the world generally. In Bethge's words, "This 'borderline case' is . . . an example of being Christian today."

But then how, through such collaboration with the worldlings' sin, are the church's believers being church? For that, as Bonhoeffer sees it, is what they are in their solidarity with the world as it is: not just private, isolated Christians but representatives of the church of Christ, though hiddenly. But then all the worse, how as the church's representatives are they really any different from those who do not (yet) acknowledge Christ? Where is there here any meaningful entry of the *church,* let alone of Christ, into the world? Bonhoeffer's answer employs the extravagant picture of worldly Christians as agents of "atonement." As penitent and forgiving co-sinners, these Christian collaborators infiltrate the state with that exclusive churchly authority which the state does not have, the all-inclusive, sinner-including authority to *atone.*

Bonhoeffer pondered how in the New Testament the Christian "who suffers in the power of the body of Christ suffers in a representative capacity 'for' the Church." "For while it is true that only the suffering of Christ himself can atone for sin, and that his suffering and triumph took place 'for us,' yet to some . . . he vouchsafes the immeasurable grace and privilege of suffering 'for him,' as he did for them." By the end of his days, Bonhoeffer must have seen that this "vicarious activity and passivity on the part of the members of the Body," this "immeasurable grace and privilege," extended also to himself.

The quotation just cited comes from *Cost of Discipleship.* But already in his doctoral dissertation, *Sanctorum Communio,* Bonhoeffer, barely out of his teens, was writing about "the love which of its own free will is ready to incur God's wrath for its brother's sake, . . . which takes its brother's place as Christ took our place for us." Bonhoeffer there recalls how "Moses wished to be blotted out of the book of life with his people, and Paul wished that he himself were accursed and cut off from Christ, not in order to be condemned with his brethren, but to win communion with God for them; he wishes to be condemned in their stead."[47] Years later, less than a year before his execution, in his poem "The Death of Moses," there is the line: "God, this people I have loved." As Bethge assures us, by "this people" Bonhoeffer "did not mean the Church, but Germany."[48] And of this people, he writes, "that I bore its shame and sacrifices / And saw its salvation — that suffices."[49]

The way Bonhoeffer retrieves Luther's doctrine of the two kingdoms is as a "polemical unity."[50] By contrast, what Bonhoeffer repudiates, as he believes Luther also did, is a "thinking in terms of two spheres" *(Räumen)* or "spaces."[51] It would be tempting, as the literature about Bonhoeffer betrays, to misunderstand his objection as if he were against the *two-ness* of the kingdoms. He is not. Their *Unterscheidung* is essential. That they are "opposites" *(Gegensätze)* is essential to their "unity." Else it would not be a "*polemical* unity." What Bonhoeffer objects to is a two-ness which regards secular and Christian as "*ultimate static*" opposites, as "*mutually exclusive* givens."[52] And the trouble with such mutual exclusiveness is not that that discourages all interest in unity. On the contrary, what ensues is a "*forced unity*"[53] which subjugates one opposite to the other in some imposed system, either sacred or profane.

Moreover, when secular and spiritual are construed not as polemically unified — the way, I would think, two debaters in a dialogue are unified — but instead as mutually repellent spheres whose unity has to be forced, then one of the two, alas, tends to be identified with "Christ" and the other with "the world." That restricts the reality in Christ to merely a partial reality. It forces people to abandon reality as a single whole and to seek either Christ without the world or the world without Christ. But it is the whole world that Christ has won for himself. There are not two realities, only one: his. All that is real is real only in him. Granted, not all that is real in Christ *(Christuswirklichkeit)* is yet "realization" *(Wirklichwerden)*. Though the

47. Dietrich Bonhoeffer, *The Communion of Saints* (New York: Harper and Row, 1963), 131.
48. Bethge, *DB I,* 791; *DB II,* 888.
49. Bethge, *DB II,* 888. From "The Death of Moses."
50. Bonhoeffer, *Ethics,* 199.
51. Bonhoeffer, *Ethics,* 196.
52. Bonhoeffer, *Ethics,* 198.
53. Bonhoeffer, *Ethics,* 198.

world is included in his reality, it only very partially recognizes that. That part of the world which does recognize itself as his is the church, *das Christliche.* "What is Christian" is not identical with *"das Weltliche."* Though the two are one reality as Christ's, they still are polemical opposites.

On the other hand, what is Christian — that is, what is church — by no means exhausts what is Christ's. For Bonhoeffer that distinction, too, is decisive. "The dominion of the commandment of Christ over all creation is not to be equated with the dominion of the Church."[54] That is what a triumphalist church forgets, as the Roman church did in expanding its ecclesiastical power over the secular. That is why Luther polemicized in behalf of secular authority. He "was protesting against a Christianity which was striving for independence" from the secular, but which thereby was also "detaching itself from the reality in Christ."[55]

Of course, the reverse also happens, as the militant secularism of the Nazi Antichrist brazenly illustrated: *das Weltliche* forcibly denies its dependence on *das Christliche,* only dramatizing thereby its renunciation of Christ. To this great divorce the church contributed when, as in *Pseudo-luthertum* after the Reformation, "the autonomy of the orders of this world" is counterposed to "the law of Christ."[56] As this escapist distortion of Luther's two-kingdoms theology showed, "any attempt to escape from the world must sooner or later be paid for with a sinful surrender to the world."[57] Bonhoeffer's critique of this "so-called Lutheran" doctrine of the two kingdoms has been widely and enthusiastically advertised. And that definitely was one, though only one, of his favorite examples of post-Reformation "thinking in two spheres."

There is a second example of post-Reformation "thinking in two spheres" which Bonhoeffer almost always mentions in the same breath with his faulting of the "pseudo-Lutheran" doctrine. But this second culprit is frequently purged from the citations by Bonhoeffer enthusiasts, particularly by those with Barthian proclivities. As a result, it is less well known that Bonhoeffer, perhaps especially in his later years when he became increasingly critical of his own Confessing Church, mounted strong objections against "ecclesiastical theocracy" or, as he also called it, "Enthu-

---

54. Cf. Bonhoeffer, *Ethics*, 299-300.
55. Bonhoeffer, *Ethics*, 199.
56. Bonhoeffer, *Ethics*, 196.
57. Bonhoeffer, *Ethics*, 200.

siasm" *(Schwärmertum)*. In the same sentence in which he commends Luther for protesting "with the help of the secular and in the name of a better Christianity," Bonhoeffer adds, "So, too, today, when Christianity is employed as a polemical weapon against the secular, this must be done in the name of a better secularity." "Above all it must not lead back to a static predominance of the spiritual sphere [*Sakralität*] as an end in itself."[58]

For Bonhoeffer the classical form of this "ecclesiastical theocracy," itself a version of "two spheres thinking," is that "scheme of the Enthusiasts" in which "the congregation of the Elect takes up the struggle with a hostile world for the establishment of God's kingdom on earth."[59] In face of such Enthusiasm, Bonhoeffer agrees that "there is good reason for laying stress on the autonomy of, for example, the state in opposition to the heteronomy of an ecclesiastical theocracy."[60] True, the church must raise questions, for example, about "certain economic or social attitudes and conditions which are a hindrance to faith in Christ and which consequently destroy the true character of [humanity] in the world." (As examples Bonhoeffer mentions "socialism or collectivism," but first of all "capitalism.")[61] However, "the Church cannot indeed proclaim a concrete earthly order which follows as a necessary consequence from faith in Jesus Christ."[62] On the one hand, the church's "negative" strictures against those social attitudes which subvert faith in Christ do need to be made "by the authority of the word of God," as "divine," as "doctrine." On the other hand, the church's "positive contributions toward the establishment of a new order" are not doctrine but "Christian life," "earthly," "not by the authority of God but merely on the authority of the responsible advice of Christian specialists and experts."[63]

The "enthusiastic spiritualism" which Bonhoeffer faults as an instance of "two spheres thinking" he finds exemplified in the Anglo-Saxon countries and particularly in the United States. In the development of American democracy the dominant influence, more dominant than Calvinist ideas of original sin, was the spiritualism of the Dissenters who took

58. Bonhoeffer, *Ethics*, 199.
59. Bonhoeffer, *Ethics*, 196.
60. Bonhoeffer, *Ethics*, 362.
61. Bonhoeffer, *Ethics*, 361.
62. Bonhoeffer, *Ethics*, 360.
63. Bonhoeffer, *Ethics*, 361.

refuge in America: "the idea that the Kingdom of God on earth cannot be built by the authority of the state but only by the congregation of the faithful." True, Bonhoeffer concedes, America too is "suffering from severe symptoms of secularization." But there "the cause does not lie in the misinterpretation of the distinction between the two offices or kingdoms, but rather in the reverse of this." And what is that? Answer: "the failure of the enthusiasts to distinguish at all between the office or kingdom of the state and the office or kingdom of the Church."[64]

That, too, we recall, is a form of "two spheres thinking." And in this case, too, it "ends only with the total capitulation of the Church to the world." Bonhoeffer finds that documented by "the New York church registers." "Godlessness remains more covert. And indeed in this way it deprives the Church even of the blessing of suffering and of the possible rebirth which suffering may engender."[65] So we return to Bonhoeffer's (Luther's?) doctrine of the two kingdoms. It is a solidarity of the suffering church with the suffering world, both suffering from their common sin. In that solidarity between two "polemical opposites," the church is represented not as an ecclesiastical theocracy, whether of the left or of the right, imposing its agenda upon the state, though it does call all society to account for its subversion of faith in Christ. Nor in this solidarity is the church's most positive contribution the "earthly" wisdom it offers toward "a new order." That, too. But the church's "immeasurable grace and privilege" is through its servantlike disciples in the world. It is their unique authority, as church, penitently and forgivingly to "atone" for their people — and for now, arcanely. With that comes "the possible rebirth which suffering may engender."

Might this Bonhoeffer, both in his life and his writings, qualify as a "responsible interpretation" of Barmen, specifically on the embattled issue of reprioritizing the authorities? For he does describe the church's battle in its entirety, not only as a *Kampf* amongst the *Kirchen* to exclude the innerchurch secularization of the gospel — that, too, and first of all, though only as a *Vorgeplänkel* — but especially that major battle, that *Kampf um das Christentum,* in which the church contends for the world as sinner among sinners, but atoningly as suffering servant.

---

64. Bonhoeffer, *Ethics*, 104-5.
65. Bonhoeffer, *Ethics*, 105.

CHAPTER 6

A Philippine Revolution:
From Patients to Agents

Part One: Historic Ironies of Filipino Faith

A Vatican II Reformation?

The 1986 revolution in the Philippines invoked as its battle-cry, "People Power" *(lakas ng bayan)*. It was more than a slogan. It evokes a potent image of actual accomplishment, a historic street scene in Quezon City demonstrating the immense, if uncertain potential of the Filipino people. Here is one eyewitness's exuberant description of that scene. Indeed, it is more than a description. It is also, as I hope to explain later, a confession of faith.

> The revolution took place a short seventy-seven hours between February twenty-second and twenty-fifth. The miracle of EDSA [*Epifanio de los Santos Avenue*]. Unarmed men and women, by the tens and hundreds of thousands, attempted to play peacemaker between two warring military camps.[1]

> On the one hand, EDSA was crowded with armored vehicles of the Marcos loyalists sent to Camp Crame to enforce Marcos's rigged election.

1. Francisco F. Claver, S.J., "The Miracle of EDSA: Reflections on the People's Shallow Faith" (March 13, 1986). Unpublished paper. The paper replies to priests who boycotted the snap elections.

On the other hand, holed up inside Camp Crame were the defectors, the troops, who (with Defense Minister Juan Ponce Enrile and General Fidel Ramos) had cast their lot with the election's rightful winner, Corazon Aquino, and were now preparing for a last-stand shootout with the approaching tanks.

In between, on the street called EDSA, were the thousands of "unarmed men and women."

> And they succeeded. They stopped tanks. They silenced guns. They tumbled an entrenched dictatorship. And their only weapons were rosaries, crucifixes, religious images of the Virgin and the Holy Child — and a vulnerability born of faith.[2]

It is this "vulnerability born of faith" to which I want to return, but not directly.

Eventually, in the second part of this case study, we shall have to deal with the sheer hyperbole of these confessors' self-explanation. See what we have achieved, they exclaim more in amazement than in boasting. See what has been done by us, of all people. Their language leaves no doubt that it was all an extraordinary divine intervention: their intensified language about "revolution" and "miracle" or about rosaries and crucifixes as "weapons." But while it was all the doing of God, it seemed, all the more ironically, to be their own doing as well — that is, if "faith" can be understood as a kind of doing. "*They* succeeded, *they* stopped tanks, *they* silenced guns, *they* tumbled an entrenched dictatorship." By faith they did. Our question will be how such a large-scale effect can be credited to such a modest and vulnerable agency as faith. It is one more theological question about the nature of confessing, this time how confessing redefines victims from patients into agents by virtue of their faith. To that we shall return in Part Two.

First, let me try to account historically for this Philippine "People Power." By that I do not mean to diminish the miraculousness of "the miracle of EDSA" except to disclaim that that event was a sudden, unprecedented bolt out of the blue. On the contrary, it had a prehistory. Even as a Christian phenomenon, and in large part it does seem to be that, *lakas ng bayan* ["people power"] was anticipated by earlier developments. The ele-

2. Claver, "The Miracle of EDSA."

ment of "miracle" may still be here in the way "power" is credited to people's faith out of all proportion to their faith's inherent causal efficacy. It recalls the traditional Christian wonderment called "forensic justification." But that ironic disparity between the meagerness of faith and what all is "reckoned" to it, that "surplus value" of faith may still figure within the continuities of history.

One example from recent Filipino history to which we shall here confine ourselves is the Basic Christian Community (BCC) movement.[3] That form of church life at the grassroots (Filipinos says "bamboo-shoots") is one of the five portents which Karl Rahner, leading mentor at the Second Vatican Council, later foresaw as shaping the future church. Here we shall be reviewing the BCC movement in the Philippines as that developed over the twenty years between the mid-sixties and the mid-eighties. Those are the years of the Marcos government and, at least as significant, the years following the Second Vatican Council. These two sequences converged in the Philippines to encourage a volatile Christian populism. One of its main themes is the participatoriness which comes with faith and the unusual potency of such popular participation.

My account of the BCCs is based intentionally on that of the same eyewitness I just quoted, Bishop Francisco Claver, S.J. His is not the only account, of course, and in fact it is one that might be contested by critics both on the political left and the political right, the adherents both of "Marx and Marcos." And not just the secular political left as such. Also the *Christian* political left. By listening selectively to bishops like Claver and his likeminded colleagues in the Catholic Bishops' Conference of the Philippines (CBCP), Bishops Fortich and Vidal and others, we necessarily mute alternative voices like those of Fr. Edicio de la Torre or Sr. Virginia Fabella, as well as many a Christian confessor among Philippine Protestants. Many of these sought to make their witness precisely by boycotting the so-called "February Revolution," though some of them in turn came to regret their abstention and said so publicly. For that matter, the bishops whom I have chosen to sample are themselves regarded as far too left-leaning by many Filipinos, both in church and state. And with most of

---

3. Much of Claver's writing on the BCCs is from a talk he gave in January 1986, at the Philippine Bishops' meeting on "History of Philippine BCCs." Cf. Mary T. Fitzpatrick, F.C.J., *Bishop Francisco F. Claver, S.J., 1972-90, On the Local Church* (Malate, Manila: De La Salle University Press, 1995).

these bishops, as they admit, conversion away from a hierarchical mentality to a Vatican II interest in "reformation" was slow in coming and quite reluctant. So there is no wish here to exaggerate the progressiveness of the CBCP, even today.

However, a position like Claver's, in addition to being readily accessible in print, does reflect some of the more "revolutionary" changes both in the ecclesiastical hierarchy and in the Aquino government. That privileged position of influence, of course, saddles such a theology with an added burden of responsibility once its adherents come to power — a burden we shall ponder in the third and final part of this case study. But the thing about a position like Claver's, which is most germane to this study, is that it illustrates one of the features of a confessing movement, which the Philippine revolution also gives signs of being, with Claver as one of its most articulate confessors. In such movements, Christian *confessio,* whatever else it is, is an appeal for and to the oppressed. Notice, an appeal not only in their behalf, as advocacy, but also directly *to* them, engaging them as participant actors newly responsible for their own history.

It is Claver's claim — again, I would call it a confession — that Basic Christian Communities, though of course they have been elicited and shaped by subsequent events in those two decades of Philippine history, in their origin are a "creation of Vatican II inspiration." "The triggering mechanism" for the BCCs was not Latin American liberation theology, which came later and is in its own way another form of Iberian Catholicism recreated by Vatican II.

"The initial impetus" for the BCCs came from Vatican II in its emphasis on the church's task of "socially transforming the world," most importantly its emphasis on lay participation.

> For important as all [the Council's] other ideas may be in re-defining the Church's mission . . . , the manner of putting them into practice could well have been done in a pre-Vatican II manner — hierarchically, uncollegially, without much reference to the action or thought of the laity. Injecting a participatory ethic, as Vatican II did, into the ordinary life and working of the Church — made for a qualitative difference . . . in its very being [and action] as Church. . . .[4]

4. Fitzpatrick, *Bishop Francisco F. Claver.*

And since Claver goes on to argue that what finally impels the BCCs' participativeness is their "faith," their Christian faith, let me round out his historical thesis by suggesting that that, too — not just the emphasis upon participation, but the deeper emphasis upon faith — was likewise anticipated in the Second Vatican Council.

If so, could it be that in this one respect at least, Vatican II turns out to be at long last that "general, free and Christian council" which the confessors at the time of the Reformation had urged Emperor Charles V to urge the Pope to convoke? Four centuries too late, perhaps. But in its new appreciation of the biblical accent upon faith, the Second Vatican Council certainly outdid, and did more spontaneously, what the sixteenth century Council of Trent had done only guardedly and sometimes grudgingly. Not all Catholic historians would agree with the one who saw in Vatican II "a revolution that brought to an end the Tridentine Era of the Church and the whole fortress mentality characteristic of the Roman Catholic Church since Trent." But it is hard to contest his further claim that "the seeds of a democratic revolution were sown at Vatican II," particularly by the role it accorded the whole people of God as believers.

The fact that Vatican II's reemphasis upon faith should now emerge in the Philippines is almost too paradoxical a connection not to dramatize. Especially so, when one recalls that it was Charles V's son, Philip II after whom the Philippines were named, who so single-mindedly devoted his reign to the extirpation of Protestantism by Inquisition and conquest, whose "Christianization" of the Filipinos contributed tragically to their heritage of national dependency, further to be exploited by the later colonialist policies of the U.S. Filipino dependency, blamed for that country's "damaged culture," sets its poverty in adverse contrast to its flourishing East Asian neighbors like Japan and South Korea and Thailand and Hong Kong and Singapore, whose economies have grown with far fewer natural resources than the richly endowed Philippines. The latter had been called by one of Aquino's own economic advisers "the basket case of Asia."

It is hard to imagine an unlikelier environment — or on second thought, perhaps, a likelier one — for the Christian preoccupation with faith and what faith entails for believers' initiative in society. Historians have found it odd that in all of Asia, where Christianity began, the only predominantly Christian nation is this impoverished, dependent Philippines. That may in time seem less odd if, as John England and others have alerted us, not just Asia but the Philippines as well is the place to watch for new and "living theologies of *confession*."

If the initial impulse for Basic Christian Communities in the Philippines came from Vatican II's stress on people's firsthand participation, and behind that, its stress on their faith, what is likewise true is that this impetus eventuated in the BCCs only under the peculiar circumstances of the next twenty years of Philippine history. The circumstances have been not only peculiar, in the sense of unique to the Philippines, they have also been ironic. The quality of historical irony is prominent in Bishop Claver's telling of the story. And the irony in his story is not just aesthetic, though it is that. Finally, it is theological irony. Claver as much as says that the story of the BCCs — and because of them, the story of the "revolution" — cannot be accounted for strictly in terms of human agency and human design, but begs an explanation larger than ourselves and often in spite of ourselves. Nevertheless, it was also "our" doing. That is the strange disproportion of faith.

One is reminded of Karl Barth's wry recollection regarding the part he had played in the so-called Barthian revolution: the church-bell tolled and awakened the sleeping village because he, staggering up the dark stairway of the belfry, had accidentally clutched the bell-rope thinking it was the railing. Luther similarly observed in retrospect that the Reformation came about as his colleagues and he had sat in Wittenberg drinking beer. Developments in the Philippines were nowhere as leisurely as that — nor of course were they in Safenwil or Wittenberg — but they were equally unplanned. This is all the more ironic in a movement that concentrates on popular self-determination. Ironic it is, though not contradictory, as we shall see, given what Claver means by faith.

Irony: The BCCs and the FFF

Consider as one example of an ironic turn of events the role played in the BCCs by the Federation of Free Farmers (FFF). This organization had been founded in the early fifties by Jerry Montemayor independently of the church, and "deliberately so." It was not until years later, in 1967 — two years after the close of the Second Vatican Council, but notice, one year before Medellin — that the Roman Catholic Church of the Philippines held a Catholic Rural Congress in Cagayan de Oro, and at that congress "firmly if quietly decided to go to the barrios." "Up till then [the church's] pastoral work was *poblacion* oriented — which means that most, if not all, of its attention was being put on what amounted to the more privileged classes of Philippine society."

Because of this post–Vatican II redirecting of the church's attention to the poor, pastors cast about for ways to implement the Rural Congress's call to go to the barrios and thus discovered the potential of the Federation of Free Farmers. Until it was "discovered" by the churches, the FFF had been very much a struggling organization.

> Fortunately by then Montemayor had himself come to the conclusion that the Church was important for his scheme of social reform. When the Church started giving its support to the FFF, the organization perceptibly began to grow by leaps and bounds to become at the start of the 70's a real power to contend with in the local politics of many a province, especially in Mindanao.[5]

Here already was irony. Two organizations — one struggling but experienced, the other established but inexperienced — reverse their previous aloofness toward each other out of new-felt mutual need. The result was that the FFF gained political power from the church and the church gained an image of compassion for the masses from the FFF.

But the irony does not end there. Later, when martial law was imposed, the FFF ceased to be an independent social organization and, at least at the national level and in its top leadership, became a pawn of the Philippine government. When in 1973 the government announced the first referendum, "word came from the FFF national office to vote 'yes' to martial law. That suggested *yes* vote sounded the death-knell of the FFF as a credible and effective organization for agrarian reform."

Was it not precisely in local and regional FFF seminars that rank and file members had been taught to be methodically "critical," critical about martial law itself and about the fear it engenders? So it is understandable that these local groups were at first puzzled, then disillusioned by what they perceived as the FFF's contradiction of its own principles in its "weak-kneed capitulation to government pressure."

Membership in the FFF dropped off to "ridiculous lows." At its next

---

5. Fitzpatrick, *Bishop Francisco F. Claver.*

national convention in Tacloban its leaders dismantled the organization. Many of its middle-level leaders "were arrested under most mysterious circumstances and the suspicion was strong that this was done with the active support — if not connivance — of the organization's top leadership." However,

> the training for leadership that the old FFF was noted for was not, with the death of the organization, a total waste. The products of FFF leadership training seminars moved into their home communities, became the nucleus, more often than not, of incipient BCCs, bringing with them into BCCs a strong social consciousness.[6]

That was essentially the same social consciousness, notice, that had been called for by Vatican II but now, ironically, was being sharpened by experienced disillusionment to become more intentionally critical and local.

Irony: The BCCs and Persecution

Quite as ironic as the part that the Federation of Free Farmers played in bringing Vatican II to fruition in the Basic Christian Communities is the part played by persecution from the Marcos regime, especially as that persecution extended more and more to the lay leaders of the BCCs and to the BCCs themselves. "Instead of stifling them," Claver marvels, "the persecution only served to strengthen them and the whole Church through them."

> If from 1972 to 1975 it was mainly priests and religious who were protesting the government's rampant abuse of human rights, in the later seventies and up to now [1986] it is ordinary people who have taken up the task of prophetic protest. . . .[7]

And though they are the "most vulnerable, [they] persist in their courageous protesting despite the heavy price they have had to pay for it." Claver's use, again, of the word "vulnerable" recalls his earlier expression, "the vulnerability of faith." And his use of the word "protest" recalls Henri

6. Fitzpatrick, *Bishop Francisco F. Claver,* 37.
7. Claver, "History of Philippine BCCs."

de Lubac's reminder: to "protest," in its primary but by now archaic sense, means much the same as to confess, as in protesting one's faith. That in fact is what made ordinary Filipino believers vulnerable to persecution by the regime, their confessing their faith.

But persecution not only by the regime. The official church bears its own share of guilt for the persecution of its members, at least by acquiescence or default. Claver faults those among his fellow bishops who have conducted a kind of "smiling persecution" of their own. To them his word "persecution" must seem exaggerated, but not to "those [bishops] who have seen their people harassed and punished, shot and murdered, simply for doing what their faith required them to do as a community of believers."

The fact that the government has felt it necessary to persecute the BCCs as subversive — or for that matter, the fact that "elements on the Left" have tried to exploit them for their own brand of revolution — proves "how BCCs have become a potent force in Philippine society simply for the fact that they are Christian *and* ecclesial." Claver underscores that in order to sustain their effectiveness the BCCs must remain both Christian and church, even in face of persecution from their own Christian *and* church authorities. That, too, is ironic.

Irony: Marxist Reason and BCC Faith

A third sample of irony in Claver's account of the BCCs is the way in which they have had to transmute their own earlier Marxist ideology into a consciously Christian process of "discernment." When in 1975 in Baguio City Canon Francois Houtart of Louvain conducted a month-long seminar on structural analysis, the markedly Marxist form of social analysis that Houtart was propagating was in turn promoted enthusiastically throughout the Philippines.

Eventually, the Marxist orientation of Houtart's way of analyzing society came to be questioned and other modes of social analysis were sought and tested.

> That those efforts were made at all brings to the fore another aspect of the BCCs that cannot be stressed enough, namely, that they are first and foremost *communities of discernment*. What this means is simply that BCCs will not only analyze the human situation they are in: they

will have to bring their faith to bear on what they have analyzed — and on their very mode of analysis — and let the light of faith suffuse and sublimate the light of human reasoning.[8]

In an earlier day Luther's "On Secular Authority — To What Extent It Should Be Obeyed," a contemporary of Machiavelli's very different *The Prince,* had noted how political reason is "unfettered" by faith. Faith frees such reason to be also more critical. Similarly, Claver observes, "social analysis is an enduring aspect of BCCs, but from an all-pervasive perspective of faith that makes Basic Christian Communities *Christian.*" The *aggiornamento* of Vatican II opened the church's windows to the modern world, inhaling what blew in, including Marxism, but also re-inspiring it and giving it back Christianized and churched. Yet none of this happened, apparently, in a way that even the most conciliar Filipino bishops could have predicted.

The delicious irony of it all may be evident enough, especially to confessors like Claver and his fellow bishops who put such great store in faith. But so do others like Ed. de la Torre for whom it is axiomatic that "Christianity is faith, not ideology." Faith, as Claver insists, "is what makes or breaks the BCC." "The faith" is the BCC's *"raison d'etre,"* "basic to its being and operation." Without Christian faith, these local communities degenerate into "purely political groups under the guise of being Church." It is understandable, therefore, given such allowance for faith, why the BCCs would be convinced that their own historical development was scarcely their doing, why they would shrug off their own initiative in that history with a kind of cosmic "aw pshaw" and credit it all instead, as Claver does, to the "Holy Spirit." That good-natured pleasure at being trumped by a God who knows better and cares better than we, would be what one might expect if the BCCs are essentially what Claver insists they are, "faith communities."

What one might *not* expect, may I suggest, is that the selfsame faith which so relishes minimizing its own human agency, should at the same time do the apparent opposite, assume almost godlike responsibility. "The poor are now to participate fully in the life of the Church, and indeed not as *objects* of the Church's concern but as *subjects,* who 'in *faith*' function as active, thinking *creators . . .* of their own destiny." This, Claver concludes, is the really "deeper significance" of the events he has recounted, namely, that

8. Claver, "History of Philippine BCCs."

"they carried forward [from Vatican II], as no other development in the Church up till then had done, the primal notion of a participatory Church." How so? By "putting the responsibility of its evolvement on every least member of that same Church." That such human participativeness rather than historical passivity should accrue from faith may be the biggest irony of all. To that we now turn.

Part Two: Weak Faith Yet Real Revolution

Faith "In" and "About"

Let me retrieve from our opening paragraph the phrase with which Bishop Claver explained "the miracle of EDSA," namely, "the vulnerability of faith." Others have spoken about "the vulnerability of the Cross," which amounts to the same thing. "For in the vulnerability of the Cross," says one Filipino account, "is our power to rise as a people." The vulnerability of Christ becomes the vulnerability of his liberated believers. That is no passive, servile vulnerability but, on the contrary, a vulnerability with unique power, including political power. So unique is it that it is accessible only to faith. But then faith is accessible to everyone, not only to this or that elite, but to "the people" *(bayan)*. Indeed, that seems to be one of the most powerful features of this faith, its sheer inclusiveness. Even the most vulnerable in Filipino society may, through faith in the cruciform Christ, see their vulnerability transmuted into power — a power, that is, which is Christ's own.

What is it about faith, according to these Philippine confessors, that endows its ordinary subjects with such extraordinary power? That question could be understood as asking: what or who is the sufficing object of their faith? Whom do they find to be so trustworthy that they would entrust themselves to be revolutionized by him? (The extravagantly Marian piety of the people might expand the question to read, "and revolutionized by *her*?") To that question the answer from Philippine liberationists, at least from those like Claver, is remarkably traditional, not uncritical but traditional. The One in whom they believe is the Trinitarian God who, incarnate in the human Jesus, died and was raised for the benefit of others, as those beneficiaries — sinners all — come under the power of the Holy Spirit. In this sort of episcopal theology, popular Marianism is well sublimated and not noticeably in competition with Christ or Trinity. It is all there, the catholic tradition intact: Trinity, incarnation, perhaps even vicarious atonement, a high sacramental realism in the means of grace and, at the center of everything, cross and resurrection.

Exactly because the answer is so traditional — the answer, I mean, to the question, on whom is their faith targeted? on what sort of God? — we may be lulled into overlooking an extraordinary feature, a potentially revolutionary feature in this otherwise traditional faith. The form in which we have put the question may be underasking their faith. A more expansive form of the question would be, not only whom is their faith *in* but also whom is all their faith *about*? God is indeed the One they believe in, but not the only One their faith is about. Faith is also about people. Faith is about people because God in Christ is about people. Exactly because of this God they trust, they therefore trust that people are what God's Christ treats them as being, a precious creation and inviolable.

We are reminded of the confession by Martin Luther King Jr. that with Jesus people are "somebodies," not "nobodies." A joint pastoral letter was issued by the CBCP from Tagaytay City scarcely a year after Ninoy Aquino's assassination, entitled "Let There Be Life." It is a ringing call for faith in face of an almost overwhelming unfaith. Unfaith in this case was the pervasive national cynicism about the value of human life, an unfaith that had gotten accustomed to violence as inevitable, indeed as practically normative, an unfaith that comes to regard killing — whether the so-called "salvagings" by the government's "secret marshals" or the "liquidations" by the National People's Army — as expectable and dismissible under the alibi "political." The Christian antithesis to this unfaith is a counter-faith, not just a Christian ethic or moral reflex, but Christian *faith*, courageous enough to trust what to all appearances is hardly obvious, namely, human beings' "unique dignity stemming from [their] creation in God's image."

Notice how explicitly Christian is the bishops' reasoning for this faith in "human dignity." Their reasons appeal directly to the gospel of Christ. "First, Jesus the Lord became [human] to save all [humans] — all without exception, without distinction as to race or color, social class or personal worth, . . . no matter how depraved, how oppressive or sinful." "Secondly, by becoming incarnate, Christ further ennobled [humanity]. . . . He identifies Himself with the very least . . . to the extreme point of giving His own life for them in order precisely for them 'to have life and to have it to the full.'" "Thirdly, everyone of us, by baptism, in baptism takes upon himself [or herself] the burden of furthering Christ's redemptive task, . . . being totally men and women for *others* — even to the giving of life itself for them." "This," say the bishops, is what "Christ has set for us, and it is only in faith that we can fathom its meaning, accept it and attempt living its implications to the full." Faith in Christ necessarily entails faith about his people, all people.

On second thought, it might be said after all that faith, for these Filipino confessors, is not only faith *about* people but also faith *in* people, if only in a derivative sense. One bishop argues for "an obvious conclusion for the ordained leadership of the Church," namely, that faith in the Holy Spirit must also be *faith in the people* among whom [the Holy Spirit] breathes and moves and lives."

The Same Object of Both Faith and Criticism

There is small danger, so far as I can tell, that such "faith in the people" is likely to become idolatrous, even in the modern mode which Habermas and others have identified, namely, the replacing of God with humankind as the bearer of history. Any such over-estimate of humanity is prevented, if by nothing else, by the selfsame bishops' indictments of their people's sin, and by implication their own sin. The same pastoral letter, "Let There Be Life,"[9] crackles with a most searching, self-revealing critique of Filipino inhumanity, indeed sub-humanity, a progressive defacing of their own divine "image." So incriminating is the evidence there is no wonder that to continue to affirm people's resemblance to God must indeed require faith.

"If we [Filipinos] indeed have such a high regard for life [as we are touted to have], then why is [life] treated so cheaply among us?" If "we are basically a people of peace," as we claim, "why the maiming and killing at the least . . . provocation?" "We are a people of great sensitivity. . . . But [then] why the insensitivity to the suffering we inflict, . . . the harm we cause to others by our acts of unconcern?" "Hunger can kill just as easily and systematically as bullets and guns." (In the Philippines, according to

---

9. "Let There Be Life: Joint Pastoral Letter on the Sacredness of Human Life and Its Defenses," *Pastoral Letters 1945-1995*, 582-89, ed. Rev. Pedro C. Quitorio III (Manila: Peimon Press, 1995). Read in all Catholic churches of the Philippines on July 22, 1984.

figures from UNICEF, four hundred children die each day because of ill-
nesses linked to malnutrition.)

All this has left "deep scars on our people's memories," a lasting burden "on the nation's conscience," "unsettling contradictions in our collective psyche as a people." "Possibly there still remains in our way of life, our
culture, forms of thinking, modes of behaving that hark back strongly to
our pre-Christian past." "Possibly we harbor in [the] darkest depths [of
our collective psyche as a people] devils that so far have defied the exorcis-
ing force of our Christian faith." We Filipinos are, no less than others,
"born with the sin of Adam and hence prone to evil."

One might suppose that after such a devastating, all-leveling denunciation, any surviving confidence in human dignity would be contradictory and hollow. At any rate, it dare not be said that when it comes to "critical thinking" or "critical analysis," which are high priorities amongst the
Marxists but also in Basic Christian Communities generally, the Christians
are at a loss for a criticalness of their own, including self-criticalness. On
the contrary, the faith they profess, though it may seem to be at odds with
their discouraging critiques of human perversity, outdoing even the ideological, structural critiques by the Marxists, seems rather to be the very resource — their faith does — which liberates them to be as critically realis-
tic as they are.

That, for them, is itself an important aspect of Christian liberation.
Faith enables self-honesty and thus illustrates what was said earlier about
the BCCs as communities of "discernment": they are to "let the light of
faith suffuse and sublimate the light of human reasoning," not least of all
socio-critical reasoning of oneself and one's people. Precisely because critique is not the last word, but deliverance from it is — precisely because
"every human being born with the sin of Adam and hence prone to evil" is
the same human being who in Christ is "eminently redeemable" — can the
critique be suffered, suffered out of existence, freely. As another episcopal
letter put it, what Christ frees us for is the "truth," even when the tyrannical most powerful plausibility structures of our society then put that critical truth in turn "on trial" and condemn it (and us) as "subversive" and
"criminal."

That is "the vulnerability of faith" or "of the Cross." Faith communities, surviving daily as they do the most mortifying criticism of all, God's
own, are freed to absorb other lesser criticisms, no matter how unjust, yet
in the same way that the divine criticism was met by God in Christ. He

who is the object of faith is also the object of the ultimate criticism, and the one because of the other. And how was it that he so trustworthily met that criticism? He did so in the conviction that the guiltiest culprit, the cruelest adversary, is still meant to live and not die, and to that end is to be loved outlastingly — and, almost surely, sacrificially. The point is, therein lies the faith communities' superior power over merely political and economic power.

Vulnerable, Yes, but Powerful?

For years theologians in the Philippines have decried that country's popular, quietistic Christologies, "The Spanish Christ" whom Unamuno had referred to as "this Corpse Christ," the morbid preoccupation with his agonies and burial — *Cristo Entierro* (Christ Interred). Possibly such fatalistic Christologies were motivated, so say some analysts, by the Filipinos' own excessive fear of dying, "the sovereign preoccupation not to die." The alternative Philippine Christology we have been sampling in this case study, "faith" being its chief corollary, including "faith in the people" of God's love, seems instead to move deliberately against the fear of death, against acquiescence in oppression, against counting the cost. Not that there is in this recent Christology an absence of *theologia crucis*. Hardly. But "the vulnerability of the Cross" now gains its power only in view of Jesus' pre-crucifixion biography, his love of the people which earned him that cross, and in view of his resurrection. This cross ensued from a real life, and from this cross real life accrues. And that life, so believed, makes for victorious vulnerability.

Take, for example, one prominent theme that has come up within the BCCs for "critical analysis" or "discernment," namely, what Tagalogs call *lakas*: power, pull, clout, influence.[10] It is said that ordinary Filipinos are more political than other people and that this is largely due to the high value they place on *lakas*, to the point of being uncritically enamored of it. In addition, there is the tradition of strong loyalty ties in the patron-client relationship between the *malakas*, the very powerful, and his dependents or followers, with a deeply inbred sense of their *utang na loob*, their moral

10. Francisco F. Claver, S.J., "Church Power and the Revolution (Episcopal Reflections)," *Pulso* 1, no. 4 (1986).

indebtedness. Admittedly, there are also indigenous countervailing values, like *awa* (mercy) or like *delicadeza* (gentleness), which serve to restrain the tyranny of *lakas*. Still, there can be no doubt that the crimes of the former Marcos regime were an excess of *lakas*, hence, with strong and virtually demonic reinforcement from the normative culture.

Consequently, a priority for the local Christian communities of discernment, according to one report, "is the need to look deep into our Christian tradition and see how faith and the complex of values that are born of faith can correct the negative aspects of our concept and practice of *lakas*." This is seen as the first step in the long process of Philippine "value transformation" or, as it is also called, the church's own "reformation." For, as this report continues, the very fact "that the Church . . . because of its prominent role in the recent revolution is now being called . . . *malakas* forces us to wonder whether in fact, not only in appearance, the Church of the Philippines has become too political and *malakas* in the cultural acceptance of the term."

That being a clear and present danger, the challenge is so to deploy the contrasting "power of the Kingdom," which is "essentially non-violent," that "our exercise of the power of the Kingdom will [never] be debased to using it merely for base political ends" of *lakas*. But that, once more, requires prior discernment:

> With ever widening and deepening discernment in the Church, we all — bishops, clergy, religious, laity — will begin fully to see what evangelical power is, . . . to try to plumb deeper the mystery of the Paschal Mystery in our lives as Christians.[11]

"For in the vulnerability of the Cross is our power to rise as a people."[12]

Yet is it politically meaningful, even morally meaningful, to speak of such vulnerability as "power"? One would hardly need to be a cynic to perceive that, given the enormity of organized economic exploitation and the persistent violations of human rights in the Philippines today, the very minimum that is needed in the way of power is the power to withstand evil, not endure or tolerate it, the power to counter, to oppose, to fight

---

11. Claver, "Church Power."

12. Cf. Franciso Claver, S.J., "Kibawe's Empty Tomb," *Sojourners* 10, no. 8 (8 August 1981): 8-9.

back. But isn't that retaliatory sort of power the diametric antithesis of what the Christian confessors there are extolling as the "vulnerability of faith," the meekness of Christ? How could such meekness, however confident the faith from which it springs, possibly be a match in any practical, consequential sense for the systematic violence it is everywhere up against? Or are practical consequences to be dismissed as unimportant so long as one stands one's ground and makes a good confession of the faith? But then if it is a function of confessing that victims are changed from patients to agents, from objects to subjects, isn't it fair to expect that their new subjecthood is historically consequential?

The question is hardly foreign to Philippine confessors. Therefore, the first thing that must be granted in reply is that one does not need to be a cynic to sympathize with the question, nor should it be ruled out as lack of faith. There is for the Christian Filipino, faced with violent evil, an honest dilemma, and evidently one of the initial objectives in the BCCs' process of critical discernment is to come to terms with that dilemma. As an "ordinary means of redressing wrongs," says Claver, "I doubt violence is Christian." "This is where we as Christians differ most," he thinks, "from communists, even if we may be one with them in our desire to right injustice, to uplift the downtrodden, to give power to the masses."

> "Put your sword back in your scabbard. Turn the other cheek." These are hard sayings of Christ, but they do point, I believe, to something that is at the core of Christianity: not repaying evil with evil.[13]

That is one firm pole of the dilemma, called forgiveness.

"But does this mean," Claver asks, identifying the opposite pole, "that when we suffer violence we must meekly give in? Allow ourselves to be trampled upon?" What would be wrong with that? His answer is remarkable. What would be wrong with that is that in that case we would be denying "our dignity as children of God" and would be selling out for mere survival. No, and this *is* the other side of the bind Christians are in, any "decrees or government policies that in one way or another infringe" upon people's God-resembling humanity, "and hence by that very fact are acts of violence," must be opposed, disobeyed.

13. Francisco F. Claver, "The Violence of the Meek," in *Third World Liberation Theologies: A Reader,* ed. Deane William Ferm (Maryknoll, N.Y.: Orbis, 1986), 337.

But then how to oppose the violating of God's children without violating the violators, who likewise are God's children? How to practice "not repaying evil with evil" yet to do so "effectively," that is, toward correcting evil? In short, Claver asks, "what is Christian?" His answer: "some act, I should think, like David's toward Saul — the violence of the meek."[14] "The Lord put you in my power, but I would not raise my hand" (2 Samuel 26:23). Thus did David do violence to his persecutor Saul: the violence of the meek. "This is not just a nice phrase, a clever paradox," Claver explains. "For the action comes from strength. It also comes from gentleness, the strength *and* gentleness of Christ."[15]

Examples of such "violence of the meek" are the people's boycotting of the government's imposed referendum, their speaking out critically about the dictatorship, their striking for humane wages in industries that enjoy special privileges. There is no question but that such actions are disobedient, that they disrupt the general order, and that they incur costly penalties. This

> violence of the meek . . . Christ practiced even unto Calvary. He violated the Sabbath law to correct its unjust man-made prescriptions. He criticized public authorities openly for their twisted interpretations of the law. He gathered the people together against the wishes of those in power and spoke to them of *the* kingdom that was to come.[16]

And when, like Christ, some of Bishop Claver's church workers were hauled before a military tribunal, and, like Christ, accused of "inciting to sedition," who should turn out in their support but the people of the Bukidnon diocese. "They came by the hundreds last Saturday, in token delegations from parishes and barrios, from farms and hills, to show their solidarity" with the accused.

"Their message . . . will not be lost on the Pilates and the Herods, the suborned witnesses and the Palace Guards of Bukidnon."[17] So then the violence of the meek does work results, perhaps even in the adversary? So

---

14. Claver, "Violence of the Meek."

15. Claver, "Violence of the Meek."

16. Claver, "Violence of the Meek."

17. Francisco F. Claver, S.J., "The Stones Will Cry Out," in *Third World Liberation Theologies: A Reader,* ed. Deane William Ferm (Maryknoll, N.Y.: Orbis, 1986), 339.

"we trust," says Claver. David "could have used the other kind of violence — the killing, hurting kind. He did not. And it made Saul think. It made Saul persecute David less." To the detached observer, that may seem like small compensation for David's faith, for his "violence of the meek": all it yielded him was that Saul persecuted him "less." Who could possibly mount a revolution on that?

The "Surplus Value" of Faith

I conclude this second part of our case study with a paradoxical observation: whatever public accomplishments are claimed for faith, the claims are always exaggerated; or so it seems. Far more is attributed to the believers' believing than it deserves credit for, at least on any critical analysis of historical cause and effect. But isn't that one of the most persistent audacities of the Christian confession? A desperate father appeals to Jesus in behalf of his epileptic boy and, although the father himself admits he is as much unbeliever as believer, Jesus credits the father's faith as though that were responsible for the boy's recovery (Mark 9:20-27). Elsewhere Jesus announces, "Daughter, your faith has healed you" (Mark 5:34, 10:52), or even, "Your faith has saved you" (Luke 7:50), when any perceptive theist could have told us that what accomplished the healing or the saving was divine providence or, at the least, Jesus — but not these ordinary believers. They, to all appearances, were but objects of divine compassion, not participant, co-responsible subjects. Yet it is as subjects, almost as if they were gods, that they are commended.

Abraham, it is said, "believed" — though, as the story confirms, not all that clear-headedly — and "God counted it [his ambiguous faith] to him [the whole Abraham] as righteousness" (Genesis 15:6). The apostle Paul grounds the whole of our justification, our right and power to live, on such faltering Abrahamic faith of sinners (Romans 4:9, 22; Galatians 3:6). John likewise isolated what "is the victory that overcomes the world," namely, "our faith" (1 John 5:14). The writer "to the Hebrews" explains the heroes and heroines who

> conquered kingdoms, enforced justice, received promises, stopped the mouths of lions, quenched raging fire, escaped the edge of the sword, won strength out of weakness, became mighty in war, put armies to

flight, . . . received their dead by resurrection, . . . were tortured, refusing to accept release, . . . were killed with the sword.[18]

And how did they so prevail? "Through faith."

Max Stackhouse, investigating human rights violations in the Philippines, inquired of Filipino lay workers and preachers what message they were bringing to their people that "empowered them to go on." One answer was: "from Paul — justification by faith." What did they mean by "justification by faith"? Answer: "you alone are responsible for your commitments." But how can they reconcile such swaggering confidence — "you alone are responsible" sounds almost as blasphemous as "your faith has saved you" — with the facts of their own ironic history? Had not Claver made a special point of how, in the development of the Basic Christian Communities, so much of their success seemed independent of or even in spite of human agency? Still, it is the same Claver, who with his fellow confessors, attributes everything to faith. It is as if Christ, whom the believers credit with their success, returns the compliment and shares the credit with them. And why? Because they so much as trusted him, however tenuously.

For us to apply Karl Marx's category, "surplus value," to faith in Christ might strike even our Philippine confessors as carrying the irony too far. After all, Marxists intend the term pejoratively. So it does seem a dubious compliment to pay to faith, even worse to Christ, who *is* that faith's surpassing value. For Filipino Communists, "surplus value" connotes exploitation, a landlord's getting something for nothing out of his alienated workers. For instance, in Angyap, a party-controlled village on the Island of Samar, the Communist Party of Philippines' "Social Investigation and Class Analysis" exposes the farmer Pedro as "rich," meaning he earned thirty to forty-nine percent of his income from the toil of others — his unearned "surplus value."

Still, while the analogy limps, isn't Christian faith in its own way a getting something for nothing out of the labor and suffering of Another? And isn't that its scandal? The revolutionary difference is that in this case the One whose labor the believers "exploit" invites them to do just that, and invites them out of strength — "gentleness and strength." Their "struggle" (a big word in Philippine liberation theology) is to trust that

18. Hebrews 11:33-37.

scandalously sacrificial love. But even when their trust falters, it is still replete with "surplus" results — incommensurable healing, salvation, righteousness, victory, the moving of mountains — all of which are simultaneously reckoned, "valued" as their doing. Their doing, that is, by faith. If nothing else, this Christological use of "surplus value" might serve as one more "suffusing" of Marxist "reason" with Christian "discernment."

The so-called "miracle of EDSA" was boycotted by some Christian leftists on the grounds that it was not a "real" revolution, seeing that it had been led not by "the true revolutionary class" but merely by the middle-class *burgis*. But that was not the only objection. The political complaint was compounded by a theological one. The real, spiritual reason the bourgeois demonstrators had to settle for such a "nonviolent," inauthentic revolution, so the leftist objection goes, was that their *faith* had been too "superficial," too "shallow." To which Claver replied:

> The faith of the people was shallow? I guess the charge is correct. But I cannot help thinking that that shallow faith — and tiny like the biblical grain of mustard seed — was of the kind that moves mountains.[19]

"Precisely because of those two facts ['It did not square with the sacred tenets of *the* revolution, and the faith of the people was shallow'] the miracle of EDSA was even more of a miracle."

Part Three: Saints Return to Sinnerhood — As Saints

Widow with Sword

The "miracle of EDSA" was followed, as it was bound to be, by the "morning after." As the media around the world did not weary of pointing out, after the party comes the hangover. "The honeymoon was over." "After the revolution comes the *Realpolitik*," as *Time* magazine put it, "and happy-ever-afters soon dissolve."[20] The Christian confessors in Manila had had their moment of euphoria, their "self-congratulatory fit," and now that

19. Claver, "The Miracle of EDSA."
20. Pico Iyer, "Cory Aquino Leads a Fairy-Tale Revolution, Then Surprises the World with Her Strength," *Time* (January 5, 1987), 22.

they had gotten what they had wanted, "power," they were finding it an embarrassingly mixed blessing. Barely eight months later, Denis Murphy could observe, "As international readers know by now, the Filipino people did not live happily ever after. . . . Over 1,000 soldiers, rebels and civilians have been killed since then in clashes between Government troops and the Communist-led New People's Army (NPA)."[21] Murphy was writing just as Aquino's own military had attempted an armed coup against her. *The New York Times* might have spoken better than it knew, "Saints return to being sinners." But they might just return to sinnerhood, I would add, *as saints.*

If only the Philippine confessors had not been so trusting in accepting responsibility for the "miracle." For by the same token they now had to accept blame for its inglorious follow-through.

> The day after her victory, Aquino found herself in charge of one of the world's most desperate countries, saddled with a foreign debt of $27 billion, 20,000 armed Communist guerillas and a pile of government institutions that bore her predecessor's monogram.[22]

She and her co-confessors had the dubious fortune of winning the revolution, a further trial that most confessors in the church's history have been spared. We have said that confessing entails an appeal *to* the oppressed as well as *for* them, luring them through their response of faith into responsibility for their whole history. Corazon Aquino, one of Marcos's most visible victims, was one of the oppressed whom the gospel had been spoken not only for but to. She responded, as she said, with "the gift of faith." But in her case that faith response soon incurred a responsibility so onerous and cruciform as to implicate her in her people's most abject sins.

It was one thing for the confessors to speak out against persecution from the underside and to suffer it innocently as witnesses to Christ. It was something else suddenly to find themselves seated in the seats of the persecutors, being held responsible for inflicting injustice that previously they had had the moral luxury of only suffering as victims. The widow Aquino, whose husband apparently had been assassinated by the government, was now herself the government by whom other wives were still being wid-

21. Denis Murphy, "Key Decision in Manila," *America* 155, no. 6 (September 20, 1986): 116.

22. Iyer, "Cory Aquino Leads a Fairy-Tale Revolution," 22-23.

owed. True, all confessors as believers are credited with "surplus value." But only some of them — those who, as we say, "come into power" — are then trusted with a still heavier burden, the sins of the whole people, to be borne as the president's own sin, no longer innocently, but as the just due of a major collaborator. In short, these confessors-turned-authorities, Christians with secular power, are chosen to bear a surplus *dis*-value. In the bargain they may even have to forego the public dignity of confessor-hood, often appearing indistinguishable from ordinary hypocrites and compromisers. This privileged ignominy is usually reserved, by definition, for laypeople.

Corazon Aquino, once acknowledged as "one of the Catholic church's most notable lay leaders," had borne memorable witness to the Christian way of nonviolence versus a national weakness for the opposite. As confessor, she had. But as president, she was herself drawn into exercising that violence and, all the more because of her previous confessional stand, having to justify it. Undoubtedly, for her to resort to killing or the threat of killing militated against what she deeply believed to be the way of Christ. The fact is, not only did she accede to the demand for force, she enacted it, involving herself conspicuously in whatever guilt that entailed. Of course, her critics, including many of her former supporters, would not let her forget that. They may well have been right. Where they may have been wrong is in their failing to see that what she did was at least as much their doing, probably theirs first of all, whose will she was in some measure obliged to execute.

As for widowhood, an evocative symbol in recent Filipino rhetoric, who are all the women whom Aquino's government is blamed for widowing? They are, poignantly for her, the very widows with whom she most personally identified, those like herself whose husbands have died at the hands of the military, including widows of rebel insurgents. She admitted an affinity with these insurgents, not because of their insurgency perhaps, but because of their and her common lot as victims of dictatorship. Marcos in a campaign speech had scoffed, "What qualifications does she have [for the presidency] except that her husband was killed?" That cynical remark turned out to be prophetic in ways he did not foresee. "Looking around," she said, "I may well not be the worst victim, but I am the best known." Her identification with victims of the military probably had something to do with her early releasing of political prisoners and her negotiating a two-month cease-fire with the insurgents. However, when that proved ineffectual and the killing persisted on both sides, she proceeded, as she had threatened she would have to, to "take up the sword of war" against the insurgency. Immediately, she incurred from the left the accusation of "militarist" and "dictator." The charge was extreme but understandable.

So were the charges from the opposite side. The military for its part accused Aquino of "softness" and "weakness," for which they were paying in casualties of their own. Mourning his losses, one officer complained, "we can match [the insurgents] widow for widow." And it was not only the soldiers' own lives that were threatened by the Communists, but also the lives of their families back home in the countryside. The officers were drawn from the rural middle class and the enlisted men came from the same peasant stock as the foot-soldiers in the Communist New People's Army. "The Aquino administration," wrote Richard Kessler, an otherwise sympathetic reporter, "does not seem to grasp the military's concern." On the other hand, when Aquino granted commanders "maximum leeway" in protecting their troops, Gareth Porter, also one of the sometime supporters, faulted her for being "afraid of the military."

The nonviolent widow who was dedicated to reversing Marcos's reign of violence was soon likened to him, and not only by her detractors. Moreover, there were times when the very thing which differentiated her from Marcos was her resorting to force in ways that even he did not, firing on her own troops. On the one hand, she seemed increasingly to resemble Marcos: when "Mrs. Aquino's palace troops opened fire and killed twenty demonstrators," said Francis X. Clines, hardly one of her detractors, "that was a black mark needing greater investigation, considering her reputation as an improvement over the past." On the other hand, there were times when, exactly to improve on her past, she seemed to have to out-Marcos Marcos. Her friend Joker Arroyo admired how different was her response to the August twenty-eighth coup attempt from that of Marcos, who on a similar occasion had hesitated to fire on rebellious troops. "Go ahead, shoot, shoot," she is quoted as saying, "I am not going to be another Marcos."[23]

To focus on Aquino's widowing "sword of war" is to focus on one extreme, of course, and then only to emphasize a point. The point is not that

23. Seth Mydans, "The Embattled Mrs. Aquino," *The New York Times* (November 15, 1987).

public office brings moral dilemmas, or that Aquino was only doing what she had to and therefore is exonerated. For the sake of our argument it would be quite conceivable that her blame was deserved, and that it would have been deserved even if she had had no other choice. That liability comes with the sort of inferior power she inherited as president. It is the sort of power that Christians traditionally have associated with the grim symbol of the sword, though it need not, and usually does not, involve anything so bloody as that. (We have seen this in prior chapters in this book.) This sword-like, retributive power, indispensable and divine as it is, is inferior because it operates by appeal to sinners' self-interest. Therefore, although it uses their sin for the benefit of others, or even for their own benefit, it also inflicts deep hurt in the process, even death, and in any case is powerless to recreate humanity at its core. This latter and more radical task, so the Christian gospel claims, requires God's contrary and preferred power, forgiveness.

But is that superior power of forgiveness — "not returning evil for evil" — any longer within the public competence of a president qua president, however Christian she may be personally? By consenting to the humiliation of cooperating with her constituents in their fallenness, must she not suffer many of the same strictures upon her power that limit them? Their grief over past hurts, or the unrepentence of those who perpetrated the hurts, may render them simply powerless for forgiveness, either to confer it or to profit from it. But if so, isn't she correspondingly disempowered to effect reconciliation, seeing how she has subjected herself to depending on their capacity for response?

Eventually Aquino did seem to swallow her bitterness over her husband's assassination and adopted a more conciliatory stance toward the military. She admonished a crowd in the central Visayan city of Cebu, "What we need now is to support the military. . . . Let's forget the past." To that, however, one Filipino observer replied, "It's fine for her to forget the past; she has power. But what about some poor farm widow whose husband was murdered by soldiers?" That reply is plausible for its pathos but not as literal truth. For is it true that Aquino by becoming president somehow acquired "power" to "forget the past," let alone to get her people to forget it? Wasn't it rather the case that whatever power of forgetting and forgiving she might have had previously, as a Christian, was now being thwarted by the body politic's incapacity to hear it — except as betrayed or pious duty, not as emancipation? *Can* they hear it? If they cannot, neither can she make it happen. That limited is her presidential power by their enfeebled power to respond. So long as "poor farm widows" do not have that power to forget (if they do not) neither would their president have the power to get the nation's past forgotten.

And what if the widows did have the power to forget? There would still be the assassins who were being forgiven. Would they have the power to utilize that forgiveness as anything more than license to persist? Must not their resistance to reform compel a president not to "forget the past" but all the more vigilantly to recall it, keeping alive the "dangerous memory"? Whatever the killers' limits, Aquino was now constricted by those same limits. That came with her job description and her constituency.

The restraint of the saint, her *ex officio* accommodation to the people's sin, mightn't that itself be a saintly mode? Though it is not so much the mode of the confessor, it may be a further stage to which some confessors are promoted as they reinfiltrate a fallen world with its inferior power and try to reinvigorate it from within. That is the incognito, ignominious sainthood that characterizes not Christians as churchlings, as explicit confessors, but Christians as baptized worldlings sustained by the church, at that treacherous frontier where church transmutes into Kingdom. It is the ambiguous dignity peculiar to the lay calling. The widow Aquino, by accepting the presidency, may have taken on more of her widowed nation's lot then she realized, its own crippling disabilities as her own limitations — and blame. Indeed, one would think that the blame alone would have been enough to finish her. For the very Marcos whose diametric antithesis she had been as confessor and, so she hoped, even as president, she was soon blamed for resembling. Not always unjustly. That, too, came with the presidency.

Partnership with Sin

On the other hand, to labor the metaphor of widowhood one more time, apparently there is a part of Philippine society to which the metaphor is inapplicable, namely, the church. As Manila's Cardinal Jaime Sin put it, "The moment the church as an institution marries a political system she becomes a widow in the next generation." The metaphor recalls the church as the Bride of Christ. That Bridegroom the church would lose were it to become wedded instead to "a political system." But notice the qualifier, "the church as an institution." The mix with politics, which is sure to widow the institutional church, is nevertheless appropriate to the church's lay members. "Partisan politics," the cardinal explained, "should be left to the laity."

Leave aside whether the Philippine "church as an institution," next to the government the country's largest landowner and one of its biggest corporate investors, has ever managed for long to stay unmarried to "a political system," including Marcos's, not to mention Cardinal Sin's current suitors, "the greed of capitalism and the atheism of communism." Leave aside whether Aquino's election could ever have prevailed without the bishops' published endorsement (authored chiefly by Claver), or whether the crowds would ever have jammed EDSA had not Cardinal Sin called them out, or whether either of these ecclesiastical interventions, both of them opposed by the Vatican, would ever have materialized without the mounting threat from "a political system" on the left — and its highly politicized church workers. Leave aside whether these churchly identifications with the Aquino administration, then and since, are necessarily "political" (Fr. Vincent Busch) or "moral" rather than "political" (Cardinal Sin) or "a moral responsibility first, then a political duty" (Bishop Claver).

Whatever, the Philippine Catholic "church as an institution," so reads an "Episcopal Reflection" on "Church Power and The Revolution," must henceforth exert its political power only "in a subsidiary way," "receding somewhat from its high visibility in the recent past in its work for justice." The latter-day church must recognize that "the people are now actively asserting themselves as responsible citizens — which was not the case through most of the martial law period when the Church had to assume a more forceful stance in its prophetic role." President Aquino, a symbol of the new laicization, put the matter more bluntly, "I am glad that the church thought it necessary to relate to the present time and not just remain in the dark ages." Although even after her election, church leaders continued to enjoy "irresistible political clout," an expression used by Fr. Antonio Lambino, one of Aquino's "little presidents" — her so-called "Council of Trent" — she seemed to see her dependence on them as more transitional. "We have not been able to really bring about justice for all, so there is still a need for [these spiritual advisers] to be involved." In any case "after Vatican II," she said, "the church seems to be more relevant as far as the laity is concerned. . . . It seems that, before, the church was just prohibiting you from being so many things."

Not that this new burden of lay responsibility, Aquino's "so many things," should now strike laypeople as an unalloyed pleasure. Her own case is bittersweet proof to the contrary. For what are those "many things" now incumbent on lay Christians as never before? To hear Cardinal Sin tell it, what "should be left to the laity" and less to "the church as an institution" is what he called "partisan politics." But is that the thing about politics that puts it off limits for the institutional church, its partisanship? Isn't that the very thing for which Fr. Ed. de la Torre has faulted the church, "We fear to be one-sided"? Surely, as Sin himself would insist, the church must take sides on "moral" issues in the political sector, and may even have to identify with a particular segment of society. Fr. Bienvenido Nebres, the Jesuit provincial superior in the Philippines and one of Aquino's advisers during the election campaign, acknowledged the church's "partisanship." "Toward the end it was no longer a question of supporting Aquino or supporting Marcos, but going for the people." Already in 1981 it was to hundreds of thousands of poor Negrenses that Pope John Paul II announced, "Yes, the preference for the poor is a Christian preference."

Rather, isn't the forbidden partisanship, forbidden to the institutional church but not to its members in the "world," the latters' strange and dangerous partnership with the world's *sin?* With that sin the church, in its public proclamation, can make no compromise but must be unsparingly critical of it, so as to omit none of it from atonement and absolution and liberation. Not that the church does not eat and drink with sinners. What else is the church but that, a banquet of sinners celebrating their freedom under the new immunity of Gospel-and-sacraments? But then follows their risky redeployment back into the old reality. There any power for good has to make the most of a bad situation, at best perfecting the art of the possible. There Christians, too, ineligible for any special exemptions because of their faith, are judged on their own merits and, being found in solidarity with other sinners, are no less subject to criticism, even from their church. It is precisely for that hazardous service, in fact, that they are said to have been freed. One can scarcely fault them for preferring to forego such a privilege, or fault the institutional church for distrusting them with such vulnerable liberties.

It is no wonder, as A. Lin Neumann reported, that Corazon Aquino "often seems ill at ease with the office she now holds." "I would much rather have been a religious leader," she said, "than my present position." From the beginning she admitted, "I don't like politics," but she has always made clear that her dislike is not a matter of taste so much as a moral aversion to complicity and compromise. When advisers chided her for being too honest, she lamented, "I don't want to be dishonest." "I've always been for the truth," but now the truth had to be abridged, seeing how impossible it had become to correct every falsehood. "As the Commander in Chief I could not go all over the country and say, 'Look, this is not true.'" She learned to her regret that even friends must be sacrificed, "people to whom I owe so much or who are really my strongest or most loyal supporters," when political necessity required her to tell them, "I'm very sorry, but I have to ask you to go." One friend plied her with a copy of Machiavelli's *The Prince,* which upon rereading she found, "It isn't me. I tried to find something there I could adapt, but . . . it isn't like Gandhi's work. . . . I really feel that that was what I was cut out to be."[24]

The other side of President Aquino, and both sides seem essential to her spirituality, is that she has also grown to appreciate the godly necessity of political power. Inferior to the gospel as that power may be, and typically manipulative, and though her exercise of that power continually incriminates her and could cost her her life, nevertheless it has become her divine vocation for the sake of the people. Odd as it may seem, that suggests that coercion and compassion for all their difference are politically inseparable. "I was not used to power before," she told a Filipino interviewer. "Now I know that, being President, you can really use power — not only for war."[25] Warlike she has learned to be when necessary. Yet she insists on believing that force and "love" not only can coexist in the same Christian person, but must be politically co-enacted, the one reinforcing the other. Just how is far from clear, much to the bewilderment of the public and especially the public press.

The Carnegie Endowment's Richard Kessler, for his explanation, finds a clue in Scripture. "She's a very biblical type of person. But it's not from a Hallmark card. It's a saintliness as in the Old Testament. On the one hand, you pardon your enemies; on the other, it's an eye for an eye, a tooth for a tooth."[26] As an explanation, the analogy falls short. Seth Mydans of the *New York Times* wished that Aquino had learned better to "blend" what she had learned from Gandhi with some needed "lessons from Machi-

24. Mydans, "The Embattled Mrs. Aquino."
25. Mydans, "The Embattled Mrs. Aquino."
26. Iyer, "Cory Aquino Leads a Fairy-Tale Revolution," 29.

avelli" and he feared that her very softness was tolerating "an escalation of lawlessness and violence."[27] Mydans's own newspaper, equally at a loss to explain Aquino's style, found it harder than he did to conceal admiration. "How Corazon Aquino must enrage her foes: she refuses to fight like a man." The editorial attacks "the frantic attempt by far left and right alike to discredit her for the disorder each is trying to provoke," and then predicts: "Their schemes might succeed if only Mrs. Aquino played by the rules. Her refusal to do so marks her as a real revolutionary, a genuine original and a democrat." My own guess is, Aquino the Christian, presiding over a nominally Christian nation, stoops to dealing with "world" on its own terms only insofar as, and not before, it proves itself incapable of responding to what she calls "peace." Her version of the formula: "First, talk, in keeping with my pledge to negotiate a peace that respects law and democracy; and then fight, should it fail."

Questionable, Answerable

Let me close by suggesting two gains that were made under Aquino's leadership, both of them gains in the people's participativeness. It is too early to judge whether these gains outweigh the losses, but both gains illustrate the central thesis of this chapter: confessing is an appeal not only for but to the oppressed, calling them to faith and, through that original response, encouraging them to bear fuller responsibility as agents of their history.

The first of the two gains in this direction is that under Aquino, far more than under her predecessor, people are exercising their responsibility as the government's critics, specifically her critics. Not only has there been more freedom to criticize, there has been more criticism in fact, more criticism per square inch in print and electronic media and in the open air, more broad-based criticism, more multilateral and less one-track, pro as well as con, more nuanced. It is as though the critical give-and-take of the Basic Christian Communities and the communist cells had suddenly become nationalized (unlike Communism), engaging the President's Cabinet as well — "a cabinet composed of people you could not invite to a party together" — and sparing Malacanang Palace least of all.

One might hope that as civil criticism proliferates, it would become

27. Mydans, "The Embattled Mrs. Aquino."

more and more informed — in the language of the BCCs, more "discerning" — and more practically consequential. Meanwhile, one cannot help but be impressed with the phenomenon of a maturingly critical public opinion, somewhat as Luther was. He marveled that never before had so much of public life become subject to the judgment of the people, *sub iudicio nostro*. Why, even an ordinary peasant had come to discern that his calling was as godly and dignified as that of a monk. It is worth pondering whether in both instances, the Reformation and the Philippine "revolution," this formation of a critical "common sense" did not owe something to an antecedent confessing movement, given the latter's emphasis upon participant response.

It seems that President Aquino especially opens herself to question, not in the sense that she is eager for criticism, and surely not in the sense that, by comparison with Marcos, she leaves more to criticize. The fact is, she has made herself questionable, and in both senses of the word. First, she continues to give her critics just cause for questioning whether she truly is effective or not. But questionable in that sense Marcos was too. The difference is, secondly, that under Aquino the critics are *able* to question her. Better yet, they are *enabled.* Her very style seems to invite criticism, favorable as well as unfavorable, almost irresistibly, and not merely because her style is unconventional. Then why? She counts on people not to be afraid of her. "Hardly anybody," she thinks, "fears Cory Aquino. In Marcos' days, so many were afraid of him. . . . I don't know if I can count ten people who are afraid of me."

Why is she unlikely to inspire fear? Because, as she explains, she herself is not basically fearful. Not anymore. Again and again, she has warned Marcos and others not to mistake her softness for cowardice. "I may be many unattractive things, but I'm no coward." If not, then what? "You acquire power either through fear or through love, and the power which you get through love lasts much longer than that which is acquired through fear." Perhaps then, if she is right, it is her fearlessness born of love that enables her people in turn not to fear her. But then to be critical of her? Apparently so, freely and publicly. In fact, for President Aquino, once uncritically adulated by millions "as a sort of Blessed Mother, a redeemer," that "image as a savior has faded."[28] That is just as well. Still, as of this writing, Denis Murphy's observation still holds. She "has the full

---

28. Iyer, "Cory Aquino Leads a Fairy-Tale Revolution," 22.

backing of an overwhelming majority of people, who *know her weaknesses yet support her.*"[29]

The criticism of Aquino which she occasions could in time come even from the church, the church which helped install her. Consider Fr. Niall O'Brien, whose heart-rending story about the Philippines under Marcos had to be written in exile in the U.S. because Marcos had banished him, and then only after first holding him in prison on a false charge of murder.[30] In a recent interview, the same Fr. O'Brien complained that the conditions of the Filipino poor had not improved under Aquino, and in this respect he likened her administration to Marcos's. (It should be noted that this influential critic was now back as a priest in the Philippines, speaking out, thanks to the Aquino election.) From the beginning, Bishop Claver has warned publicly that if Aquino should abuse her power, "I am sure the church will become critical of her."[31] Fr. Lambino, her close adviser, told the press that if need be he would have to distance himself from her. "The close embrace of the state is never too healthy for the church."

Evidently, Aquino is prepared for such isolation, even worse. Her mother-in-law may have been right, "Ninoy's [Cory's husband's] assassination was his fate; the presidency is hers." But that prospect seems not to threaten her, "because," as she had reminded Marcos, "I am not alone." "God has placed me in the presidency and I have no fear for my life." That ultimate Partnership, transcending even the "embrace" of the church, evidently frees her from fear and for love. That could be contagious, nerving her constituents to speak out against a president they simultaneously hold in affection, meanwhile leaving her explainers at a loss. "People have concluded that someone up there is supporting her in her shaky throne." Strange that that should have been said by Blas Ople, one of Aquino's most outspoken critics.

What is the second gain accruing from this Christian confessor's casting her lot with the questionable game of politics? Answer: the way she has expanded the game's circle of players and thus raised its stakes. The term

29. Denis Murphy, "Aquino's Biggest Problem: The United States?" *America* 158, no. 2 (January 16, 1988): 33. Italics Bertram's.

30. Niall O'Brien, *Revolution from the Heart* (Oxford: Oxford University Press, 1987).

31. Cf. Francisco F. Claver, S.J., "The Church and Revolution: The Philippine Solution," *America* 154, no. 17; "The Church and Revolution: The Philippine Solution (Part II)," *America* 154, no. 18.

ordinarily employed to describe this achievement of hers is "democracy," as if it were basically a popular redistribution of power or rights. It is that, of course. But is it not, at least as significantly, a redistribution of responsibility? Responsibility is here meant as roughly synonymous with accountability or answerability and, as with our previous word "questionable," answerable in two senses: both *obliged* to answer and *able* to. Response-able. I have been suggesting that Mrs. Aquino has succeeded in rendering herself questionable. Really, "questionable" is the same as "answerable," in converse. The same one who is open to question is by that token one to give answer, for instance, a president. What I am suggesting now is that this same President Aquino who has made herself publicly questionable (or answerable) has also begun to draw more and more of her people, her questioners, into bearing responsibility with her. Their questions to her become increasingly questions for which they too must answer.

The implication is that one of a people's most fundamental rights is the right to be held responsible for their lives and history. It is a daunting right in any case and one which, for them even to want it, necessitates a "people power" like *faith* perhaps more than any other power. It has been said of democracy that it gives people the government they deserve. To restructure their governance so as to edge them into maximum feasible accountability must require, I would think, pacing them up to their spiritual limits. (In my own country it is a challenge we greet and seldom meet.)

In that light, implicitly a theological light, recall the democratic reforms instituted by the Aquino administration during its first two years, what Mydans regards as "her major achievement": a reinstating of liberation standards of human rights; a successful national referendum for a new constitution (vehemently opposed by both left and right, including almost two-thirds of the armed forces, led by Aquino's Defense Minister Juan Ponce Enrile) trimming the president's powers which had multiplied under Marcos; democratic elections of congress, of governors, of local officials. As government becomes critically questionable by more and more of the governed, more and more of them in turn become structurally answerable to that same critical process. It is a development that Paul in his Epistle to the Romans could not have imagined he was anticipating. Viewed cynically, it could be called Aquino's revenge, the way her questioners are sucked into becoming co-answerable with her. Viewed hopefully, it is taking people seriously as historical agents, as respondents on a witness stand, not just as victims and dependents.

Take the case of land reform, one of the Philippines' most desperate needs and from the outset one of President Aquino's announced priorities: an agrarian law that would not only redistribute lands, but also provide peasant farmers with necessary support services such as credit and technical assistance. That is a promise on which her actual performance has been most questionable (in both senses) and on which, by way of comeback, she has countered by returning the responsibility to the electorate as a whole. (Just how democratic she was in getting her own brothers and sisters, something of an aristocrat dynasty, to sell the family's vast sugar lands to their plantation workers is not clear.)[32]

Her new constitution includes a mandate for redistribution of land, which mandate was then complied with by her presidential decree, Executive Order No. 229. However, the constitution also prescribed that the "priorities and reasonable retention limits" (on landowners) should be legislated by Congress. Consequently, many of those decisive details fell to that legislative body instead, where they ran amok of its conservative majority, still tilted toward landlords and the old political elite.

Aquino has been condemned for impeding land reform by such a consensual process. By contrast, some of the most successful programs of economic reform in Asia have begun under conditions of military control or revolution in which political resistance was simply swept aside. Aquino, too, so runs the criticism, ought not to have waited for a democratic constitution and legislature, but instead ought to have moved quickly during the first months of her administration while she still had the dictatorial powers inherited from her predecessor. But that, she insists, is exactly the concentration of power and responsibility she eschews. One exasperated American editorial, scolding her for being such a "novice" in her assertion of power, threw up its hands and exclaimed that the "salvation" of Philippine democracy would finally have to fall back on "the people once again showing their determination to have it." The editor seemed to have missed

---

32. Claver indicated in personal correspondence to the editor, "She did push through with a land reform program, but contrary to what Bertram wrote, she was unable to have her family put their landed estate under land reform — for which she was severely criticized. The family got out of the need to give the land to their tenants by the subterfuge (it was actually allowed by the law) of forming with their tenants some kind of share-holding company. The family however did not comply with the provisions of the law and the court recently decided to force them to agree to dividing the land among the tenants" (April 29, 2006).

the irony that that was precisely Aquino's policy all along, though admittedly at a terrible cost in prolonged poverty and hardship.

President Aquino's extension of responsibility to the people by means of the electoral process has won some strange converts, some of them perhaps more grudgingly accepting than actually converted. On one end of the political spectrum is Juan Ponce Enrile, Marcos's former defense minister, who by "an accident of history" ("the EDSA miracle") became also Aquino's defense minister until she fired him after his reputed linkage with coup attempts, corruption charges, and civil rights abuses. When finally he lost his bitter battle against her plebiscite for the new constitution, even he would profess: "I take great pride as a Filipino in the triumph of the democratic processes in our country; we accept the verdict of the people." Indeed, a few months later, those "democratic processes" elected him to the Senate, a new vantage point for his opposition to the president. Could this be what was meant by our earlier quotation, democracy gives people the government they deserve?

At the other end of the political spectrum is Bernabe Buscayno, who did not win a seat in the Senate. What is impressive is that he ran for it at all. Buscayno founded the New People's Army and was imprisoned for nine years until being freed by Mrs. Aquino. To take advantage of the "democratic space" she was offering, Buscayno and some of his comrades, who until then had been operating mostly underground, were emboldened to enter the electoral process and to campaign for public office. They did so as candidates of their new Partido ng Bayan, a legal party though it espouses many of the same elements as the outlawed Communist party. For these candidates even to acknowledge their party affiliation (many of them dare not) is an act of courage since the label is "a magnet for harassment and violence." Frequently they are crushed by the financial resources of their wealthy opponents, and their sympathetic voters are disenfranchised.

Though the violence these candidates encounter comes mostly from the militant right, it comes also from those hard-liners within the Communist underground who still prefer an armed struggle over a parliamentary one and are not above purging from their ranks those who opt for nonviolent responsibility-taking. But taking responsibility, sad to say, does not exclude taking the consequences. Some observers compare the democratic ferment on the Philippine left to that which occurred among Roman Catholic traditionalists following the Second Vatican Council. "Corazon Aquino presents the left today with questions of war and peace [and questions, I would add, of the public bearing of answerability and question-ableness] that are equally difficult to handle" as those which "the church leadership at the time of Vatican II often found difficult to control."

It must have been Karl Marx's old dogma that responsibility for history rests in the hands of humankind and not in a transhistorical "invisible Hand" which prompted Bishop Claver to reply that, for Christian faith, the two — The Hand and the hands — are mutually not exclusive but implicative. Corazon Aquino said she could understand why Moses' followers, whose exodus from bondage had been handled by a divine "Hand which they could see," would despair when that visible Hand was suddenly withdrawn.

> But I cannot understand the despair of a people whose deliverance was worked by God through the work of *their own hands,* as those whose hands were made strong by the power of their faith.

Accordingly, "strengthened by Christ's promise," she once told an American audience, "when you lift up your hands to implore another miracle, look at your hands, for it is from thence that the answer will come."

CHAPTER 7

A Time for Confessing; or,
When Is the Church a Confessional Movement?

There are nine theses to "a time for confessing"; here, only the first two of these will be explored in greater detail.

Thesis One: The church is a confessional movement whenever it has to take the stand against secular authority, especially its own, in order to testify that for the church one gospel-and-sacraments is authority enough. *Satis est.*[1]

Thesis Two: The question, "When is the church a confessional movement?" needs to be asked nowadays if only because of the dilemmas these movements are posing.

Thesis Three: A confessional movement is authorized to list within its ranks, and to list by name, those confessors who took their stand in times past, provided it confesses what they confessed, that our Lord's one gospel-and-sacraments is all the church has ever needed to be one long, unaging church. "We who are walking in their footsteps intend by the grace of God to abide by this confession" (FC X, 18).

Thesis Four: A "case for confession" — unlike, for example, a baptismal confession or evangelistic testimonials — typically occurs in a situation of oppression, that is, when the one gospel-and-sacraments is so compromised by superior secular authority (usually church authority) that this oppression becomes Christ's call to Christians to disobey and to give reason for their disobedience, the way accused defendants must "upon a witness-stand" *(in statu confessionis)* as though they were on trial (FC X, 3, 14-16, 22-23, 27-29).

1. AC VII.

Thesis Five: However, it is not against these more obvious "adversaries," the secularist ecclesiastical oppressors, that the testimony is directed so much as it is directed to those other Christians in the courtroom who have not yet taken the stand, to encourage them to do so while there is still time. ". . . The entire community of God, yes, every individual Christian and especially the ministers of the Word as the leaders of the community of God, are obligated to confess openly, not only by words but also by their deeds and actions . . ." (FC X, 10).

Thesis Six: That there ordinarily are such things as adiaphora — that is, otherwise neutral issues which do not require taking a stand against them — is important for Christian freedom, for it is still true that the gospel-and-sacraments is the church's only non-negotiable.

Thesis Seven: Yet the special calling of a confessional movement, ironically, is to demonstrate that all sorts of otherwise secondary circumstances, "*even* adiaphora," can become priority issues for the church's very life or death. In such a "time for confessing," even adiaphora may cease to be adiaphora at all and suddenly become inseparable from the gospel-and-sacraments itself (FC X, 3, 14, 15).

Thesis Eight: Adiaphora are defined as church practices "which are neither commanded nor forbidden in the Word of God" (FC X, 1). But the "Word of God" in this case does not mean Scripture, for in Scripture God does explicitly command such practices as circumcision, the sabbath, women's head coverings, all of which the confessors, however, regard as no longer binding but optional or even as the "precepts of men." What *is* commanded by God and is never optional is what he commanded through Jesus Christ his Son, to proclaim his gospel and administer his sacraments — in every situation and irrespective of the cost.

Thesis Nine: What ultimately makes confessional movements confessional — that is, what gives them reason "enough" for being — is the reminder of who their Judge-behind-the-judges ultimately is and who their own Confessor is before that Judge. "As he values his soul's welfare and salvation, every Christian is obligated" not to "yield and conform" in such a "time for confessing." For "we are to be particularly mindful that Christ says, 'So everyone who confesses me before men I also will confess before my Father who is in heaven.'"[2]

---

2. Matthew 10:32; FC X, 16-17.

Detailed Commentary on the Theses One and Two

Thesis One: The church is a confessional movement whenever it has to take the stand against secular authority, especially its own, in order to testify that for the church one gospel-and-sacraments is authority enough.

A.

By "secular" authority I mean the authority which governs life in this age *(saeculum).* And life in this age does have "all things visible and invisible," "me and all that exists, body and soul, food and clothing, family and property,"[3] synods and seminaries.[4] With so much life there must be authorization for it. Moreover, life in this age is always aging: bodies perish, also church bodies, seminaries go out of business or into exile,[5] even exile can pall.[6] With so much aging, that too must be authorized, and by the same authority.

"Secular" is not the opposite of churchly. Churches, too, not only society, need secular authority. Churches dispense life — employment to clergy, press coverage to churchmen, payments to banks, devotional literature to widows — for all of which the churches have to exact life in return: service from clergy, newsworthiness from churchmen, risk from banks,

---

3. *Small Catechism,* First Article of the Creed.

4. Editor's note: This is specifically indicated here in regard to the confessional crisis in the Lutheran Church–Missouri Synod. Bertram would consistently insist that seminary professors are paid to teach (by secular authority), but *what* they are to teach is *the gospel.* Likewise, in the case of pastors, Bertram would contend that they are "servants of Christ" (Galatians 1:10) for the sake of their congregations, but that congregations are not in turn the masters of the ministers who serve them.

5. Editor's note: This is a reference to the formation of Concordia Seminary-in-Exile, those who were exiled from the Concordia Seminary campus in St. Louis in 1974. Eventually the name of the seminary was changed to Christ Seminary-Seminex.

6. Editor's note: Bertram's reference to the "pall" of exile would come into focus as a serious and contentious matter, maybe even a *status confessionis,* when Seminex voted in the early 1980s to deploy its faculty and staff to the seminaries in Austin, Berkeley, and Chicago. In the wake of this development, Bertram himself continued to commute between Chicago and St. Louis to continue the work of Crossings with his colleague Edward H. Schroeder (who did not deploy, for confessional reasons, with the other faculty).

mites from widows. Both operations, both the dispensing of life and the taking of it, are by the same secular authority, also in churches.

"Secular" is also not the opposite of sacred. It is God's own authority, his right to run the old creation, both to create it and simultaneously to make it old and die. Being his authority, it is by definition fair, though saying that is mostly a matter of faith. Secular authority — call it the divine Law — is God being fair, giving people and peoples what they have coming to them. True, in practice it almost never works that way, seeing how fragile and exploited this Law is. Think of the Holocaust or apartheid or the wrongs, just the ecclesiastical wrongs, which some of you are suffering (and inflicting) all in the name of his Law. Is this fair — of God?

Maybe not, but God's day will come, his Day of Fairness. When it does, alas, nobody — no person or institution — will be able to stand that much fairness. *That* "oncoming future" is bad news. Isn't that the trouble with God's secular authority: we yearn for it since none of us can live without it, but when it comes we cannot live with it either?

No wonder we lust to make secular authority into something it is not and is not meant to be: good news, a gospel, a saver of life. And what abets that blind lust for law (Paul would call it "zeal") is precisely that it comes on such high authority. Is there any more terrifying abuse of secular authority than the religious abuse of it, also in Christian churches, especially when they conspire with other secular authorities like the state or the economy? In face of such theoretical alliance who could doubt that secular authority must be God's way of saving?

To be saved by the authority of this age is alluring for another reason: secular authority is enforceable authority. The life it provides — the livings and livelihoods, a pastor's pension or a congregation's good name — is life which can always be threatened and taken away. Because of the claim it has on our lives, the right to foreclose on them, secular authority is coercive and hence enforceable.

Most of all, though, what makes secular authority look salvific is its essential fairness. To give folks their due, especially with theological legitimization and with enforceable sanctions, is after all only fair. But that is all it is, fair. And fairness, though saying so seems blasphemous, is simply not enough. *Satis non est.*

B.

The other authority, what I have called "gospel-and-sacraments," is by contrast with God's secular authority not all that fair. But it is considerably more conducive to life. Unfairly enough, at least to God, this authority does not give people what they have coming to them, namely, exile and death — at least not ultimately. That, quite shockingly, is assigned to God instead. And what God has coming to him — love and life — goes instead to the world. Call it the "Happy Exchange" or — as Luther might have called it had he spoken American — the "Sweet Swap."[7]

It is true that Christians — who are the only ones who believe this "foolishness," as Paul called it[8] — really have no more authority for believing it than Jesus did. So good do they find this news, this "gospel," that they are willing to believe as he did that his authority for it is God's own. They believe that by what Jesus did God has trumped his own authority, his own fairness toward this *saeculum*, rendering it old and eventually obsolete. In the history of Jesus as God's Christ, for those who accept that as their own history, God's oncoming Day of Fairness has been scooped and upstaged by a still more ultimate future, Jesus' own, and by quite another brand of fairness — that old word can still be used in this new context, except now as a Christian pun. That is, Christ's new alternative to exile and death is resurrection and life — "for those who are in Christ Jesus"[9] — but through the wringer of crucifixion — also "for those who are in Christ Jesus." Not all that fair, perhaps, but good. And the Spirit in which Jesus commends this alternative to us, being God's Healing Spirit, persuades always without coercion.

When Christians claim that the authority of this gospel supersedes God's other, secular authority, aren't they demeaning secular authority? If they are — and let us admit it, often they are — they are then demeaning God himself, whose age this old *saeculum* still is and for which he dearly cares to the point of his own Son's death. For Christians to sell out secular authority, God's passion for fairness, just because it is not salvational, is as perverse as those who make such authority salvational. In fact, both par-

---

7. Editor's note: The phrase "sweet swap" was actually created by an anonymous Seminex student as a synonym for the "happy exchange."

8. 1 Corinthians 1:18-25.

9. Romans 8:1.

ties, zealots and anomists, are but flipsides of the same fallacy (and usually of one and the same person). Both assume God's *nomos* can deserve our lives only if it can save lives, otherwise not.

The gospel, to the contrary, liberates from that fallacy. By placing our lives beyond reach of God's *nomos*, his gospel liberates us to live for secular fairness, not only to live for it but to die for it, knowing that death, though fair, is not the Father's last Word. With secular authority so relieved of all soteriological pretensions and with such unbribable agents working to make it happen, fairness has a chance in the world.

By emphasizing the "*one* gospel-and-sacraments," the only one that is "enough," I am recalling the apostolic warning that there are after all other, rival gospels that need to be exposed for the counterfeits they are. What makes these gospels so credible in the church is that they are virtually indistinguishable from the real thing. They too preach Christ and quote Scripture. They too are capable of sincerity. They can marshal the most persuasive ecclesiastical authorities in their support. They may even make a show of secular fairness, though just as likely they may not, and that may be the first telltale sign of their falsity as gospel.

In any case, the one invariable fallacy of these gospels is that they always represent the Christian gospel *plus* something else besides. As if that gospel were not really enough and needed to be reinforced or safeguarded or guaranteed by some condition other than the inherently winsome goodness of God's pity at the cross. And that extraneous condition, whatever it is — whether doctrinal or ethnic or liturgical or organizational — is always some form of secular authority, some further criterion by which people can still be evaluated in terms of what they have coming to them, some sanction which can be enforced. However, that is a case where more is always less. Gospel-plus is never gospel at all. Having no authorization from Christ, such gospels fall under the only alternative, God's secular authority, according to which they are "accursed."[10]

In such conflicts with pseudo-Christian gospels, what is at stake, remember, is the Christian gospel itself, the church's — no, the world's — "one gospel-and-sacraments." But when that is the issue, then no one but the church can contend for that gospel. In other conflicts, the issue may be the need for basic human fairness. On that battlefront, the church seldom needs to fight alone and can count on many a secular ally, often more

10. Galatians 1:8-9.

skilled in that form of God's authority than the church is. But when the gospel is on the line, then no one else but the church has the means or, what comes to the same thing, no one else has the authority to contend for it. After all, the only authority there is for the gospel of Christ is that gospel itself, Christ's gospelling the world. What else is the church but that, Christ's body gospelling the world? For the church to stay one and whole, and to stay that way for the world, only one thing suffices, the one gospel-and-sacraments. *Satis est.*

For that battle no other authority can help. Though the church does have other kinds, secular kinds of authority as well and needs to have them (payrolls, communication systems, pecking orders, influence, convention votes) these are utterly impotent when the gospel is the issue. All these can accomplish — these secular forms of authority — is to save church bodies. But never the church. Still, that is the hardest thing for the church to learn. Indeed, that *is* the battle for the gospel, the church's struggling to believe and teach and confess that all it finally needs for staying together is its Lord's one gospel-and-sacraments.

And confessional movements, what are they? What else but the church's *satis*-sayers trying to drive that same lesson home, and to learn themselves? For doing that, they too have no other authority — and what a wretched, vulnerable authority it seems to be — than their Lord's authorization to do as he did, to live for the world and die for it and to count it all gain — Good News.

C.

Consider, finally, that other set of terms in Thesis One, above. I refer to the courtroom terminology, "take the stand," "testify," "confessional," and even the word "authority." The church is here pictured — as it is in Article X of the Formula of Concord and, of course, long before that in the New Testament — as being a church on trial. In previous paragraphs, we spoke of the church's contending for the gospel against pseudo-gospels as a conflict, a battle. But "in a time of confession" that battle is more like a case at court. The adversary is still false gospel, gospel-plus, legalized gospel. But now, in addition, the pseudo-gospel is represented by superior secular authority, more often than not the church's own authorities, with the result that their legalistic gospel is linked with official power and becomes not just an occasional aberration, but church policy, publicly enforceable.

These ecclesiastical authorities now stand in judgment as secular magistrates would and, whether they recognize it or not, the defendant whom they have arraigned is the whole church of Jesus Christ. Oh, I do not mean that there literally are ecclesiastical trials, actual forensic proceedings, with formal charges and evidence and judicial verdicts. Sometimes there are, but even then, these are often so rigged as to never allow the gospel even a fair hearing. Just as often there are no trials at all except perhaps through a controlled church process, for fear that the authorities' own pseudo-gospel might be *cross-examined*.[11] No, this metaphor of the courtroom is more a theological construct, re-picturing the actual current situation according to the perceptions of faith. Here the church's "witness stand" is merely the concrete historical situation in which at the moment the gospel is being oppressed. To call the situation by such a prestigious name, a *status confessionis,* is to take what is to all appearances a ridiculous

11. Editor's note: Bertram may well be making an autobiographical reference to the process under then LCMS President Jacob A. O. Preus II. "In September 1970 Preus appointed a fact-finding committee to interview faculty members as to their beliefs regarding Scripture, Lutheran confessions and other theological issues. Those interviews began in December and continued, under faculty protest, until March 1971. Preus's assessment of the results led him to issue a document euphemistically known as the Blue Book in which he charged that certain unnamed members of the Concordia faculty were teaching false doctrine. That report was received by the Board of Control, the seminary's governing body, which conducted its own interviews of faculty and announced that it could find no professor guilty of heresy. Tietjen reproduces several verbatims from those interviews as well as a chart delineating the vote count — to commend, correct or abstain — for each faculty member. Though some votes were close, no professor was judged to be in need of correction. Dissatisfied with the Board of Control's verdict, Preus took the matter to the Missouri Synod's 1973 annual meeting in New Orleans. The convention adopted a resolution which declared that there was indeed heresy at Concordia Seminary and accepted Preus's 'Statement of Scriptural and Confessional Principles' for establishing doctrinal parameters for the entire church. Efforts were also begun to remove [Concordia Seminary President John] Tietjen from office. The New Orleans convention called upon the seminary's Board of Control to deal punitively with the president. In late 1973 the board, now dominated by a pro-Preus majority, voted to suspend Tietjen. When he refused to accept their ruling and threatened legal action, the board delayed its suspension of the president. In other sweeping actions, the board set the mandatory retirement age at 65, thereby removing several long-term faculty members, and required all professors to submit their course syllabi for examination by the governing body." Bill J. Leonard, Review of John Tietjen, *Memoirs in Exile: Confessional Hope and Institutional Conflict* (Minneapolis: Fortress Press, 1990), *Christian Century* 107 (November 21-28, 1990): 1096-98.

and petty ecclesiastical hassle and dignify it with the image of a cosmic tribunal — what in truth it is.

Before this intimidating tribunal, the church is being asked whether in fact it does not agree, as its actions seem to betray, that the one gospel-and-sacraments is *not* enough after all and therefore in need of outside secular intervention. The court waits for a reply. The moment for the church to answer this interrogation, the "time for confessing," is agonizingly short and not postponable. In that fleeting historical moment, the church has no choice but to be the *satis*-sayer and thus do what otherwise it would almost never dream of doing, renounce its own secular authority, and then only because the latter was replacing the gospel. The best confession in such cases includes taking the consequences, although — as Luther reminded — "never in silence."[12] The Answer is too good to be silenced, in view of whose it is.

Thesis Two: The question, "When is the church a confessional movement?" needs to be asked nowadays if only because of the dilemmas these movements are posing.

A.

They pose a dilemma, first of all, for the gospel's kind of authority and, second, a dilemma also for secular authority. In relation to the gospel, such movements truly do help to liberate it from its secular pseudo-gospels. On the other hand, these same movements, once they come into secular authority of their own, are themselves apt to forget that for the church the gospel is enough.

Confessional movements pose a corresponding dilemma for secular authority as well, also for the church's secular authority. On the one hand, they do expose the salvational pretense of such authority. On the other hand, once given some secular authority of their own, these same movements forget how that authority can be liberated and so in their cynicism they either reject it anti-institutionally or exercise it with a bad conscience and furtively.

Nowadays we often decide for confessional movements or against

12. Cf. Chapter One above, under "martyria."

them so automatically that we overlook these dilemmas they entail. All the more reason to be clear about what confessional movements truly are. Else when we do discover how ambiguous they are, we are prone to shrink from them and plead neutrality, which usually has the practical effect of discrediting them — and thus reneging on our own witness.

B.

To illustrate how ambiguous confessional movements can be, both in their evangelical and in their secular dimensions, consider those Lutheran and Reformed movements in nineteenth-century Europe and America, which were explicitly called "confessional." They refused to be coerced into sub-gospel commitments by their secular authorities. The authorities they opposed in the name of the gospel may have been, as in this country, simply the legitimate officials of their own denominations. I think, for instance, of the Princeton Presbyterians in the struggle with their General Assembly. In Europe, on the other hand, the authorities who needed to be opposed were the officials of the state as well as of the church — for instance, the Venerable Company of the Canton of Geneva, or the king as *summus episcopus* of the Prussian Union, or the Conventicle Law of the state church of Norway.

But these movements also leave us with a question. Would they have objected if what the secular authorities enforced had been the genuine gospel, which by its very genius abjures enforcement? Or would these confessional movements have stood up for the freedom of the gospel if they themselves had gained control of secular authority, denominational or governmental — which eventually they almost all did in one form or another? Their record is ambiguous. For instance, there was that movement of confessional Lutherans — later to be called The Lutheran Church–Missouri Synod — who in protest originally against the Prussian Union came into exile in the American Middle West. For a long time they managed to keep their two kinds of church authority — evangelical and parliamentary, spiritual and coercive — in a remarkable balance. As their constitution read, "All matters of doctrine and conscience are to be decided only by the Word of God, all other matters . . . by majority vote." By that distinction the synod is now obliterating, revealing its death as a confessional movement.

The most visible confessional movement of our time and one which has left all of Christendom in its debt was the Confessing Church (at first called the "confessional" church) in National Socialist Germany. This movement arose — as the Missouri Synod did, originally within the Prussian church — as a combined Lutheran and Reformed protest against the pro-Nazi, state-favored "German Christians." The movement's confession, the Barmen Declaration, set a bold distinction between the authority of the church and the authority of the state, especially that state authority which on the basis of blood and soil aspired to saviorhood.

But did the Confessing Church recognize how radically this same distinction applies — the distinction between the authority of the gospel and secular authority — right within the church's own mixed bag of authorities? And did the Confessing Church remember how in ecclesiastical structure itself these disparate authorities can be coordinated after all and still reflect the authority of the gospel?

On that score some of the very leaders of the Confessing Church already had premonitions of their movement's shortcomings.[13] Dietrich Bonhoeffer wondered, how would his own church develop once Hitler was gone? What new shape would it assume, to be forced or enticed to assume? He feared that there might be a "premature new organization of the privileged wielding power," and without a "recasting, returning and a chastening purging."

Were his suspicions confirmed? Well, less than a year after he had written these words, so Eberhard Bethge informs us, "The church people from the confessing church [came together] to plan what the new structure of the German church should be. . . . They founded the so-called Evangelical Lutheran Church in Germany." "All privileges came back," says Bethge, "more than we had them before" — church taxes and all. "So we made the *epoch* of the confessing church just an *episode*. . . ."

But Bonhoeffer's misgivings were directed not only against *"die Lutheraner,"* but even against his mentor, Karl Barth, whom he also blamed in part for this deterioration, and who he feared was making "a law of faith" and making the Christian revelation a matter of "like it or lump it."[14] That does smack of a confusion of authorities, doesn't it? And mightn't there have been the seeds of that confusion — we ask with the luxury of hindsight — already in the Barmen Declaration?

13. Cf. Chapter Five above.

14. Bonhoeffer, *Letters and Papers from Prison*, ed. Eberhard Bethge (New York: Macmillan, 1972), 286, 328.

Still, if those were the ambiguities that were done in the green tree, what will be done in the dry — among us, the aftergrowth? And who of us dare point the finger without earning the same in return, particularly since few of us are likely ever to seal our confession with our blood?

C.

A similar dilemma which our confessional movements reflect is their tension between the doctrinal and the ethical. Are they actually confessional movements at all, whose foremost concern is the sufficiency of the uniquely Christian gospel-and-sacraments? Or is their concern primarily ethical, essentially the issue of human fairness, getting for people what they have coming to them, a concern which these movements share with all who are under God's secular authority, Christians and non-Christians alike? If the latter is the case, might these movements not misrepresent themselves — and overly spiritualize themselves — by adopting the label "confessional"? On the other hand, if they truly are confessional, can they do justice to the doctrinal priorities without letting that diminish attention to the moral injustices which almost always accompany controversies of this sort?

To illustrate that dilemma between the doctrinal and the ethical, consider the following example. Inside the Lutheran Church–Missouri Synod, where legalism has effectively become synodical policy, an opposing movement has raised its voice. Members of this movement, too, refer to themselves as a "confessional movement," deliberately invoking that term so as to remind the Missouri Synod of a pledge it once made: "The Lutheran Church is not merely one denomination among others but is a confessional movement within the whole Body of Christ." This sentence is from the former Missouri Synod's *Mission Affirmations*,[15] whose chief author was Martin Kretzmann, then active in Lutheran World Federation mission offices. The sentence here quoted was suggested at the time (1965) by William Danker, another of the Missouri Synod's world-mission experts. He in turn has been inspired by a recent article in *The Christian Cen-*

15. "The Mission Affirmations," Section III, "The Church is Christ's Mission to the World," adopted at the annual convention of the Lutheran Church–Missouri Synod in Detroit in 1965. Cf. Appendix to "The Mission of the Christian Church in the Word" (St. Louis: Commission on Theology and Church Relations, 1974).

tury, "American Lutheranism, Denomination or Confusion," written by Missourian-at-Yale Jaroslav Pelikan.[16]

The confessional movement arising out of that Synod has taken form in such counter-organizations, all of them closely collaborative, as Evangelical Lutherans in Mission (ELIM), Seminex, Partners in Mission, and now, outside the Synod, the Association of Evangelical Lutheran Churches. When did this recent phase of the movement become strictly a confessional one, at least according to the definition here? Not when Missouri faculty came under fire for their (very conservative) use of the historical-critical method or for their "gospel Reductionism."[17] Those differences might have been accommodated mutually. No, the confessional issue really surfaced when the Concordia Seminary students and faculty and thousands of others from a wide theological spectrum within the Synod refused their synodical authorities the right to impose any other criterion for faithful ministry than the one gospel-and-sacraments, which (according to the Augsburg Confession) is "enough" and anything more than which is less. Moreover, at least in my judgment, it was that confessional challenge to synodical authority more than any other difference that evoked from synodical officials the wave to purge and other reprisals. Even those reprisals were not what made the movement confessional, though they did help.

This movement, too, suffers the characteristic ambiguities, necessitating a reminder of what a confessional movement is. For example, there is in the movement a constant undertow toward minimizing its confessional purpose in favor of moral protest. In view of the injustices committed, that impulse can hardly be falsified. But that also reverses the movement's unique priorities and could soon secularize it out of existence as confessional. Even the movement's official newspaper, *Missouri in Perspective,* has on occasion made that mistake. A recent editorial in that paper claimed "that the 'exiles' stand has been based primarily on ethical, not doctrinal, grounds." Secondly, members of the movement sometimes ex-

16. Jaroslav Pelikan, "American Lutheranism, Denomination or Confusion," *Christian Century* 8 (December 25, 1963): 1608-10.

17. Edward H. Schroeder, "Law-Gospel Reductionism in the History of the Lutheran Church–Missouri Synod," *Concordia Theological Monthly* 43 (April 1972): 232-47; Cf. Commission on Theology and Church Relations of The Lutheran Church–Missouri Synod, *Gospel and Scripture: The Interrelationship of the Material and Formal Principles in Lutheran Theology* (St. Louis: Concordia Publishing House, 1972), 7-9.

press the moral complaint that they are "sick of fighting," which — if that is truly what they were doing all along, fighting — is understandably sickening. But that may also reflect a misunderstanding of what the fighting is all about. Thirdly, others want to quit and "get back to the church's real mission," implying that that is separable somehow from what they have been calling "confessing." But then perhaps all they ever meant by confessing is essentially a moral protest, secondary to "the church's real mission." All three examples characterize conscientious people who have left the Missouri Synod as well as those who have not but who, in both cases, find their confessional movement bewildering and for that reason dismissible.

Take another example. In July 1977 the Sixth General Assembly of the Lutheran World Federation resolved emphatically against apartheid and did so on explicitly confessional grounds.[18] It declared "that the situation in southern Africa constitutes a *status confessionis*. This means that . . . the churches would publicly and unequivocally reject the existing apartheid system." But notice why: "on the basis of faith and in order to manifest the unity of the church." To be sure, the Assembly left no doubt that the only "basis" needed for "the unity of the church" is still the "faith," our Lord's one gospel-and-sacraments, since "under normal circumstances Christians may have different opinions in political questions" and still be one church. Yet there come times when "political and social systems might become perverted and oppressive" to the point where what they violate is that very "faith," the one "basis" of "the unity of the church." For the church in such circumstances to be apathetic, William Lazareth told the Assembly, is not only "ethical disobedience" but "ultimately theological heresy." Now saying that is one thing, making the point clear, the confessional point, may be something else. That task demanded the Assembly's most strenuous efforts. Bishop Manas Buthelezi (I say to his credit) made the confessional point this way: "Those who deliberately shun worshipping together cannot legitimately claim that they belong to one church." And that is, isn't it, a matter of the gospel?

Confessionally, the case is classic, and prone, of course, to all the classic temptations. The sorest temptation, no doubt, will be to shift the battle against apartheid away from confessional grounds to primarily legal-ethical grounds, if only because these are so much more provable and enforceable. With something so obviously unjust as apartheid, that will be

---

18. Cf. Chapter Four above.

the aspect of it, its sheer unfairness, which will be most tempting to capitalize on. And, of course, if that were all that were wrong with it, that would be the point at which to concentrate all our energies. And all the appropriate means for combating such evil (economic pressure, public opinion, governmental influence) which are available to an organization as secularly powerful as the LWF and which it has no choice but to employ — these could easily become its major preoccupation, pitting it against the secular tyrannies on their own terms. But if that were all the LWF did against apartheid, or even almost all, its present confessional message would be muffled. The message might go out instead that the church must not be for some sinners after all, at least not for very sinful sinners, and that it does indeed have some other basis for including the people it does than the one gospel-and-sacraments, some selective criterion according to which people are admitted to the church of Christ according to what they have coming to them. For the LWF to keep testifying that apartheid so strikes at the gospel itself that *that* authority above all is the one to be invoked against it — that will take some doing by us all.

I have confined myself here to confessional movements which have publicly been described by that nomenclature. Not for a moment would I want to suggest, however, that similar movements are not occurring elsewhere in the Christian church with or without the designation "confessional." I think, for instance, of movements afoot (at least as significant as those I have mentioned) inside the Roman Catholic Church — from Vatican II to Cardinal LeFevre to last year's Call to Action Conference in Detroit and the National Conference of Catholic Bishops' (NCCB's) response to it — or inside the Episcopal Church — its controversy over ordaining women being, I gather, penultimate to a deeper issue of authority — or inside the Presbyterian Church in the United States, and so on, to name only a few examples from within single denominations. There have been confessional overtones also in trans-denominational movements such as those described recently by the Strasbourg Institute for Ecumenical Research: the "charismatic," the "action-centered," and the "evangelical" movements. As a case in point, consider this country's *Battle for the Bible* controversy in which both sides have identified, for instance, with their counterparts in the Missouri Synod. The whole vast ecumenical movement, moreover, sometimes precisely when it has subordinated particularist "confessions," has shown some sign of being also a confessional movement, though usually quite ambiguously. Some of the most fascinating movements of all are those apparently secular movements like the American civil rights movement or something like Amnesty International or Bread for the World, not identifiable as such with the Christian church and yet not conceivable without it either.

But this amorphous conglomeration of movements only reemphasizes the need for basic clarity on what a confessional movement is. Surely it is not every Christian movement that is out to reform church and society or even that, in doing so, appeals to Christian standards. But neither, so far as I can tell, could a confessional movement *not* be such an ethical movement as well. It must by its very nature involve a protest against abuses of authority, which, whatever else they are, are always also immoral. But the grounds on which a confessional movement ultimately protests are something else besides, something uniquely Christian, the very gospel-and-sacraments without which the church cannot — though secular society well might — operate. In fact, as I am contending here, based on the so-called adiaphoristic controversy of sixteenth-century German Lutheranism, the point is made that the church may at times need to resist its secular authorities *even if* their impositions are not otherwise wrong, so long as these authorities would force the church to misrepresent its own gospel-and-sacraments. But saying that only thickens the plot.

It goes without saying that in such cases the only weapon the church has for resisting, as church, is this one gospel-and-sacraments itself, that being "enough." But then, come to think of it, hasn't that been one of the central dynamics of some of those other movements, too, which are usually described — under-described — as being merely "nonviolent"? For instance, Dr. Martin Luther King Jr. did indeed speak of "the way of nonviolent resistance,"[19] tempting everyone to concentrate attention upon his adjective "nonviolent" and to forget his noun, "the way." But King knew better than most of us what Paul in 1 Corinthians means by "the more excellent way" and what John's Gospel means when it personifies "the Way" as Jesus our Lord. But then "the way" becomes something considerably more than merely nonviolent. Might it not even be confessional?

D.

But the biggest dilemma of all in our confessional movements, I believe, is their relative rightness or wrongness. Not one of those movements to

---

19. Cf. Chapter Three above.

which I have alluded either was or pretended to be infallible. Neither, I suppose, have they all been as humble as we might wish them to be. Shouldn't they issue at least some confession of repentance as well as of faith? Still, when the Confessing Church attempted that in its October 1945 Stuttgart declaration of guilt, it was criticized as being unconvincing. Nevertheless, that very feature of confessional movements — "Who are *they* to be pointing the finger!" — may be the one thing more than anything else which accounts for their ambiguity. Namely, people who themselves are demonstrable sinners, and are that perhaps most demonstrably in the way they criticize others, nevertheless have to bear the overwhelming burden — more overwhelming even than any loss of "goods, fame, child, and wife" — of being for once in their lifetimes embarrassedly, mortifyingly right. My own observation is that most of us, and most of us for reasons of conscientious humility, find exactly that burden too crushing to shoulder: that known wrong-doers should be made a laughing-stock by being made to stand up for what is absolutely right. But then, doesn't it become just that much more urgent to recall *whose* rightness it is they are being made to represent? And if that makes them look like fools for his sake who bear his rightness as an "alien righteousness," and drives them to act recklessly as if they were going to live forever when all the world can see how obviously they and their movements age — well, then maybe that very ambiguity is of the essence of their confession. But have you noticed how shamelessly they laugh, as if the joke on them were ultimately on someone else — "who died for them and rose again"?

*   *   *

"Seminex Was about Risk"[20]

Seminex was also about risk, the obvious risks but then also one risk which is not so obvious. There have been the obvious risks: the risk of being fired and put out on the street, the risk of lawsuit, the risk of being not only misunderstood but scorned by the church press, by one's classmates and friends and even family, the risk of one's own kids being embarrassed and

---

20. An address by Robert W. Bertram on a public day of recognition for the ministry of Seminex at Lutheran School of Theology at Chicago, December 11, 1987.

disillusioned by such a messy church (and such a messy Christ), the risk of having closet supporters feel sorry for us rather than stand up and be counted, the risk of feeling sorry for ourselves, the risk of becoming wearisome bores to those in the church who felt themselves above all this, the risk of turning cynical and quitting and in the bargain missing out on this chance of a lifetime, the risk of being scarred for life also psychically and maybe spiritually and of losing years off one's life, the risk of forgetting that the one thing at stake really was the gospel, the risk of assuming that now that it's past it should be forgotten. These are the obvious risks not to be minimized but also not to be exaggerated, especially by comparison with that one biggest risk which is not so obvious.

The most hazardous for the people of Seminex and for their whole confessing movement has been the risk of blasphemy. What if, in making their confession so loudly and publicly, calling God as their witness, speaking judgment on others as the enemies of the gospel, and reducing all hope to the promise of cross and resurrection — what if, by so doing, they have been misrepresenting God? That is a grim prospect. Of course, to try too hard to avoid blasphemy is to run the opposite risk, apostasy. That is, what if instead of confessing the faith at this *kairos*, this moment of now-or-never, they held their peace — the "Peace which surpasses all understanding," the Peace "not as the world gives"? That risk of apostasy was equally hazardous. The choice between the two, between blasphemy and apostasy, was humanly impossible. But that does not mean it was impossible altogether. Finally, the only thing Seminex had to go on was faith. So in faith we commend the outcome, including our own outcome, to him who risked everything, who died for us all (also the opponents) and rose again.

Postmodernity's CRUX:
A Theology of the Cross
for the Postmodern World

THESES ON "C IS FOR CRITICISM"

Introduction

Note 1: This is the first of a four-part series entitled "Postmodernity's CRUX." That overarching title is meant as a pun, a serious pun.[1] On the one hand, *crux*, which is Latin for *cross*, refers to the heart of Christianity. On the other hand, the English word "crux" means the heart of a problem. For instance, we say, "That is the crux of their argument," their bone of contention. What is the connection between these two cruxes? Just this: a major dilemma for the postmodern world, its burden, its crux, is its dependence upon Christianity. Postmodernity seems unable to live without Christianity, but neither can it live with it. Now, we ask, is the reverse also true? Is it so that Christianity (at least Christians) cannot live either with postmodernity or without it? If so, what accounts for this dilemma? Might the crux of the problem be the cross of

1. Editor's note: Due to the dichotomy that is often drawn between modernism and postmodernism today, a brief word of explanation is in order regarding Bertram's use of the two terms in the present work. He did not make much of the distinction between the two; his ambivalence was due to his theological understanding that the root of criticism, already inherent in the Enlightenment, is not displaced but only enhanced differently in postmodernity. Therefore, he often uses the terms "modernism" and "postmodernism" interchangeably, while at the same time recognizing some differences between them (as, for example, in Thesis 5 below).

Jesus the Christ? Then again, might that also be part of the solution? Obviously, there have been a vast variety of answers to these questions.

Note 2: "CRUX" serves also as a four-letter acronym:

C is for Criticism
R is for Revelation
U is for Universality
X (the Greek letter *Chi*) is for Xristening (i.e., Christ-ening)

Here are four dominant themes not only in Christianity but in modernity as well. And all four themes reflect, each in its own way, "postmodernity's crux" as described above. These are the four themes we shall pursue in the series which follows, beginning with "C is for Criticism."

Note 3: The particular form in which the four themes are presented, namely, in the form of "theses," goes back to a tradition in medieval university life. A student would take the final qualifying exam in the form of a public "disputation," for which a professor had prepared "theses" on the topic at hand. The theses may or may not have represented the professor's own position on the topic. Either way, they were to be responded to by the student, pro or contra or some of both, but in any case with a well-reasoned, convincing argument to support the response given. That is, the student was expected to "dispute" the professor's theses, though "dispute" need not mean *refute*. It could. But it could also mean that the student strengthened the theses or elaborated or documented them more than the professor had in their bare, concise original wording. The theses were numbered for easy reference during the disputation.

Note 4: The present theses on the topic of "Criticism" are based, in part, on a long passage from the Apostle Paul's Second Letter to the Corinthians, 2:14–7:4. The reader would be helped to understand the following theses by consulting this original source in the New Testament. Why just this passage? Because it is a classic source of Christianity's emphasis upon the cross, the *Crux Christi*. That brings us back to where we began in Note 1, above.

I. Criticism: A Hazardous Responsibility

1. One of the riskiest assignments we have inherited from the Enlightenment and before that from the Reformation — more or less, from the Christian tradition itself — is the assignment to be critical: the universal human responsibility to evaluate all authority, also political and religious authority, critically.

2. What is most risky about that is that if our criticism is consistent it is bound to overshoot, attacking the very Creator, the ultimate authority, thus we discredit ourselves with blasphemy in the process.

3. Yet it is from the Creator that our assignment comes. Being images of God, the primal Critic, being critics is part of our natures. We cannot *not* be critical. But neither dare we incur blasphemy, hence self-incrimination and doom. Just by carrying out our historic calling as postmoderns, thus as critics, we risk incurring final, terminal criticism ourselves.

4. During the sixteenth-century Reformation, Luther was dismayed to discover that the most authoritative institutions of his society, especially monasticism and the papacy but even the state, were now coming under the "judgment" of ordinary people. By the eighteenth century the Enlightenment was accepting that practice as normative, demanding that we all "dare to think" for ourselves, critically (Kant).

5. By now even those who yearn valiantly to get beyond modernity, as "postmoderns," seem doomed to fail at least in one respect: they still are as driven as ever to be critical, thereby perpetuating one of the deepest drives of modernity.

6. Modern critique, of course, must always be informed: a knowledgeable electorate, a free press, universal education, open to continual correction. But that we all must exercise critical judgment and must act upon it has become not only a right but a universal "responsibility" (itself a modern word.) We *have* to be free enough, enlightened enough, bold enough to "respond" on our own.

7. We are to respond not only by answering for ourselves to those who challenge us but also by cross-examining them in turn, and their authority.

We have no right to let ourselves be taken in, even by those who mean well. We are obliged to talk back. But to *every* Authority?

II. Free Choice?

8. How then do we avoid judging God, whose creatures these are which we are constrained critically to question: these authorities, these traditions, these fellow humans, most of all ourselves? For doesn't our criticizing them reflect upon their Maker?

9. One way out of this dilemma, the favorite way for moderns, is to pretend that human creatures do what they do *freely,* that is, free of God's making them do it or even God's wanting them to. For aren't there things which they make and do, alas, which no self-respecting God would, which therefore cannot be God's doing? If so, aren't these humans at least minimally self-made?

10. That way God would not need to be blamed for them. Some wag has quipped that the self-made man relieves the Almighty of an immense responsibility. On this theory God is in the clear, being now free of criticism, that is, insofar as the ones being criticized would no longer be God's fault. God would also be free to *do* the criticizing (some criticizing) with a clear conscience, so long as God is not faulting God's own creatings.

11. For if God *were* to condemn the very creatures God has made, that would be outright contradiction, contradicting all that is reasonable. And surely reasonableness is one of our most distinctively human mandates from the Creator.

12 Worse yet, if the Creator were to be so contradictory as to turn against the creatures themselves, and to expect us too to join in that critique, that would make God — not just our rationality but the Creator personally — look very bad. So bad, in fact, that that contradiction has scandalized many moderns into atheism.

13. Consequently, to avoid that contradiction — to avoid that self-contradictory God! — why not be good sports and shift any hint of blame

from God to ourselves, even if that means arrogating to ourselves some measure, at least some tiny measure, of "free" self-creation, therefore some guilt?

III. Neither God nor Us off the Hook

14. On second thought, is that theory of self-made humans any less contradictory, any more reasonable than the first theory about God as the "Maker of *all* that is, visible and invisible"? By fencing off some small corner of creation as our doing, not God's, do we really take God off the hook?

15. Sure, God might then be credited with allowing us some "freedom." But what sort of freedom? Freedom from God? That is free? And for what? For committing creational suicide?

16. No, Luther replied. That way out of the dilemma, humans pretending to be free to create themselves and thus to spare God, struck the Reformer as a cop-out. That was the fatal fallacy of Erasmus: attributing to humans just enough freedom to be able to transfer the blame from God onto them, accusing humanity in order to excuse God.

17. A cop-out? How so? We shall return to that later. Meanwhile, notice that Erasmus's "semi-Pelagian" solution, whatever else is wrong with it, is already a reneging on The Critical Process. And The Critical Process, remember, is an engagement with the Creator which no one may shirk, moderns especially.

IV. The Critical Process — the Law

18. Still, shirk is exactly what we do. The truth is, moderns are not as critical as often assumed, even of themselves and of one another, let alone of God. Especially not when they rely upon criticism to *save* them — as they all (we all) constantly do.

19. When the Critical Process is burdened with that impossible task, salvaging the human race, then compromises and shortcuts have to be made

in that process. Then only so much critique is allowed as the sinner can stand — "as the market will bear," as will "play in Peoria."

20. It is time to call the Critical Process by its biblical-theological name, the Law. More on that later. For now, though, what we are saying is that even the Law of God gets shortchanged in order to spare the fragile, guilty human creature.

21. When the Critical Process has to double as savior, it is no longer free for its major task: to tell the whole, the mortifying truth. Else who could be saved — that is, by criticizing them? Even when the Critic is God? Especially then. The divine Law also cannot save. It does the opposite. It alienates, finally kills. Clearly that is counter-creative. Then what is God to do? Lie?

V. Veiling the Truth

22. We do not dare say "lie" when the Critic we are speaking of is God. When God spares us the full truth about ourselves, it is advisable (also biblical) to speak of the truth as being "veiled" (2 Cor. 3:13ff.). All the same, if the truth is being veiled even for the sake of salvaging what is left of creation, isn't that still a blunting of the truth, a concession to sin?

23. Granted, such concessions have to be made if life is to go on, if the social order is to sustain any civil viability. That is the hard reality which was acknowledged in the Reformation concept, the "civil function" of the Law. Nonetheless, the Law in its *usus civilis* is the divine original vastly compromised.

24. That sorry fact about us, that we so much as need the truth to be veiled in order for us to survive, is an even grimmer reflection on us. That we are fallen is bad enough, that we cannot face how *far* we have fallen is even worse. This second, further judgment upon us — that is, upon our incapacity to face the full truth — is the Law in its "theological function" *(usus theologicus)*. That is the depth dimension of the Law that usually gets veiled.

25. Paul, for instance, explains why Moses had to "veil" the unbearable "glory" ("glory" might better be spelled "glow-ry") of his countenance when relaying the divine Law to his people: because of their "hardness of heart" (2 Cor. 3:7-18; cf. Exod. 34:29-35). Jesus is reported to have said the same thing earlier, namely, that the only reason Moses had allowed divorce was as a concession to his people's "hardness of heart" (Matt. 19:3-12).

26. Moses' toned-down Lawgiving was a case of *usus civilis.* Jesus' and Paul's exposing of Moses' guilty secret was *usus theologicus.* The former is obviously more bearable. The latter, because it is so unbearable, is what has to be veiled. That, to put it crassly, is the cop-out: not God's but ours.

VI. Misunderstanding/Misrepresenting the Law

27. When the Law, the Creator's Critical Process, is conveyed to us — and by us! — only in the filtered, dumbed-down version of its "civil function," the temptation for us is overwhelming to infer that that must be all the Law there is.

28. What really was intended as sub-normative (the Law in its veiled, civil compromise) is then misunderstood to be the norm. That misunderstanding is a theological version of what Daniel P. Moynihan has called "the normalization of deviancy." Modernity is roundly guilty of that.

29. So is the modern church. As often as not, this church is an institution which one critic has lampooned as a "not-for-prophets corporation." Dietrich Bonhoeffer found that flaw also in the mainline churches of America. "Protestantism," he called them, "without the Reformation."

30. In the process, God too comes to be thought of, falsely, as being less than critical. In the public mind God is then rendered incapable, for example, of "wrath," of truly righteous indignation.

31. Instead, God is then simply assumed to be "love," by definition, yet an uncritical love, love which has to falsify the bitter truth about the loved ones in order to love them. That sort of love is not even morally respectable.

32. Gone, then, is one of the most basic features of human truthfulness as well, what Scripture calls "the fear of God." Oh, people still fear as much as ever, though now perhaps more cryptically. They fear all sorts of things and powers and persons, sometimes as dreadfully as if these were gods — everything *except* God, whom they dare not acknowledge to be fearsome. Else their lie about God's "love" would be exposed.

VII. Living a Lie; Avoiding the Law's Criticism

33. The upshot is that moderns have succeeded after all in overshooting and have in fact attacked the very authority of God; specifically, they have attacked God's authority to be critical. They have done so, however, not openly and forthrightly — say, in the form of outright atheism — but deviously. They have subverted the Creator's authority by means of pious flattery.

34. By imagining God as "love," as cheap love, they have deconstructed any thought of an offensive God and any impression therefore of being blasphemers themselves, hence any appearance of being unsaved. Is that appearance trustworthy? Stay tuned.

35. One thing is sure: modern people, maybe modern Christians especially, are failing badly the historical vocation they have been given: to be, like the very Creator, critical. They may compensate by being, instead, hypercritical or hypocritical, which is quite something else from being genuinely — shall we say, penitently — critical. Thus the Critical Process degenerates into a carping, whining "culture of complaint."

36. Moderns may rationalize their uncriticalness theologically by invoking Jesus' advice, "Judge not lest you be judged," as their alibi. They may fantasize that even God has taken that advice personally.

37. However "Christian" the excuse, the vocation of moderns to be critical is simultaneously being betrayed, often with their religious authorities providing cover with comforting ideologies. This is a first, major form of "modernity's crux."

VIII. How Critique Also Saves — Somewhat

38. The objection, so far, has been this: moderns have been living a lie, a self-contradiction, on the one hand priding themselves on their God-ordained criticalness, on the other hand reneging on the very criticalness to which they are called. But the premise for our objection went deeper. We claimed that the *reason* why moderns renege on their vocation to be critical is that they idolize the Critical Process, turning it into something it is not intended to be, a *way of salvation*. Isn't it?

39. Is it really true that critique is not saving? Doesn't the Johannine Jesus himself claim to have come to "save" the world, not to "condemn" it, and claim to do that exactly by means of the "truth"? Indeed, his promise that "the truth will make you free" has long been a motto even for moderns who in no way believe in him as a savior. And isn't "the truth" critical truth, impartial and unsparing, letting the chips fall where they may? Doesn't that save?

40. The answer depends on what we mean by "save." Take the phrase, "save the world." But then distinguish between saving the world's sinners and saving the sinners' world. Granted, that is a very crude distinction, subject to many qualifications and exceptions. But at least we might use the distinction to say this much (though the Johannine Jesus doesn't say this): the sinners' *world* might be "saved," even if its sinners are not, by means of the Critical Process.

41. Call that kind of world-saving a "secular" form of salvation or, to recall the "civil" function of the Law, a civil or social form of salvation. That is saving what Christians call "the Old Creation," at least for awhile. To save the ozone layer, we are told, think critically about emission standards. To save time, reevaluate your work habits. To save the world's hungry children, critique our consumption of food. To save money, critique greed. In that sense, critique does save.

IX. Still Left with the Critical Process

42. Admit all that, namely, that the Critical Process or the Law does accomplish a kind of secular, provisional salvation, and for that purpose is utterly

indispensable to the "world," really to the Creation itself. Admit also that every human being within this world, sinner or not, according to the measure of his or her capacity, is called to be God's co-creator precisely as God's co-critic. Admit, finally, that the same criticism we are expected to employ applies to us as well.

43. Now, having admitted all that, even the most uncritical moderns are still critical enough to admit the opposite as well: that the Critical Process, much as we may idolize it as a savior, fails badly in that role. It doesn't remotely succeed in saving the sinners' world, to say nothing of the world's sinners.

44. The Critical Process may be the best thing the world has going for it, perhaps even the Creator's noblest creation. Even so, as world-saver it is definitely overrated. And moderns know that. Yet they also don't believe it. They don't dare.

45. Especially they don't dare believe that when they recall that, biblically speaking, the Critical Process is the Law, that is, the Law of God. And to criticize the Law of God is almost indistinguishable from criticizing God.

46. That borders on blasphemy, overshooting the creation and striking the Creator. That all but intimates that the Creator lacks competence or, in the language of Paul, lacks "righteousness." Oh, one might still alibi that this Creator must be righteous enough "in himself," personally, in some transcendent, otherworldly dimension. But in the world? If there is a righteousness of God in the world, surely it has eluded many a modern's search for it.

47. That search (and its Quarry) will be joined in the next series, "R is for Revelation."

THESES ON "R IS FOR REVELATION"

I. Retrieving "Revelation"

1. Theologians since the Enlightenment have so overused the biblical theme of revelation, and often in such sub-biblical ways, that the term has become "inflated." It has proliferated in currency and depreciated in value.

2. So much so that critics seriously suggest declaring a moratorium on the term. That is unlikely to happen soon. The bolder course would be to regain for the concept of revelation its original biblical force, notably as it was employed by Paul.

II. Does Revelation Save?

3. Today's revelationist theologies assume that the only thing the world has ever needed in order to be "saved" is to be shown that it already is saved. If so, we really must not need all that much saving, just a recognition of a salvation which obtains anyway, regardless of whether we believe it.

4. What we need, presumably, is not that God will forgive us — that, it is assumed, God is doing in any case — but only that God will reveal that forgiveness to us, assuring us how well off we already are.

5. If that were true, then, whether we are convinced of God's love or not, whether we accept it or reject it, loved we would still be. It is as if the world were unconditionally elected and that grace were irresistible, no matter how much the world may resist that grace.

6. Beginning from that dubious premise, revelationists are left to busy themselves with only one change, a change of human hearts and minds, an attitudinal change in our relationship to God.

7. Still, within revelationism even that change makes little difference in the end. For in revelationist theologies the only decisive relation is not our relationship to God but God's to us, which allegedly has never needed changing in the first place. That relationship is assumed to be fixed — by definition, gracious.

8. Thus the "revealing" of divine grace seems to be the only project left to promote, though even that makes little difference ultimately. That is why the idea of revelation, though currently it abounds in theologies everywhere, has drastically lost its original cash value and has become inflationary.

III. Getting Loved

9. What this revelationist half-truth forgets is how *inter*-personal the biblical love is. Inseparable from *God's* loving is the part *we* play in it, precisely as the beloved.

10. Consider this biblical view. Just negatively, if those whom God promises to love should disbelieve the Promiser, then they are not in fact "getting" loved. What they are getting — and from God! — is the opposite.

11. Conversely, it is exactly in their trusting the Promiser that the promised love comes true. Of course, they do not *make* it come true. The love is always of God's making. But neither does God love without the loved ones' receiving it, without their *getting* loved — which is what faith is.

12. Note the analogy to human promising. A bride promises to love her husband, and means it. But suppose he distrusts her. Then, not only is he deprived of her love. Her love itself shrivels to nothing but her private feeling, a solipsism. *Her* conscience may be clear. But is *he being* loved? If so, only in a way that discredits him. Is that love?

13. Grace is like kissing. God does not do it alone. Unilaterally? Yes. Even passionately. But not ineffectually, not without the beneficiaries' receiving it. The kiss is not thrown or blown or forced or slept through. In one measure or another, sooner or later, it is accepted, enjoyed. If not, whatever "kiss" there was becomes instead a judgment upon the recipient.

IV. Two Prior Questions

14. There are at least two prior questions about revelation which revelationists neglect, though Paul did not. First, *as what* is God revealed? Only as gracious? Not also as wrathful? Second, is it *only God* who is revealed? Aren't we as well?

15. As to the first question, as Paul knew well, there is also a revealing of God which is anything but saving, namely, the revealing of divine condem-

nation. That revelation, too, must be faced. Yet it cannot be faced except on pain of death.

16. As to the second question, Paul reminds us that it isn't only God who is being revealed, whether in wrath or in mercy. So are we being revealed, either as infuriating or as endearing. Indeed, it is only as we heed God's revelation of *us* that God's *self*-revelation occurs.

V. Divine Wrath

17. On the first point, that God is revealed also as wrathful, Paul leaves no doubt.

> "For the wrath of God is revealed from heaven against . . . the wickedness of those who by their wickedness suppress the truth" (Rom. 1:18).

18. That *is* the divine wrath, that God *lets* them be wicked and, what is more, lets their wickedness keep them from knowing the truth about themselves.

19. What probably does not need revealing is that there is "wickedness." What does need revealing is that very truth which we suppress, namely, that this wickedness of ours is allowed by God. That is God's wrath. Exasperated, God lets us do it. That is the dreadful discovery — or uncovering, unveiling. "*God* gave them up" (v. 24).

20. Human, truth-suppressing wickedness implies not just an absence of God but an absenting of God.

21. That is the hard point, however, which is so incredible, most of all to revelationists, namely, that our suppressing the truth by our wickedness has the active acquiescence of the Creator, who indignantly leaves us to our untruth.

22. And because that is so offensive to piety, this deeply suppressed truth about God's wrath has to be "revealed," literally unveiled. Without that

revelation we moralize our sin, arrogating it exclusively to ourselves, denying any thought of God's angrily letting us have our way.

VI. *Contradiction in God?*

23. The starkest theological antithesis is not, as we often pretend, between
"sin and grace," namely, between something *we* do (sin) and something
God does (grace). True, that antithesis would be stark enough.

24. But no, starker still is the corresponding antithesis between something
God does (judgment) and something *God* does (mercy.) It is the antithesis,
as Paul puts it, between divine Law and divine promise, between God's
cursing and God's blessing.

25. Notice that the antithesis between God's wrath and God's mercy is real,
not illusory. It isn't as if God only seems to be wrathful but really is only
loving, or as if wrath is just a temporary disguise until it is unmasked, disclosing the kindly God behind it. The judgment which is revealed is no less
real than its opposite, mercy.

26. Nor is it a matter of two gods, a demonic one who accuses and a pitying
one who forgives. If that were the case there would not be a problem
within God, only between gods. But no, both actions are the doings of one
and the same righteous God.

27. But then doesn't this revealed antithesis of wrath versus mercy, Law
versus gospel, imply a contradiction within God? Perhaps.

28. Still, need that be offensive? Mightn't it even be Good News? Isn't it a
marvel that out of *love* for us God is willing even to incur contradiction?
After all, God *could* have avoided such inner conflict by sticking just to the
law and being done with us.

29. And isn't the greater marvel this, that God finds a way, as Paul says, to
"reconcile" the contradiction (2 Cor. 5:18-19), and at immense personal
cost, even if that entails being triune in the process? Think what an embarrassment that has been to God's unity and consistency.

VII. Understandable Denial

30. Revelationists typically evade Paul's antithesis by construing "wrath" not as God's real self, which for them can only be love, but rather as a passing — stern, yes, but passing — "form of grace."

31. Once the divine wrath has thus been domesticated, it becomes instead a kind of interim "tough love," a merely tactical means for bringing sinners to their senses — and never anything but such a means.

32. Would that the Critical Process were always that benign. Or always that temporary.

33. Granted, the divine wrath is seldom manifest for what it is, a killer. So it is understandable, just on empirical grounds, why revelationists might shrug off Paul's and other biblical writers' depiction of God's anger as exaggerated.

VIII. Moses' Face Veiled

34. Paul senses how extreme his claims about divine wrath must seem, especially to the religious establishment. And he accepts the burden of proof. He appeals to the establishment's own writings, to the story in the Book of Exodus where Moses descended from Sinai to present his people with the newly revealed Law (2 Cor. 3:7-18).

35. So blinding was Moses' brightness as a result of his recent encounter with the Lord that he had to don a veil in order to spare his people the withering glow of the Law's "glow-ry."

36. With that allegory Paul dramatizes a universal condition that still prevails: the Law always comes to us "veiled." Its fierce "condemnation" of us has to be muted, actually belied, in the process of transmission. Else we in our weakness could not tolerate the law's mortifying truth even minimally.

37. Moreover, this veiling of the Law, a concession to human weakness, is a compromise to which the law's own Author is party. God colludes with our veiled minds and deliberately conceals the full truth of our condemnation.

38. The only alternative, it seems, would be for God to lift the veil from the Law, as a bullfighter lifts his red cape from the path of the charging bull. But then the price of truth would be the goring of the crowd downfield. Instead, for the moment, the veil stays between and the people's fate remains hidden from them.

IX. Divine Quandary

39. God, so to speak, is in a quandary. On the one hand, by keeping the lethal truth of the Law veiled, the Creator in the short run spares sinners from immediate annihilation.

40. But on the other hand, that very veiledness only deludes them into imagining that the Law is survivable and, worse yet, that it is viable, a way to life rather than what it truly is, a "ministry of death" (v. 7).

41. Sinners are still destined for death. But in spite of that they live under the illusion of a wrath-less, fulfillable Law. Can God be party to that deception and still be honest, "righteous"?

42. On the other hand, can God be "open" with us (4:2), unveiled, without destroying us?

X. Christ the Unveiler

43. It is in Jesus the Christ, Paul declares, that the Law's veil has at last been lifted (3:14-15) but not in the way the bullfighter's red flag is lifted to let the bull come charging through.

44. Rather, Christ lifts the veil by interposing himself in the Law's line of fire. He absorbs its scorching blast for those who stand downwind of it, as a heat-shield absorbs the lethal radiation.

45. In his death, where "one died for all," sinners now confront the fatal "glow-ry" which was directed against them but from which they have now

been spared. In him, their stand-in, "the ministry of death" is executed and, only then, revealed for what it always was: death-dealing.

46. But simultaneously with this life-consuming wrath there is revealed the diametric opposite of wrath, the far "greater glory." In the same Christ "who for their sake died and was raised" there glows God's surpassing, wrath-absorbing *mercy*. Indeed, that is the mercy happening, Christ extinguishing our death in his.

47. In one and the same action, as God's "blessing" overcomes God's "curse," *both* are revealed for what they are: real curse which in Christ alone is trumped by real blessing.

XI. What Is Not Revealed

48. Notice what the unveiling in Christ does *not* reveal. It does not reveal that the divine condemnation never was real in the first place, that all along it was merely a false face, an imaginary scowling "mask over God's smiling face" underneath, a tactical fiction on God's part to sober us. Certainly that is not what Luther intended by that metaphor.

49. The revelationist fallacy trivializes not only divine wrath but Christ as well. It reduces him to *only* a revealer, a mere messenger of a foregone conclusion. As if God's mercy toward us would be in effect anyway with or without Christ. As if all he does is make a prevenient mercy *known* — a show and tell. This is the Christ of the Gnostics.

50. Not only does the revelationist fallacy under-employ Christ. It disemploys the Holying Spirit. To put all our Christological eggs in the one basket of "Christ the Revealer" ignores a prior question: And who, pray, reveals Christ? His death is not Good News self-evidently. If it were, what need would there be of the Spirit?

XII. Reconciled

51. What Christ's lifting the veil does reveal is how deadly the Law's "ministry of death" truly is — and apart from him still is — and, moreover, how

altogether "new" therefore must be God's "reconciling to himself" two diametric opposites (5:17-19).

52. The opposites are, on the one hand, "the world" which in all honesty God finds infuriating. On the other hand is God "himself" who, though he yearns to love this world, yearns to love it not cheaply or permissively but in all honesty. That is a quandary. How to reconcile these opposites?

53. Among revelationists the verb "reconcile" in 2 Corinthians is usually subjectivized to mean, God's winning back our confidence and love. Thus, God's "*reconciling* the world to himself" is understood as in marriage counseling, inducing the alienated spouse (us) to once again trust him. That way it is up to *us* to feel favorable toward God.

54. A more apt analogy from modern life, a more objective one, would be the reconciling done by an accountant, "reconciling" two sets of books which do not jibe, or balancing a frustrating checkbook. Or an investigative reporter tries to "reconcile" — to square, to harmonize — the facts with the witness's contradictory testimony.

55. In 2 Corinthians it is God who is reconciling "the world" — an utterly unacceptable, dishonest world — "to himself," an utterly honest God, in the sense of making the two *jibe!* God longs to square these two polar opposites, "the world" and "himself," yet to do so honestly. Why? So that in all honesty ("righteousness") God can love that world.

56. It is in the history of Jesus the Christ, says Paul, that this infuriating world at last becomes honestly lovable to God, "a new creation." How so? By God's "not counting [sinners'] trespasses against them" but instead "for our sake" making Christ "to be sin who knew no sin" (5:17, 19, 21).

XIII. Revelation Begs Reconciliation

57. Since this whole change happens "in Christ" it is *to God* that it happens. "For God was *in* Christ." Whatever conflict there may have been in God is now settled — again, *in God*. What occurs in Christ occurs not outside of

God. For it is *"God"* who was doing the "reconciling" "to *himself,*" squaring the world, shall we say, with his own conscience.

58. More pointedly, whose honesty is it which is here at stake? Whose "righteousness" is here on the line — not only which is being revealed but which here and now, in this world, is on trial? Whose righteousness? Paul's answer: not merely ours but the very "righteousness of God," whose loving the likes of us seems anything but righteous.

59. But the shocker in Paul's answer is that *we* are to be "the righteousness of God." Notice, the point is not just that we are to be righteous ourselves. That, too, but that is another kind of Pauline language, the language of "justification." Here the talk is about *God* being righteous — and that *we,* of all places, are where God becomes that.

60. Theodicies ask, Where in the world is God being righteous? Not: where is God's righteousness merely being *revealed?* But: where is God's righteousness coming into existence? Where? In Christ and his believers. In that worldly process where Christians are becoming, there the inner-worldly righteousness of God is also becoming.

61. It is only when and as the divine opposites, curse and blessing, wrath and mercy, are in Christ historically *reconciled* that there is any *revelation* of mercy. Indeed, only then is there any actualized mercy to be revealed. Apart from that and prior to that historic reconciliation, the revelation is at best anticipatory.

XIV. Being Reconciled

62. But God's reconciliation "in Christ" does not conclude with the death and resurrection of Jesus. True, it was then and there (past tense) that "God was reconciling the world to himself." But what still remains is for the world, us, to suffer ourselves to *be* reconciled — or not.

63. And true, as of God's reconciling in Christ, "everything old has passed away; see, everything has become new." But our *seeing* that newness is in-

trinsic to our being included in it. That is why Paul says, "If anyone is *in Christ*, there is a new creation" (5:17).

64. Both possibilities persist: to accept that in Christ we are honestly made plausible to God; or instead, not to accept that and thus to forfeit such plausibility. In the one case the God-world reconciliation succeeds and is so revealed. In the other case, there is no reconciliation to be revealed, seeing it is spurned.

XV. One Aroma, Two Scents

65. What prompts some to allow themselves to "be reconciled," that is, to believe, and others not? Paul is frank to admit that the difference lies not in themselves alone but also in the revelation itself. The very idea of God's unveiling the Law in Christ, to his hurt and to our advantage, strikes people differently.

66. To some people, as Paul says, the God-world reconciliation in the cross reeks of death and morbidity, hence is obnoxious, and for understandable reasons right within the Christ event itself. Such a reaction, though understandable, reveals the reactionaries — if not to themselves, at least to believers — as "perishing."

67. To others, however, the same original odor, "the aroma of Christ," comes across as joyous and vivifying, "a fragrance from life to life." They thereby, in view of their quite different response of faith, are revealed as "those who are being saved."

XVI. Revealing Us

68. Hence it isn't only God who is revealed. So are God's believers. Or as Paul says to the Galatians, "*faith* [is] revealed" — revealed for what it is, namely, as justifying, as the birthmark of junior deities (3:23-26).

69. This revealing of faith — notice, not just a revealing *to* faith but *of* faith, disclosing its wondrous clout — recalls how in the Synoptics the compli-

ments that Jesus pays to faith sound almost idolatrous: "great," "has made you well," "has saved you."

70. In 2 Corinthians, faith is revealed as our "accepting" of the world's having been reconciled to God in Christ (6:1). And therewith, with our accepting, that part of the world which is we ourselves is in fact "*being* reconciled" (5:20).

XVII. Ministry of Reconciliation

71. We have saved until last the crucial missing link, what Paul calls "the ministry of reconciliation" (2 Cor. 5:18). Between God's "reconciling the world to himself in Christ," on one hand, and believers' suffering themselves to "be reconciled," on the other, there intervenes that link of love, a "means of grace," the apostolic ministry.

72. Like the incarnate "God in Christ," the apostolic ministry is likewise divine-human. Though it is obviously "we," the all-too-human Paul, who here and now "entreat you on behalf of Christ, be reconciled to God," it is no less "God [who] is making his appeal through us" (5:20). So vulnerably does God submit to human mediation.

73. The divine plea, "Accept your reconciledness," though that may be rebuffed by many, is meant for everyone. So the apostolic messenger "from now on . . . regard(s) *no one* from a human ["fleshly"] point of view" (5:16). In Christ everyone is eligible. Where there is faith there is hope.

XVIII. An Open Ministry

74. Apostolic ministers, as the name "apostle" suggests, are messengers. Though they are personally chosen for this messengership, their authority inheres in the Message they bring. Paul's "ministry of reconciliation" is "the message of reconciliation" (5:18, 19). The Message makes the messenger, not vice versa.

75. "We are engaged in *this* ministry," says Paul, as opposed to what other ministry? The opposite ministry — and there is such — is "the ministry of

death," "the ministry of condemnation." The apostolic ministry, by contrast, is "the ministry of the Spirit," "the ministry of justification" (4:1; 3:7-9).

76. However, it is not as though "the ministry of death" has simply been by-passed. It has been fulfilled, remember, in the cross of Christ and only thus superseded. Indeed, the very thing which distinguishes the apostolic ministry, namely, its sheer openness, its unveiledness, lies in its frontal and free dealing with sin, law, death.

XIX. A Readable Bodily Letter

77. Moreover, the death and rising of Christ not only marks the Message the messenger brings but even marks those who receive the Message. "*We are afflicted in every way but not crushed, . . . always carrying in the body the death of Jesus so that the life of Jesus may also be made visible in our bodies*" (4:8, 10). A quite bodily revelation!

78. Thus Paul can picture his readers, the believers, as themselves a revealing message — to the world. "You yourselves are our letter." The content of the letter is "Christ." Its verbalizer is the apostle. The One who inscribes it, not on tablets of stone but on the believers' hearts, is the Spirit.

79. This "letter," which is the believers themselves and whose content is their crucified and risen Lord now bodying forth in their own mundane crosses and easters, renders them legible. To whom? "To be known and read by all humanity" (3:2).

80. It is into believers' "hearts" that "the glory of God in the face of Jesus Christ" has "shone." Thanks to the mediating ministry of messengership, the original "glow-ry" of God's "reconciling the world to himself" in Christ now radiates into that same dark world through the cruciform and paschal lives of the reconciled ones (4:6).

THESES ON "U IS FOR UNIVERSALITY"

I. The Universalist Challenge

1. Probably no feature of the Christian gospel has been so troubling to modern Christians as the way in which that gospel limits salvation to those who believe in Christ.

2. So troubling is this limitation that many theologies, so as to exclude as few people as possible, prefer instead to redefine "salvation" in some more generic way.

3. But that well-meaning universalism only introduces a new and subtler exclusivism. In order to spread salvation wider it has to be spread thinner. The saved become more numerous but much less "saved."

4. Thus, in order to include non-Christians it may be necessary to exclude benefits unique to Christ, and to exclude Christians who insist on his unique benefits, even to exclude Christ himself — that is, the actual, original Jesus Christ.

5. For example, a typical universalism may extend salvation to all, also those who decline it, by postponing salvation till some future afterlife when presumably the decliners will reconsider.

6. But then, by that postponement, whatever salvation is left to them will already have missed out on the whole historic here and now, so essential to the Incarnation, so essential to this-worldly Christians.

7. In short, universalism harbors its own exclusivisms. In order to be inclusive it has to exclude so much! More becomes less. The conclusion is inescapable, universalism is a contradiction in terms, an oxymoron.

8. Still, that hardly relieves the Christians' embarrassment. The question remains, How to meet the universalist challenge without diluting the gospel's distinctiveness in order to expand its coverage?

II. A Scandal Inherently Christian

9. The embarrassment inheres in the Christian gospel itself.

10. True, it may be harder nowadays to conceal the embarrassment, thanks to the growing pluralism of modern societies and the new global awareness of other religions.

11. But the dilemma has always been there, intrinsic to the gospel. On one hand, faith in Christ is itself one of his supreme benefits, indispensable to all the rest.

12. On the other hand, that selfsame faith impels believers to crave that gift for those they love — in principle, for everyone.

13. So faith in Christ — that is, in Jesus Christ — is by its very nature exceptional. Yet that same faith, again by its very nature, yearns not to be exceptional but to be shared with everyone, to be enjoyed by all.

14. That might explain why no one, not even the most critical outsider, is more preoccupied with this Christian scandal than are Christians themselves. They suffer the scandal at firsthand.

III. The Dear Disbelievers

15. Moreover, the Christians' anguish comes not first of all in their encounter with other religions — there, too, yet not there most poignantly — but with those disbelievers who are nearest and dearest to them.

16. These disbelieving loved ones may or may not be religious but they have decidedly withdrawn from the circle of Christ. And their numbers are growing geometrically, especially within old "Christendom."

17. No wonder so many of the remaining Christians these days are tempted to settle for universalism. They have a most personal stake in the outcome, as Paul did with his "kinsmen according to the flesh."

18. And no wonder so many of these universalists are revelationists and sub-critical critics. What Christian today hasn't faced that temptation firsthand: rather cheapen the Gift than leave someone out?

IV. The Offense Is Jesus' Own Universality

19. It might seem that in order for Christians to be more inclusive they must de-emphasize Christ's uniqueness. Nothing could be farther from the truth. For isn't he unique exactly in his inclusivity?

20. Else how are we to explain the way the New Testament writers touted Jesus' monopoly on salvation as they did right in the midst of a very competitive religious culture yet without any sense of exclusivism?

21. Was their monopolistic claim for Christ merely an act of exuberance or insensitivity?

22. On the contrary, what for them distinguished Jesus from all other saviors was precisely that he was for everyone, not for some privileged few. He differed from all others exactly by his being for all others.

23. In almost diametric opposition to our modern embarrassment, it was Jesus' very inclusivity which made him the scandal he was.

V. Then and Now

24. But isn't that really the scandal still today, also for today's universalists: Jesus the Christ is the One for others, yet not just for some others but for all others? That is his offense, also, for moderns.

25. Conscientious, discriminating people, people with ethical and religious standards, may not want a salvation which so indiscriminately is for just anyone and everyone.

26. Jesus the Christ offends against the elitists' creed, "When everyone is somebody, then no one's anybody."

27. If everyone, even every nobody, does in Christ become somebody, then that affronts important social distinctions, say, between Jew and Gentile, male and female, slave and free.

28. Granted, such relative, cultural distinctions are not insuperable for any person of good will, whether Christian or non-Christian, and Jesus is not the only one who has helped to supersede those distinctions.

29. More drastically, however, he does challenge the deepest distinction of all: between good people and evil ones, between the righteous and the ungodly. That distinction is insuperable — except in Jesus Christ. So Christians have learned.

VI. The God of the Good

30. That all-inclusive, that egalitarian even the most tolerant moderns are not prepared to be.

31. Often what tempts us to be "universalists" at all is that we know of persons, even whole groups, who are not Christian but who by their sheer serviceableness or selfless spirituality put Christians to shame.

32. How could God, so the question goes, discriminate against such superior human beings, "the righteous," whether they be Christians or not? That question must be respected, as it was also by Jesus.

33. Still, notice how the question assumes that God must be a God of the good or, worse yet, a God of the religious.

34. That already makes God out to be far more exclusive than the God in Christ is, who is a God for sinners — therefore for everyone and anyone.

VII. Came Not for "the Righteous"

35. So then it is this very Jesus, this all-inclusive Jesus, who does exclude some people after all, namely, "the righteous." At the very least, his inclusivity causes them to exclude themselves.

36. Jesus is the Christ for all only on the prior assumption that all, even "the righteous," are sinners enough to require such an abject, sinner-level savior. But it is "the righteous," by contrast, who deny that they are that helplessly needy.

37. Instead they prefer the flattering alternative, namely, achieving their "somebodiness" on their own, with perhaps just a bit of an assist. In so doing they deny the universality of Jesus' unsparing critique of humanity, namely, that everyone without exception is as badly off — and in need of his help — as is everyone else.

38. Also, these same "righteous ones" exempt themselves from the status of nobodies only to relegate others to that status, namely, their inferiors, the "tax-collectors and sinners." The "Pharisaic Fallacy" about their God-relationship necessarily entails a corresponding fallacy about their intra-human relationships.

39. Even the most enlightened universalists today are caught in that intra-human prejudice, if only by the way they disparage their less enlightened opponents, the non-universalists.

40. This social prejudice against inferiors on the part of universalists stems from a deeper, theological prejudice, namely, that God prefers "the righteous" and, as was mentioned, that God is a God of the good. What makes that prejudice so appealing is that it is at least partly true.

VIII. Self-Exclusion

41. But is that what embarrasses Christians about Jesus' exclusivism, that by offending "the righteous" he really turns out to be a closet-exclusivist himself? No, that probably is not what occasions Christian embarrassment.

42. For in the case of these "righteous ones" isn't it rather a case of their self-exclusion, their own scandalized reaction to the Christian opposite, namely, the gospel's explicit, unexceptional universality?

43. In that case, what it is about the gospel which excludes is its inclusivity. What it is about Jesus which alienates is not Jesus himself so much as it is the unsavory company he keeps: sinners — in other words, his church. The fact that Jesus says, in effect, Love-me-love-my-church, turns "the righteous" against Jesus himself.

IX. Those Who Need No Physician

44. But doesn't Jesus himself allow for the possibility that there may be those who are not all that sick as to need his kind of physician, those who are already righteous enough to manage without him as their "friend of sinners"? He calls them "those who are well."

45. But does he offer that non-Christian option to "the well" with literal seriousness? Or is he being sarcastic? Is he perhaps saying to them: If you think you are so well, go ahead, take your chances, but in the Final Analysis we shall see (ha-ha) how "well" you really are? Is he saying to the "well" that they are already healthy enough not to need him? Or is he just taunting them with their own smugness? It is hard to tell.

46. Still, there is one way to find out whether in fact they are well: wait and see. Of course, at the end of the wait, as Jesus also cautions, it may be too late. By that time their lives will have been spent. Or misspent.

47. Meanwhile, Jesus makes both options available, only those two, and he coerces no one. If under those circumstances "the righteous" are excluded, it is by their own choosing. So he says.

X. A God Problem

48. On the other hand, the self-exclusion of those who are too good for Jesus' inclusiveness, while that may alleviate the Christian embarrassment, by no means removes it.

49. For the haunting question which persists is a question, frankly, about God. Quite apart from those who decline the offer of Christ, there are

those millions who will never have been given his offer — that is, the offer of Jesus Christ — in the first place.

50. And there are those, also in the millions, to whom Christ's offer may indeed have been presented yet never in its native winsomeness but only in some legalistic or cheap distortion at the hands of off-putting messengers.

51. For that matter there are those, likewise in the millions, who may well have heard the Good News in all its winsome goodness yet who, just because of that, found it too good to be true.

52. The question finally is: where for all these millions is the grace, the persuasive grace of God in Christ, not to mention the "means of grace" through which his persuasion comes? In a word, where is Christ's God now?

53. Stated more personally, if we quite undeservedly have been so favored by Christ, then why — if deservedness has nothing to do with it — haven't others been afforded the same unmerited favor? Does God play favorites?

54. As Luther dared to suggest to Erasmus, and asked Erasmus too to admit, isn't this ultimately the unbearable scandal, how could God "save so few and damn so many" — and still be just? Or still be God?

XI. Grieved About God

55. The question about the divine justice, notice, is not why sinners incur judgment. That they do, and should, and that they ALL should, is demonstrably just.

56. But that some of them, and only some of them, should be privileged to surmount that judgment through the death of Christ, and in him survive it and now already begin to enjoy his resurrected life — that seems grievously unfair.

57. And no one, as was mentioned, is so grieved by this ostensible unfairness as the Christians, all the more so when those for whom they grieve are those they love. But their grief, finally, implicates their avowedly all-loving God.

58. Most mainline "Western" theologies today prefer to avoid this griev-ance against God by redefining the problem into a non-problem, by rede-fining salvation. In the weakest cases such theologies are universalist axi-omatically, dogmatically, unquestioningly.

59. By contrast there are liberation and post-Holocaust theologies which do confront the grief which God occasions. But they ask the God-question, understandably, from the standpoint of the victims, not the privileged.

XII. Excusing God

60. In the matter at hand it is the privileged who incur the grief. Being privileged, "the elect," they do not attract much sympathy. Nor should they. What they do attract is antipathy, but most of all from themselves.

61. For instance, these Christians may minimize what privilege they enjoy by stressing that they are really "no better" than others. Probably so. But then all the worse, why are they of all people better off than others?

62. Or they may discredit the question by discrediting themselves, Who are we to say that some are saved and others not? Exactly. For that matter, who are we to say that all are saved? One is no more dogmatic than the other.

63. But the problem is, the scandal that only some are saved comes on much higher authority than ours. The scandal is not removed by our tak-ing the blame for it.

64. In short, we typically risk the fallacy which Luther detected in Erasmus, "accusing human beings [ourselves] in order to excuse God."

XIII. Versus Whom?

65. Similarly, today's Christian resists any disjunctions of "us" versus "them." Good. In fact, even when biblical writers employed that disjunc-

tion, wasn't it more as a warning against the "us" than as gossip about "them"?

66. Still, for the disjunction between "saved" and "unsaved" one need not even invoke "them." That disjunction appears already within the Christian alone, between herself as believer and herself as unbeliever.

67. The opposition between before-Christ and since-Christ, between in-Christ and outside of Christ, is vividly present in each Christian's own person.

68. The same Christian has little trouble distinguishing which of these two conditions of hers is to be fought for, versus which other condition of hers. The antithesis between "us" and "them" is first of all autobiographical, right within the solitary Christian's self.

69. To the Christian it is equally clear that the conflict within her between salvation and its opposite is not entirely of her own making. In her case that conflict is ground for gratitude, that she has been chosen for the struggle.

70. But that only reintroduces the grievous question of divine partiality, Why her? Why not so-and-so? Why not all those others? Why must they be denied the joyous struggle of the paschal Crossing?

71. Her grief, in other words, implies a "versus" not against the less favored "them" or even against her own privileged "us" — though she would prefer to blame the "us" — but finally against an unfair God.

72. Still, that "versus," that grievance against God, is explicitly forbidden. "Who are you to answer back to God?" That only compounds the grief.

XIV. Let God's (Problem) Be God's

73. On the other hand, it doesn't only compound the grief. It does something else besides. Paul's rebuff, "Who are you, a human being, to answer

back to God?" is simultaneously an ultimate comfort, a hopeful last resort.

74. The prospect of many being excluded from Christ does suggest a problem with God. But that need not be a criticism. It may also be an exhortation to faith. Then let it be God's problem. The inflection is decisive theologically.

75. Notice, the question about God is not being dismissed as illogical or far-fetched. The reason the pot may not fault the potter is not that the potter is not responsible but rather that the pot is hardly the one to point that out.

76. Attributing the problem to God, however, undergoes an evangelical switch. What begins as an attribution of complaint reverses instead into an attribution of trust. The problem is entrusted to, confided in God.

XV. From Complaint to Trust

77. Such entrustment does not set preconditions for God, except one. It does trust that God, all present appearances to the contrary notwithstanding, will in the end emerge as just. For that much, Christians believe, there is explicit promise.

78. But what trust does not prescribe is that, in order for God to be just, all must be saved, even though for now, short of the Last Analysis, there is no conceivable way that both those poles of the dilemma can be harmonized.

79. To trust that these opposites can be reconciled involves Christians in an enormous sacrifice, not so much of the intellect as of conscience, the very center of their old selves. Or if not a sacrifice, certainly a sublimation.

80. But for that, too, there is explicit promise, namely, that the dying of the old self at its very core, when it is a dying with Christ, is assured a resurrection with him, starting now. Faith, as Christianity universally claims, is that start on the new self.

XVI. Intercession

81. However, while the boon of a New Creation in place of an old one is available to believers, that is the very boon that is unavailable or unacceptable to the dear disbelievers. Meanwhile, what about them?

82. While it may be a comfort to faith that in the end God will be shown to be just after all even though not all are saved, is there nothing left to be done for those who renounce this faith and its God?

83. If the church's "means of grace," that is, its proclamation, its sacraments, its familial "conversation and consolation," or even inter-religious dialogue, are of no interest to the beloved, what is left by way of access to them?

84. And of course coercion is out of the question, as is any even slightest hint of pressure or manipulation, not to mention closed-mindedness or condescension.

85. The one last resort which immediately springs to mind is intercession, prayer for the disbelievers as advocacy in their behalf. Nor is that option to be minimized but on the contrary extolled, also as a theological resource.

86. Yet it must be admitted that prayer offers no direct access to those being prayed for but typically is done at a distance from them, "behind their backs." Prayer is not a "means of grace" in the traditional sense of that term.

87. Prayer, it has been pointed out, is our speaking to God and hence the church's second-best gift. It is not, as with the means of grace, the church's greatest gift, God speaking to us.

XVII. Vicarious Repentance

88. There are other ways by which believers intervene for their dear disbelievers, other than intercession. These other ways, though they too are third-person advocacies and not means of grace, are less distant than prayer.

89. For instance, vicarious repentance. One would think that Christians had more than enough to repent of in their own sin without taking on the additional guilt of their whole family or nation or ethnic group.

90. Yet a Moses could offer to be blotted out of the book of life and a Paul to be accursed for the sake of their people.

91. Luther could plead for a believing remnant to repent in the stead of European Christendom as a whole, so as to free it from its first Enemy, God, thus reducing the Turks to a merely secondary, manageable threat.

92. Bonhoeffer could return to his warring Germany, and certain death, in order to identify penitentially, not only with the "voiceless" victims there but with his guilty and condemned people, to co-atone with Christ for them.

93. In each of these cases, and who knows how many more, the vicarious penitents act not out of "survivors' guilt" nor by distancing themselves from the dear culprits but by joining directly, guiltily in co-sinnerhood with them.

94. With this vicarious repentance the grief against God over the dear disbelievers is transformed into an alternative, constructive use. But in the transformation nothing is lost of the original audacity.

XVIII. Vicarious Doxology

95. There is another way that Christians intervene for the dear disbelievers, and not behind their backs but elbow to elbow with them, actually face to face. Christians can do their praising for them.

96. The worst disservice to the creation is that it goes unacknowledged, under-applauded. It is in danger, Annie Dillard says, of "playing to an empty house." The extravagant efforts of the Producer to please go to waste.

97. None of the creatures are so little appreciated, especially by themselves, as are the human creatures. So benumbed are they to enjoying how they resemble their Creator that, as a consequence, they lose that resemblance.

98. Without Christ to restore the divine resemblance they have reason for disbelieving how wondrous they are — and look and sound and feel. Without Christ to re-value them they resort to auto-suggestion and self-flattery.

99. In the very midst of these dear disbelievers, not off to the side or above them, are Christ's believers, the world's cheering section.

100. And the believers cheer and compliment and approve, not deceitfully but for good reason. And their praise is not only in the dear disbelievers' stead but is directed to the disbelievers themselves, dears that they are.

101. "For from now on," as one Christian said for the rest of them, "we regard no one from a human point of view."

102. Neither are believers above being surprised, least of all about their own fate, let alone the fate of others.

THESES ON "X IS FOR CHRIST-ENING"

I. Christ Perdures

1. If ever there were a theme which seems *not* to reflect modernity, let alone postmodernity, it is that of *Christ*. But is that true? No, at least not so sweepingly true as moderns may suppose. Or as they may wish. Or as anti-modern Christians may complain.

2. Even if we count only such cultural reminiscences of Christ as Christmas and Easter, or the persistence of his name in popular profanity, or the sen-

---

Editor's note: Bertram noted on this chapter that he had hopes of even further refining: "The following theses are an attempt to understand a fourth theme in 'Christianity and Modernity,' namely, the theme of 'Christ-ening', on the basis of some of the relevant sources in Christian Scripture and tradition. The reader would do well to keep these sources close at hand as a check on the theses. See especially John 5:19-47; 8:31-38; 10:1-18; 14:1-31; 2 Corinthians 4:5; Philippians 2:5-11; the Nicene Creed. These theses, in their current state, are very much 'a work in progress.'"

sation which is still aroused by scandals or innovations in his church, we cannot help but be struck by his durability in face of the most secular forces to the contrary.

3. Jesus Christ may well be the best known and, yes, the single most depended-upon person in the world today, even if for all the wrong reasons. Without him we would have to re-number our calendar years (think of the computer glitches), whole commercial enterprises would go under, personal jewelry would have to be redesigned, so would a lot of favorite music and architecture and people's first names.

4. Indeed, those who try hardest to eliminate the influence of Christ still have to pretend that that is not what they are doing. It is still risky to oppose him publicly by name. (Ask Nietzsche or Stalin.) Confirming one of Jesus' own warnings, anti-Christ causes may even have to invoke his name to give their movements credibility — against him.

5. All of this seems like proof of what Christian Orthodoxy has called Christ's *vis major,* that surpassing power by which even his sworn enemies are compelled to acknowledge him.

6. In any case Jesus Christ does not seem to be in danger of being evicted any time soon or, if he is, of leaving quietly. It is as if this world, no less in its modernity, is still his to haunt one way or another. He has cast a spell upon it even though that may not literally be his Go(d)-spel.

II. The World's Christ-ening

7. But the question is, How can we, who are this modern world, be brought to make use of Christ — Jesus the Christ — for who he truly is? Not: how might he survive among us? But: how might we survive as his? In a word, how might we, the modern world, be "Christ-ened" — and maybe, in the process, become more authentically modern?

8. So stated, our question expands from Christology to pneumatology, from a Christian theology about Jesus Christ to a Christian theology about

his Holy Spirit or, as we might better say in this connection, his Holying Spirit.

9. The modern world is intrigued, pragmatically, with Jesus' historical results, his long-range accomplishments. In theological terms, the dominant interest is in his "work" more than in his "person." Even when much attention is given to the original (the "historical") Jesus, that is, the pre-Easter Jesus, what makes him interesting in the first place is the influence he has wielded post-Easter, really post-Pentecost.

10. That post-Pentecost phase in the Christian story which ensues with the sending of the Holying Spirit focuses not only on Christ himself (*christos*, the Anointed) but as well on *the world's being anointed* into Christ by the Spirit. Let us call that the world's holying or hallowing, its Christening.

Part One: Is the Problem Dependency? Yes. Dependence? No.

III. Reducing Freedom to Independence

11. One version of this Christening is particularly favored in the modern West: the civilizing effect which the Spirit of Jesus Christ has had in bringing the world to freedom. Characteristically, freedom — also social and economic and political freedom — is held up as Christ's richest bequest to modernity.

12. With this modern version of Christening, namely, the world as being freed, a problem emerges: freedom is mistakenly equated with independence. Before we explain why this is a problem, let us notice: moderns incur one of their gravest problems right at the point of their greatest promise, their potential for freedom. That is precisely where they most risk becoming the opposite, namely, slaves.

13. To equate freedom with independence is by itself not all that serious. That might just be a slip of the tongue. But that harmless semantic slip conceals a subtle misconception that can be disastrous. For if freedom is independence, then mustn't the opposite of freedom be dependence?

14. And then, so we imagine, dependence must be slavery. For that much we all know, that the opposite of freedom is slavery. Is this then the root of our slavery, that we depend? So we are tempted to believe. And there's the fatal fallacy, one which bedevils the modern age: If you want to be free, don't be dependent. Re-enter "modernity's crux."

15. Contrast that shortsighted modern equation (dependence equals slavery) with what in the Christian Scriptures is a diametric opposition: between the slave and the child. The slave is indeed dependent and obviously unfree. But the child, too, is dependent and nevertheless — or therefore — is free.

16. The distinction is crucial (as in "crux"). There is dependence and there is dependence. There is slavish dependence, which is bondage, but there is also filial dependence, which is liberation. In today's English we might distinguish the former as "dependency." But in biblical sources there is also, by contrast, a vital "dependence" without which no one is free.

IV. Childhood Is Prior, Permanently

17. Scripture commends childlikeness not because children are young or small or cute. They may be, but most of us at this stage are not. Yet all of us, no matter how old, are in a very real sense still children — someone's children — for the rest of our lives.

18. We are all daughters or sons of parents on whom we shall always depend for who we are — and that we are — ever after. That much we depend, at the very least. We may also depend, lifelong, on their love and approval. Especially so, perhaps, when their love and approval are wanting or withheld.

19. Being children, at whatever age, need not be infantilizing. Childlike does not mean childish. Indeed, to depend as the children we are — not as slaves but neither as self-made, roots-denying "independents" — is key to being mature.

20. At least that is the human experience, a liberating dependence, which underlies the biblical analogy of God's "children." It is only such "children"

who, being freed by their unique dependence, are entrusted with the responsibilities of maturity, as God's "heirs" and co-administrators of creation.

21. The current problem is more than terminological or conceptual. There are whole generations of disempowered moderns who, struggling desperately to be freed from old dependencies, in the process surrender also the very power to depend, therewith any real freedom.

Part Two: Christological Interlude

V. God the Child

22. However, before we can proceed farther with this pneumatological discussion, how the Christening Spirit liberates the world through a new gift of dependence, we must first review the Christological basis of that Christening: how Jesus the Christ himself is a dependent yet preeminently free.

23. Christians confess about God what all monotheists, more or less, confess about God, that God is that One on whom all things depend. That, at a minimum, defines God as God.

24. But in the second Person of the Trinity, as Christians also confess, God is simultaneously the One who depends: God the "Son." Yet this dependent God is not, for that reason, any less God.

25. On the contrary, that is exactly how the Son *is* God, namely, as God's Offspring, "eternally begotten from the Father," not created nevertheless derived ("God from God") and all the while as truly God as the Father is — the way a daughter is from her parents, descended from them yet just as human, as one candle is ignited from another ("Light from Light").

26. But then doesn't this make the Son subordinate to the Father, committing the Arian heresy, negating the "equal Godhead" of the Son? Yes and no.

27. Yes, the Son is subordinate to the Father, if only in the sense that he depends on the Father for his very being. About that the Scriptures leave little doubt. Nor does the Nicene tradition.

28. But no, the Son's dependence does not diminish his equality with the Father. That precisely is what condemns Arianism, that it infers from subordination to subordinationism.

29. On the contrary, it is the heart of the church's Christological confession that the second member of the Trinity, related to God as progeny to parent, is — not in spite of but because of that filial relationship — "very God of very God." Thereby hangs the Christian gospel, literally as Good News.

30. Granted, this filial relation of the Son to the Father affects also the Father's "fatherhood," also the role of the Holying Spirit. But not everything can be said at once. At the moment we are talking only about the Son as Son — as Child.

VI. God the Son B.C.

31. God the Son does not first become a son when he becomes human. He is, as Christians confess in the creed, "begotten of the Father *from eternity.*" At first, that assertion of faith — that the Son as Son, as dependent offspring, "pre-existed" the man Jesus — may strike moderns as needless speculation.

32. Instead we are tempted to date the Son's sonship with the onset of his incarnation, not before. And why? Not merely because we know nothing about him prior to that. That sort of healthy agnosticism, by itself, may be defensible.

33. Rather, we mistakenly assume with the Arians that to be a dependent is automatically humiliating. And so we reason, didn't the Son's humiliation begin only when he became one of us? True. But what is not true — contra Arianism — is that to be a Son at all, a dependent, is itself humiliating.

34. In the case of God the Son, being God's Child is not a demotion. Being derived does not make him a creature, he who is "begotten not made." His depending is, on the contrary, the very glory of his Godhood, whether incarnate or pre-incarnate.

35. In patristic language, a language dominated by time and eternity, there was a time when the man Jesus was not, there was no time when the Son was not. The point is that his sonship is prior to his incarnation, and prior not just temporally but also logically and ontologically.

VII. God the Son "For Us"

36. But that is *our* glory as well, that the One who eventually assumed our fallen condition was, already prior to becoming human, not only a God on whom all things depend but also a God (the same God) who on God depends.

37. It is decisive for the Christian gospel that the One "who *for us and for our salvation* came down from heaven and became incarnate" was not the Father, not the Holy Spirit, and not God in undifferentiated unity. Only the Son, God the Child, became a human.

38. For good reason. For we humans, likewise, are meant to become not God's spirits, obviously not the Son's fathers or mothers or God the Father's siblings. We are meant to become God the Father's daughters and sons, because brothers and sisters of God the Child. Else there is no Christian Story.

39. True, the whole triune God cooperates in our salvation. Indeed, we know no other reason why God (or whether God) is triune except for reasons of the world's salvation. The Trinity is "God for us" (LaCugna). God apart from us or God against us — and God is that, too — has no reason, so far as we know, to be triune.

40. Even so, though the whole Trinity does conspire in our salvation, it does so in order to restore us not to divine Parenthood or divine Spirithood but distinctly to divine Childhood.

VIII. The Son's Enslavement

41. The Son's humiliation was not that he was a Son, a dependent — that is his glory — but that he "emptied himself" of that glory, taking instead "the

form of a slave, being born in human likeness" all the way to the shame of a criminal's death (Phil. 2:6-8).

42. His condescension was to our condition, a condition of slavish dependency, in order to restore us to his condition, the dependence of free and glorious childhood.

43. Notice, our enslavement is not merely that we *feel* enslaved, a servile subjectivity, a craven spirit. Had it been only that, only psychological, we might have been freed simply by a change of heart, a conversion of mind or spirit.

44. If that were all, there would have been no need of anything so ontic, so trans-subjective as the Child God's literally *becoming* one of us slaves, except perhaps (à la revelationism) as a kind of object lesson to "reveal" or pantomime his childlike alternative to our slavish minds.

45. However, that much might have been done just as well without Jesus the Christ by the heart-warming influence of a Holying Spirit, namely, to infuse into us a new kind of "spirituality" directly, immediately.

46. But that would assume, much too naïvely, that the slaves still possess within themselves the potential for turning from dependency to free dependence, needing only the Spirit to call forth their potentiality into actuality. As if the world's "powers" would even permit their turning.

47. The contrary assumption of the biblical gospel is that there simply is no holy childhood, no godlike dependence left in this enslaved creation, not even potentially. Moreover, the whole world system, including God's Critical Process, militates against such free dependence. The only way it can imagine such dependence is as the opposite, as slavish dependency.

48. The very possibility of free and glorious God-dependents must be created in world history all over again, beginning with the dispossessing of those cosmic owners who till now have "held title" to the slaves. Hence our need of the Child God to infiltrate the old creation as himself the firstborn of a new creation.

49. But neither does the divine Son simply displace and destroy the old, enslaved creation. On the contrary, he takes it as it is and assumes it into his own being in order to retrieve it. In the language of the fourth century, what has not been assumed cannot be redeemed.

IX. The Slave's Liberation

50. Putting the world's enslavement to death by his own death, the Son is resurrected into cosmic lordship, but not simply as the same divine Son he had always been. He now returns to the Father different from what he had been before. He has in the meantime become every bit as human as he had always been divine.

51. There has been a change in the deity. The triune God in the person of the Son now has a human biography, a datable history. In the Christian Story this is a turning-point.

52. God the Child became one of us, a slave like us, who now however — an ex-slave — has the run of the household as the whole creation's "Lord."

53. Because of Jesus the Christ, the dependency of slaves has been transmuted into the free dependence of children and, if children, then heirs. Therefore, as the Christian tradition recalls, we too may "rejoice constantly that our flesh and blood have in Christ been made to sit so high at the right hand of the majesty and almighty power of God."

54. So much for the Christological review. Now we are ready to move to the pneumatological question. Given such a Christ, what historical benefits accrue to the world through the Holying Spirit, who Christens servile dependency not into mere independence but into the free dependence of offspring and heirs?

Part Three: The Problem (Continued): Fear of Following

X. "Independents" as Dupes

55. We moderns are suspicious of those in authority — parental types — on whom we have to depend. The blame seems always to lie with them, with leadership, not with followership. If only leaders were trustworthy, we suppose, the people would surely support them. Supposedly, dependability is what is hard to come by, depending comes readily enough. Is that so?

56. Granted, from its beginnings the modern age has had exceptionally good reason to be wary of authority both in church and society. (Recall the first series of theses, on "Criticism.") And true, "eternal vigilance" continues to be "the price of liberty."

57. But what is just as true, alas, is that the same modern age, so vigilant against oppression, has repeatedly been blindsided and duped by the very vigilantes who decry oppression — remember the Committee of Public Safety or "the dictatorship of the proletariat" (Robespierre) — and duped by them on a scale seldom matched in numbers and savagery.

58. Indeed, the age is remarkable for how often those who were most sophisticated and cynical about dependence were in the end tyrannized into the most gullible dependency.

59. Conversely, modern history is strewn with potential leaders — from promising political candidates to aspiring minorities and women — who deserved to be depended upon but were not, for want of followers, to everyone's loss.

XI. Being Led? Or Following?

60. Moderns fear being led, as if that — being led — were the counterpart to being a leader. No, it is not. The natural partner of the leader is not the led but the follower. And following is quite different from being led.

61. What our age remembers all too well about followers, disciples, is that in the Scriptures they are called "sheep." What we forget is that *these* sheep

can tell a good shepherd from a hireling by his "voice," can follow him through hell and high water, and can survive with him into the life that lasts. Thanks to the Paraclete, these sheep can follow right through the midst of the wolves.

62. What should have been learned by now is that it is not enough to distrust those we depend upon, or to excuse ourselves — say, by a theology of whining — as merely their victims, or to exhaust our energies in replacing them with more dependable leaders, namely ourselves. That may be true but, by itself, only half true.

63. All these cautionary efforts still lack one thing needful, the ability to depend. The question is not just, Whom dare we depend upon? The question is also, given someone dependable, how may we be discerning enough to recognize them and free enough to follow them?

XII. True, Christ Depends for Us, But . . .

64. In the Christian story, those who are Christened by the Spirit are those who are freed to depend upon God, but always God in Christ. Why God in Christ? Not only because in him God is dependable — that, too, and first of all — but because in him God also is depending, which is the very thing we cannot do. Christ is God depending *for* us.

65. The Son, with whom the Father is "well pleased," depends on the Father for his own plausibility. Yes, but that is not all. The Son depends on the Father also for *our* plausibility.

66. So confident is the Son of the Father's "good pleasure" that he dares to trust as well that the sinners he brings home with him are likewise welcomed by the Father.

67. These strays and parentless bastards whom the Son brings home are not lovable waifs but on the contrary God's enemies. Yet the Son dares to reconstrue them as the Father's elect favorites, specially entrusted to the Son as "gifts" from the Father, not one of whom the Son dare lose along the way back home.

68. This Johannine scenario requires on the part of the Father an incredibly good-natured Parent, that he should take back — yes, pursue — these orphaned ingrates as his own.

69. But just as incredible is the way the Son *depends* on that Parent, so sure that because he himself is dear to the Father he endears us to the Father as well, never mind who we otherwise are. So the story goes.

XIII. *Depending on Our Depender*

70. The story of course is incredible. The Son's tagalongs question him, "How can you be so sure we are welcome?" — knowing what they do about themselves. They may envy how trusting he is: "Would that we had your confidence — or is it naïveté?" Like a terminal patient testing her physician's assurances, they protest: "There is nothing left for us to depend on, other than that you do. Why do you?"

71. The answer to that Why, as we saw, is Christology. But there is a sequel, pneumatology: the disbelieving tagalongs, tempted though they are to prefer the safety of "independence," do begin believing — depending! — after all.

72. Still grumbling, "You, Son, had better be right," they at least depend on his being right though they are not so sure they are. Being unsure of themselves they depend on his standing surety for them. However faintly and fitfully, they trust their trustee. That already is their Christening by the Spirit.

73. The Son depends for us, yet not without his sharing — "assuming" into himself — our disbelief. As One of us, he too despairs, "My God, my God, why have you forsaken me?" Still, "he trusted him who judges justly": "Into your hands I commend my spirit" — and with the same trust he commends us. Now his trust grows on us, as his Spirit does.

74. Notice how subtly the Spirit works. The believers are freed to depend not so much *as* Christ does, in direct imitation, as *because* he does. They trust, not because he commands "trust me" but because, as his command

reveals, he trusts even though they don't. Then, because he still does — for them — they do too. So contagious is the Son's depending. They "catch" his Spirit. That is their Christening.

75. It would be misleading to call the Son our "co-dependent." More accurately, he is our pro-dependent. But his depending for us does not relieve us of our own depending. Rather, exactly because he depends *pro nobis* (for us) we can follow him in that, freed from any coercion to do so. The Christening Spirit is always the freeing Spirit.

76. The Father credits the believers' weak dependence on the Son as fondly as he credits the Son's own strong dependence on the Father. "Those who love me," says the Johannine Jesus, "will be loved by my Father" (14:21). Their love for the Son, however half-hearted, is as welcome as the Son's love of the Father. That is the Johannine equivalent of Paul's "faith reckoned as righteousness."

77. One Christian commentator marvels at this passage in the Fourth Gospel, how Jesus' followers, so plagued with doubt, can simultaneously so "please" the Father by the good judgment they show in depending on his Son at all: "the Father cherishes you because of your faith in Christ." Consequently, "whatever you speak and do will [likewise] please him," the Father.

XIV. Freedom by Faith, Depending

78. Believers count on their plausibility with God because Christ, God's plausible Son, counts on that for them. So they need no longer depend for their plausibility on any other valuers or creditors, not on parents or peers or superiors.

79. Even the best of these human authorities are co-dependent. Even mothers, let alone political candidates and salesmen and teachers, depend on being depended upon. However subtly, however against their own wills, they are ingratiating, indebting — except to those, the Christened ones, who now are free of all dependency upon them.

80. Because Christians' dependence is in Christ, who depends for them, they need not even depend on their own faith, their Christian depending. That would be fideism, faith in faith itself.

81. True, sinners are dear to God only if they believe they are. But what is endearing about their faith is the One in whom they believe, Jesus the Christ, not their believing as such. From this idolatry too, fideism, they are freed.

82. Still, all this freedom-from — freedom from dependency, freedom from enslavement to earthly creditors, idols — is only half the freedom which comes with the believers' new dependence, the negative half at that. That much is, at best, in-dependence.

XV. The Freedom to Depend

83. Simultaneously there is an affirmative, venturesome freedom as well: a freedom to depend — and to depend upon the most risky earthlings and earthly structures, even hostile ones: the political process, the market, pastors and masters, lovers, a fallible conscience, limited experience.

84. True, the children of God, who trust God the Child to ensure their viability, depend on these lesser authorities only penultimately and for something far less than viability.

85. But since God in Christ is himself an earthling, at home on the earth, his Christened siblings can detect traces of divine parenting in the most earthly, undependable parent-types (for instance, the press, the police, peers) and can respond to these with cooperation and respect — not fear but respect.

86. To respond to earthly powers not as gods but as God's, as authorities not to whom but through whom we are ultimately answerable, not needing like adolescents to compete with them but secure enough in God's favor to use them as our servants from God — so to respond to them, so freely, is truly mature response-ability.

87. For example, as one Christian catechism puts it, when the Fourth Commandment enjoins children to honor father and mother, it is not father and mother finally but "God who holds you accountable" for your obedience. But then see how that honors children, too. For they answer, as equals, to the same primal Parent as their parents do. "The subordinate person in the social order is addressed as a moral agent" (Yoder).

88. Authoritarians, no doubt, find children of God threatening. "To [Hitler] the conviction that man as a child of God is directly connected to God is a frightening notion." What unnerved Pilate was not that Jesus was insubordinate but subordinate, yet not to Pilate so much as to "the Father"!

89. For others, however, that can be not threatening but reassuring. For the Corinthians it was meant as encouragement that Paul, though he subordinated himself as their "slave," did not for a moment depend on them as his "lords." On the contrary, he was their slave "for Jesus' sake." What a relief for them to be so served without the burdens of lordship.

XVI. Favoring the Dependents

90. Likewise it is liberating for those Corinthians "who buy as though they had no possessions, and those who deal with the world as though they had no dealings with it" (2 Cor. 8). But buy they can, and deal they can, yet without having to depend on it for sheer life or for their very plausibility.

91. For their prior, higher dependence is elsewhere, in the Son on whom alone they depend to do their depending for them. Meanwhile, therefore, they can so depend on the world as to be unpossessed by it.

92. Best of all, perhaps, when they depend on the dependent God, the Child-God, these believers can reprioritize which earthly authorities they shall serve first: the hungry, homeless, lonely, those in prison, the very ones who are the most abjectly dependent of all.

93. Christians say, We favor these unlikely "authorities," the world's dependents, not because we depend on their final verdict to seal our fate, though it will do that. Rather we favor them, "these least ones," because we

depend on no one's final verdict except the Son's. And his verdict, being already assured, liberates us for nearsightedness, to see only the needy world at hand.

Conclusion: (To Be Cont'd.)

Note. What is "to be continued" is much the same question of Christ-ening, the world's Christening, which we have been pursuing: How to become so dependent as to become free — free to be depended upon by moderns without enslaving them? Most of that question we have already addressed on the basis of Christian sources, though even within that tradition we have not yet said anything about the word "christening" as it is usually understood, namely, as baptism, especially infant baptism. That would tell us a great deal about child-like freedom, also for adults. Beyond the Christian sources, however, what remains to be seen is how this Christening of the world holds up in the face of some modern challenges. For instance, think of Nietzsche's criticism of Christianity as a religion of "slaves." Or: Bonhoeffer's challenge to modern Christians to "grow up" and "live before God in the world without God." Or: in the history of this country, the heavy emphasis of its founders upon "independence." *(Sic!)* Or: the ways in which recent liberation theologies criticize "dependence" (or is it "dependency"?) and advocate "freedom." Ah yes, there is much yet to be said. (Sigh.)

Gloss #1: Baptism, Where Christening Begins

94. What is "free responsibility"? In a "world come of age" it is mature adults acting in response to God's demand though they become sinful in doing so. But such risky maturity is impossible unless first of all, like a child, it "depends on God" *(beruht auf Gott)* and, like children, can count on being forgiven (Bonhoeffer, *After Ten Years*).

I. Baptism

95. In the church of Christ all Christening begins with baptism. In English, "christening" commonly *means* "baptism." Would that the converse were

true, namely, that baptism more commonly meant Christening — not just christening but Christening, CHRISTening.

96. Of the several means of grace, the sacrament of baptism is preeminently the sacrament of dependence. For it is in this unique transaction that the sinner becomes from now on a dependent child of the triune God in Christ.

97. This initiation into the new childhood is most explicit in the catholic traditions of infant baptism. The baby does not come to baptism already a believer, a God-dependent, as participants do in adult baptism or in the Holy Communion or in the Mutual Absolution or even (usually) in the Gospel Proclamation.

98. On the contrary, the baby is assumed to be in a pre-existing state of *dependency* — dependency upon kidnappers hostile to the triune God. It is that dependency, that hostile takeover which in her baptism is publicly exorcised and she is delivered for the first time into childhood with God.

II. How Do Babies Depend?

99. So dependent is the baby upon God in Christ that he, Christ, has to depend for her without her yet even being able to join him in that, without her so much as *believing* him — yet! — baptized though she is.

100. In short, baptized infants may not yet have faith. By the same token, neither would they yet have unfaith — deadly sin, yes, but not that subjectively developed sin called unbelief.

101. Granted, many an orthodox theologian has been convinced that already in baptism infants do receive faith. With Luther, for instance, this "infusion" of faith into the infant at baptism seemed necessary for his defense of *sola fide*.

102. And true it is that a baptism which does not result in faith *eventually*, and sooner rather than later, would indeed be a failed baptism, lacking the gift of the Spirit.

103. Moreover, even if the baby herself is not yet believing at the point of her baptism, what is essential is that someone — someone quite as incarnately human as she — is then and there believing for her.

104. And that someone, to begin with, is Christ. It is he, as Head of his Body the church, who in baptism intervenes to reclaim her as his. Thus through this "water and the Word" does he assert his confidence about her, his pro-dependence in her behalf, even though she may not yet be aware of that.

105. It is not enough that the one who depends for the baptized infant is the church. Even that believing community cannot marshal the confidence needed to repossess this poor child from the powers who spirit her away from her Creator. The only one who finally suffices to depend for her is the church's Head, Christ the Child-God.

106. Still, neither is it enough that Christ depends for the baby. What good, as Luther says, does that do her? The whole purpose of God's sending us the dependent God is that we, too — we rootless "independents" — might depend with him. And for that we need not only Christ but the Christener.

107. For that reason, when the baptized baby as yet has no faith of her own, not only does Christ the Head depend for her. So also does his earthy embodiment, the Christened community. For the baby the church is the Christening Spirit's warm and ample breast, "the mother who begets and bears every Christian through the Word of God."

Gloss #2: Hallowing God's Name

108. One of the world's most urgent needs is that it be free to call God by name. More pointedly, the name by which the Christian world already addresses God needs radical hallowing — not in the name itself, as Luther explains, but "among us."

109. What makes that difficult is that traditional names for God have lost their primal power to convey the One who goes by those names. The names have lost their power not merely by the attrition of time. Worse, they have been conjured with for partisan and evil purposes. God's names are used ideologically, hence blasphemously, giving God a bad name.

110. A notorious example is the patriarchal exploiting of the divine name "Father." As the ideological motives behind that name have been exposed, fewer and fewer Christians have felt free (as the hymn bids them) "to call him Father with delight."

111. The sin is twofold. Not only is the "Father" invoked to keep people, in this case women especially, in appalling dependency. But then next, those who oppose this oppression — and who dare not! — are tempted to over-shoot, patricidally, attacking not only the so-called "Father" of the oppressors but the very "God and Father of our Lord Jesus Christ."

112. Thus God the Father is mistaken for his caricature, not only by the patriarchalists but now also by their opponents. So, this illusion the two fronts now have in common. The opponents have internalized their oppressors, self-defeating their power to oppose them.

I. God: "Mother" or "Father"?

113. Some Christian feminists have proposed substituting the name "Mother," but with mixed results. For in Christian usage God is not first of all *our* "Father" but first of all "the God and Father of our Lord Jesus Christ." So then is the first person of the Trinity to be renamed "the God and Mother of our Lord Jesus Christ"?

114. The trouble with that is that there already is a mother of Jesus Christ, Mary by name, and very dear to most Christians. To them the sweet scandal is not that God is a mother but more radically — to Nestorius's dismay — that God has a mother, as human and vulnerable as our own mothers.

115. On the other side are those who insist on the name "Father" for that reason alone: simply because it is a name, and a name is a given, an arbitrary, non-negotiable datum.

116. There is some truth to that. Names, especially names for God, are less chosen than given. And if those names currently suffer a bad reputation, the remedy is usually not in coining more acceptable substitutes, if we even could.

II. The Impasse

117. Still, in the case of "Father" — or for that matter, of "Son" and "Holy Spirit" — the name is not just a name but a title as well, descriptive of what the name's bearer is and does. "Father" is admittedly a unique, irreplaceable form of address to God. But it is also an assertion *about* God. It characterizes what God is like, that is, like a father.

118. True, this Father, the "Father in heaven," is also unlike any earthly father. Isn't that as good a corrective of patriarchalism as calling God "Mother" would be? Add to that the ancient claim that Jesus, in order to be who he was, had no need of any human paternity. Isn't that, too, a rebuff to paternalism and sexism?

119. All the same, the fact remains that to call God "Father" does imply that God in some important respect is father-like. In what respect? Answer: God's creatures, but even God the Son, depend on this God altogether for life and love as children depend on their parents.

120. Their parents? Ah, but then that could just as well describe God as "Mother." Knowing what we do nowadays about conception and birth and parenting, we know that children depend at least as much upon mothers as upon fathers.

121. So the argument has come full circle. The gender controversy over God-as-Father versus God-as-Mother, assuming that that is the real issue, returns to its initial impasse. The temptation is to settle for some stand-off compromise and to wish the debate were now laid to rest, not because it has been resolved but because it has been exhausted.

III. One Last Question

122. Still, the controversy over the divine name ought not be retired without at least one last retrospective question. Isn't it telltale that the debate has raged mostly around the first Person of the Trinity, whether as "Father" or "Mother" — that is, around the parent-like God on whom all things depend?

123. By contrast, there has been far less interest in the second person of the Trinity, God the Child, who depends.

124. Partisans on both sides, feminists and paternalists alike, have vied to claim title to that God whom power-starved people have always envied as the most godlike in the Trinity, the Creator-Parent.

125. This fixation with the God of power seriously distorts the power of God. It is a selective preoccupation with one dimension of divine power, God's power to generate dependents. It suppresses that further power of God to be a dependent, the very thing about the Son which the Father so admires and rewards and the Spirit promotes.

126. At times the debate about God's names does extend beyond the first member of the Trinity to the second and the third as well. But then too what is of interest is not just the Son's or the Spirit's gender but also their own parent-like power to command respect and confer benefits.

127. Much less appealing, presumably, is the Son's and the Spirit's dependence, their subordination.

IV. Heeding the Son

128. The foregoing diagnosis implies a contrary, more promising — the Spirit's own — strategy for hallowing God's name among us, also God's name as Father: heed the Son.

129. Heed the Son, the Spirit implores, as Son. The point is not that the Son was male, any more than that he was young or unmarried or a Jew or a product of the first century or a Roman subject, decisive as all those conditions were for his being like ourselves: a historic human being, someone in particular.

130. The point is that he is also, as the Spirit is at pains to emphasize, someone we are not but need desperately to be: God's freely depending Child. Heed that.

131. We hallow the divine name by heeding the Son as Son, not merely as a model or a commander. Still, he does command, doesn't he: "When you pray, say 'Our Father in heaven'"? Yes, but what is the force of that imperative? The appeal of it?

132. The appeal of the Spirit is that we — motherless and fatherless runaways, both slaves and "independents" — are nevertheless urged to address the Critical Creator as cherished children do. Why? Because that is what the Son has entitled us to do, being himself God's own cherished ("plausible") Child. In our behalf he is, and as one of us.

133. What is more — more Son-like — is that he depends on being God's cherished Child, so confidently that even those bastards and delinquents he brings home he depends on the Father to cherish as well, as the Son's newfound tagalong siblings. That calls for a very good-natured Parent but equally for a very trusting Child.

134. Would that we could share the Son's confidence: his confidence for us without his even having to be confident in us. If we could, that would be heeding the Son. And that is the Spirit's Christening: our sharing the Son's confidence for us.

V. Hallowing the Triune Name

135. The great desecration of God's name is not our calling God something other than "Father." That is at worst a symptom. Far worse is that macho independence of either sex which snubs the invitation of the Son: to trust as he does that he can gain us the same entree to his Father that he enjoys.

136. Conversely, hallowing God's name consists not in inventing more feminine, nurturing titles for God. (Still, why shouldn't we do that, too?) Hallowing God's name consists rather in naming why we are so certain in the first place of God's mothering, as we are. And why are we certain? Because the Son is certain. And because, by the Spirit, his certitude grows on us as ours.

Bibliography of Robert W. Bertram

by Michael Hoy

Most of the works by Robert W. Bertram listed in this bibliography are available on the website of the Crossings Community, and may be found at the following address: http://www.crossings.org/archive/bob.

Books Authored

A Time for Confessing. Grand Rapids, Mich.: Eerdmans, 2007.
"How Theology Is About Man: Luther Since Barth." Ph.D. diss., Divinity School, University of Chicago, 1963.

Books Edited

Theology in the Life of the Church. Minneapolis: Fortress Press, 1963.
The Lively Function of the Gospel. St. Louis: Concordia Publishing House, 1966.
A Reader in Military Ethics and the Ethics of Military Leadership. Unpublished anthology collected and edited for the Religious Resource Center of the United States Army, Europe, 1976-1977.

Articles and Public Addresses

"Brunner on Revelation." *Concordia Theological Monthly* 22, no. 9 (September 1951): 625-43.

"Freedom Under Law." *The Cresset* 16, no. 3 (January 1953): 21-26.

"Legal Morality and the Two Kingdoms." *The Cresset* 20, no. 4 (February 1957): 6-9.

"The Angels of Michael (Revelation 12:7-12)." *The Cresset* 21, no. 9 (September 1958): 12-14.

"Human Freedom in a Lutheran Theory of Education." *The Cresset* 22, no. 9 (September 1959): 16-20.

"The Confessions for Today's Student of Theology: A Session with Schneeweiss on Scripture." *The Springfielder* 25, no. 3 (Autumn 1961): 31-35.

"C. F. W. Walther on Law and Gospel." Reprint of "The Orthodox Teacher and the Word of God." *The Cresset* 25, no. 5 (March 1962): 11-18.

"Scriptures and Confessions: A Session with Schneeweiss." Paper presented at Valparaiso University, Valparaiso, Ind., 1962.

"Keeping the Word of God by Letting It (Him) Go to All the Trouble, and Take the Trouble (Matthew 9:1-8)." Paper presented at Valparaiso University, Valparaiso, Ind., February 27, 1962.

"Pagan and Puritan (Ephesians 2:11-18)." *The Cresset* 26 (November 1962): 17-18.

"Preface." In *Theology in the Life of the Church*, iii-iv. Edited by Robert W. Bertram. Minneapolis: Fortress Press, 1963.

"Even Rome Can Be Home." Address at the Annual Youth Workers Conference, Valparaiso University, Valparaiso, Ind., February 24, 1965.

"Be It Ever So Humdrum." Address at the Annual Youth Workers Conference, Valparaiso University, Valparaiso, Ind., February 24, 1965.

"Der heile Hauptmann." Address at the conference entitled *Menschen unter Befehl*, Evangelische Akademie Bad Boll, Germany, October 25-28, 1965.

"As the Faculty Sees It." *The Hamma Bulletin* 5 (1967): 22-24.

"Luther's Mission." *The Correspondent* 65 (1967): 2-7.

"The Great O Antiphons of Advent." *Concordia Seminary Newsletter* (Christmas 1967): 2-4.

"The Radical Dialectic between Faith and Works." In *Luther for an Ecumenical Age*, edited by Carl S. Meyer. St. Louis: Concordia Publishing House, 1967.

"Spirituality Is for Angels — The Angels of Michael." In *Ecumenism: The Spirit and Worship*, edited by Leonard J. Swidler. Pittsburgh: Duquesne University Press, 1967.

"The Doctrine of Justification Today." Unpublished address, June 27, 1967.

"Does MAP (Metropolitan Associates of Philadelphia) Need Theology?" Unpublished paper presented at the MAP Consultation, St. Louis, Missouri, December 5, 1967.

"The Complete Centurion." *Concordia Theological Monthly* 39 (1968): 311-27.

"Our Common Confession and Its Implications for Today." Featured address before the Fourth World Assembly of the World Council of Churches, Uppsala, Sweden, July 6, 1968. Printed as an appendix in the official *Uppsala Report* and in *Concordia Theological Monthly* 39 (1968): 715-21.

"On the Nature of Systematic Theology." Fragment from the meeting of the Concordia Seminary Department of Systematic Theology, November 13, 1968.

"Letting the Word Go to All the Trouble." *Interaction* (October 1969): 11ff.

"The Hermeneutical Significance of Apology IV." In *A Project in Biblical Hermeneutics,* edited by Richard Jungkuntz. Commission on Theology and Church Relations of The Lutheran Church–Missouri Synod #32. St. Louis: Concordia Publishing House, 1969.

"Immortality." Letter to Richard Jungkuntz, January 5, 1969.

"The Church and the Economic Order: Scriptural and Confessional Basis." Address, St. Louis, April 30, 1969.

"How Free Are the American Churches? A Clue from Martin Luther King." In *Begugnung: Beiträge zu einer Hermeneutik des theologischen Gesprächs,* edited by Max Seckler, Otto H. Pesch, Johannes Brosseder, and Wolfhart Pannenberg. Vienna: Verlag Styria, 1971.

"Some Friendly Warnings for the Would-Be Christian." *Concordia Theological Monthly* 42 (1971): 403-6.

"On the Care and Feeding of Enemies." *Concordia Theological Monthly* 42 (1971): 317-21.

"Sub Iudicio Nostro." Address at the Fourth World Congress of Luther Research, St. Louis, Missouri, August 26, 1971.

"A Theologian's Perspective on Economic Activities in the Christian World Mission." Address, St. Louis, Missouri, September 1971.

"Doing Theology in Relation to Mission." Address, 1971.

"The Lively Use of the Risen Lord (John 20:19-31)." *Concordia Theological Monthly* 43 (July-August 1972): 438-41.

"A Parting Peace: from the Faculty to the Graduates of 1972." St. Louis: Concordia Seminary, 1972. Co-authored with the rest of the Concordia Seminary faculty.

"The Gospel as Good News in Today's World." Address, 1972.

"Transactional Analysis . . . Redeemable for Christian Purpose?" *Seminar* 5 (April 24, 1973): 3-4.

"Piepkorn in Perspective." *Missouri in Perspective* 1, no. 5 (December 24, 1973).

"Reconsidering Lutheran Identity in an Age of Theological Pluralism and Ecumenical Challenge." *Lutheran World* 20, no. 1 (1973): 3-18.

"Informal Remarks on the Historicity of Adam." Presentation, 1973.

"Silencing the Word of God." Public memorandum to the faculty majority of Concordia Seminary, St. Louis, December 13, 1973.

"Crossings, Inc. (Saint Louis): A Proposal." Confidential paper, January 6, 1974.

"For the Faculty." A reply in behalf of the Seminex faculty to the Board of Control of Concordia Seminary, declining to be re-interviewed for possible re-employment, June 5, 1974.

"Isn't the Church Big Enough for Both of Us?" *ELIM in Missouri* 1, no. 4 (July-August 1974): 1-2.

"Confessional Allegiance and Historical Method: Conflicting Accountabilities?" Essay presented to the Conference of Lutheran Professors of Theology, Chicago, August 29, 1974.

"Ordained Into Whose Ministry?" Address to 1974 Seminex graduates at regional meetings, September 1974.

The following essays are collected and published in *The Promising Tradition: A Reader in Law-Gospel Reconstructionist Theology,* second expanded edition, edited by Edward Schroeder. St. Louis: Concordia Seminary in Exile, 1974. The first edition was published in 1973 by Concordia Seminary.

- "A Theologian's Perspective on Economic Activity in the Christian World Mission," 41G-41R.
- "Confessional Subscription," 38-41.
- "Doing Theology in Relation to Mission," 419-41.
- "The Gospel as Good News in Today's World," 40-44.
- "The Hermeneutical Significance of *Apology IV,*" 2-4.
- "How Free Are the American Churches? A Clue from Martin Luther King," 22-28.
- "How Our Sins Were Christ's: A Study in Luther's Galatians (1531)," 7-21.
- "Informal Remarks on the Historicity of Adam," 41Q-41X.
- "The Lively Use of the Risen Lord," 5-6.
- "On the Nature of Systematic Theology," 1.
- "Our Common Confession and Its Implications for Today," 33-37.
- "Pardon My Dying. A Sequel to Ash Wednesday," 30-33.
- "Transactional Analysis . . . Redeemable for Christian Purpose?" 29.

"What Is So Great About Faith?" In *Faithful to Our Calling, Faithful to Our Lord,* vol. II, edited by the Faculty of Concordia Seminary. St. Louis: Concordia Seminary, 1974.

"Those Troublesome Mission Affirmations." *Cross and Caduceus* (1974): 3.

"Who Needs Seminex?" *In Touch* (Winter 1974-75): 3-4.

"How to Be Technological Though Theological: An Answer for 'Fabricated Man.'" In *Fabricated Man II: In Vitro Fertilization.* Proceedings of the Institute for Theological Encounter with Science and Technology. St. Louis: ITEST, 1975.

"Six Steps — Give or Take One." Presentation to the faculty and students of Concordia Seminary in Exile, January 12, 1975.

"Address on Churching the Movement." Address at the ELIM Assembly, Rosemont, Ill., August 19, 1976.

"A More Excellent Way." A proposal in behalf of Concordia Seminary in Exile, January 27, 1976.

"Social Justice: A Recollection of King's 'Letter from Birmingham Jail.'" *NICM Journal* 1, no. 3 (1976): 39-53.

"Still Needed: A Confessional Movement." *Missouri in Perspective* (August 2, 1976), 4.

"Ethical Implications of Military Leadership." Outline of address at MCA Seminars in USAREUR, February 14-18, 1977.

"Confessional Movements and FC-10." Address, Munich, July 1977.

"A Time for Confessing: When Is the Church a Confessional Movement?" Address at Valparaiso University, Valparaiso, Ind., October 21, 1977.

"A Letter in Response to a Call to Teach." *The Lutheran Independent* 4 (September 1977), edited by Frank Leonard.

"A Time for Confessing: When Is the Church a Confessional Movement?" In *The Cresset: Confession and Congregation, Occasional Papers III*, edited by David G. Truemper. Valparaiso, Ind.: Valparaiso University Press, 1978.

"Transfer of Church Authority to Church Administration?" A paper delivered at the Twelfth Ecumenical Seminar of the Institute for Ecumenical Research, Strasbourg, July 10, 1978.

"Like Movement, Like Seminary." *Missouri in Perspective* (February 19, 1978).

"Assessing Movement's Future Role." *Missouri in Perspective* (October 23, 1978).

"A Christmas Crossing (Luke 2:1-20)." *Currents in Theology and Mission* 6, no. 6 (December 1979): 344-51.

"What Lutherans Confess: A Theological Course of Study in Five Sessions, Based Upon the Five Parts of Luther's Large Catechism." Presentation at the Lay School of Theology, Piedmont Circuit, Southeastern District, Lutheran Church–Missouri Synod, 1979.

"Our Theological Shape Five Years Later, or, A New Movement and a Word for It." Address, June 28, 1979.

"Re-Wording the Localist, Antibureaucratic Movement into an Intentional Confessional Movement." Address at the Annual Ecumenical Theological Symposium, Center for Parish Development, Naperville, Ill., July 1979.

"A Trans-Pluralism Trend: Might It Become Confessional?" Address at the Conference for Professional Church Workers, East Coast Synod, AELC, Garrison, N.Y., October 15, 1979.

"Responsibility: A Confessional-Ethical Splice." Address at a meeting of the Society of Christian Ethics, New York, January 18, 1980. Second edition, 1987.

"The Present Governance Structure." Memo to the Seminary Relations Committee of Christ Seminary-Seminex, March 10, 1980.

"Jesus and the Gentiles." *The Christian Century* 97, no. 28 (September 10-17, 1980): 438-39.

"An Epiphany Crossing — Programming Matthew 2:1-12 for Readers Today." *Currents in Theology and Mission* 7, no. 6 (December 1980): 328-36.

"How a Lutheran Does Theology: Some Clues from the Lutheran Confessions." In *Lutheran-Episcopal Dialogue: Report and Recommendations*, edited by William G. Weinhauer and Robert L. Wietelman. Cincinnati: Forward Movement Publications, 1981.

"A Christmas Crossing (John 1:1-18)." *Currents in Theology and Mission* 8, no. 6 (December 1981): 335-43.

"A Baptismal Crossing (Isaiah 42:1-9)." *Currents in Theology and Mission* 9, no. 6 (December 1982): 344-53.

"Ministry." Paper prepared for BEM, 1982.

"'Confession' Against Apartheid: When Faith Is Ethos." Address at the Annual Meeting of the Society of Christian Ethics, Indianapolis, January 15, 1983.

"Confessing the Faith of the Church." Address at The New Church Debate, Lutheran School of Theology, Chicago, February 7, 1983. Later published in *The New Church Debate: Issues Facing American Lutheranism*, edited by Carl E. Braaten. Philadelphia: Fortress Press, 1983.

"From Reflection to Responsible Living: Where Do We Go from Here?" Address at Valparaiso University, Valparaiso, Ind., April 27, 1983.

"Redeeming Hefner's 'Discerning the Times.'" Presentation, December 8, 1983.

"Confessing As Re-Defining Authority: Ethical Implications of Augsburg's 'Time for Confessing.'" In *The Debate on Status Confessionis: Studies in Christian Political Theology*, edited by Eckhardt Lorenz. Geneva: Lutheran World Federation, 1983.

"Chicago Theologians on BEM." Address, December 1983.

"Glory: Empty or Full? Programming the Pericope Philippians 2:1-11." Address, 1983.

"Chicago Theologians on BEM." *Journal of Ecumenical Studies* 21 (1984): 64-70. Also published in *The Search for Visible Unity: Baptism, Eucharist and Ministry*, edited by J. Gros. New York: Pilgrim Press, 1984.

"Liberation by Faith, Confessing." Address at conference entitled Liberation: Common Hope in a Complex Hemisphere, Seguin, Tex., February 22, 1984.

"Response to Wilhelm Linss on the Ministry." Letter, October 1984.

"Political Preaching: Thirty Propositions on Addressing Controversial Social Issues." Address at Institute of Liturgical Studies, Valparaiso University, Valparaiso, Ind., 1984. Published in *The Cresset* 38 (December 1984): 4-6.

"Depth of the Faith." Paper, 1984.

"Mary and the Saints as an Issue in the Lutheran Confessions." Address at the Lutheran-Roman Catholic Dialogue USA, January 1985.

"A Smithian Luther and Faith-Based Universalism." Address at the Lewis Conference, St. Louis University, October 18-20, 1985.

"Three Parables from Stavanger: The WCC's Faith and Order Commission's Plenary Meeting." Address given September 4, 1985. Published in *Ecumenical Trends* 14 (1985): 157-60.

"'Faith Alone Justifies': Luther on Iustitia Fidei." In *Justification by Faith*, edited by H. Anderson, T. Murphy, J. Burgess. Minneapolis: Augsburg, 1985.

"Recent Lutheran Theologies on Justification by Faith: A Sampling." In *Justification by Faith*, edited by H. Anderson, T. Murphy, J. Burgess. Minneapolis: Augsburg, 1985.

"Confessio: Self-Defense Becomes Subversive." Paper, January 1986. Later published in *dialog* 26, no. 3 (Summer 1987): 201-8. Response by Paul R. Hinlicky, *dialog* 27, no. 1 (Winter 1988): 66.

"A Constructive Theology of the Saints." Address at the Lutheran-Roman Catholic Dialogue USA, Burlingame, California, February 1986.

"The Confessional Situation as Eschatological and as Hypothetically Atheistic: A Comparison of Luther and Bonhoeffer." Paper, March 1986.

"Explanation-Justification: A Rung from Sharpe's Ladder." Address in response to Kevin Sharpe's *From Science to Adequate Mythology* for Ralph Burhoe and Philip Hefner's Advanced Seminar on Science and Religion at the Lutheran School of Theology, Chicago, April 15, 1986.

"Response to Jay Rochelle's 'Ends, Means and Diversions in Theological Education.'" Address at Faculty Retreat, Lutheran School of Theology, Chicago, December 16, 1986.

"Preaching Peace" (Ephesians 2:13-18). LSTC Baccalaureate Sermon, June 9, 1985. Published in *Currents in Theology and Mission* 13, no. 3 (June 1986): 155-60.

"Review Symposium on Revelation and Theology: The Gospel as Narrated Promise." *dialog* 26, No. 1 (Winter 1987): 69-71. With response by Ronald F. Thiemann.

"The Crux of Philippine Liberation Theology." Address at the Society for Christian Ethics, Boston, January 17, 1987.

"Luther on the Unique Mediatorship of Christ." Address at the Lutheran-Roman Catholic Dialogue USA, Tampa, February, 1987.

"Correlations and Crossings." *The Cresset* 51 (1987): 16-18.

"Don't Confuse Athanasius — Or God." *Currents in Theology and Mission* 14, no. 3 (June 1987): 200-203.

"Putting the Nature of God into Language: Naming the Trinity." Address at Lutheran School of Theology Faculty Forum, Chicago, May 18, 1987. With response by Paul Rorem. Later published in *Our Naming of God: Problems and Prospects of God-Talk Today*, edited by Carl E. Braaten. Minneapolis: Augsburg Fortress, 1989.

"Cresset, Correlations and Crossings." Address at the Graduate Students Association, Lutheran School of Theology, Chicago, September 21, 1987. With response by Michael Hoy.

"Two Ways Not to See the Judge (Matthew 25:31-46)." Christ the King Workshop, Lutheran School of Theology, Chicago, November 10, 1987.

"Seminex Was About Risk." Address, Lutheran School of Theology, Chicago, December 11, 1987.

"Forgiving One Another, Out Loud." Paper, 1987.

"A Philippine Revolution: From Patients to Agents." Paper, March 1988.

"The Ministry of 'the Ordained' and 'the Laity' (2 Corinthians 3-6)." Paper, April 1988.

"On Faith in Christianity." Letter to Ninian Smart of the University of Lancaster, June 29, 1988.

"Is God Triune Apart from Jesus Christ?" Paper, July 1, 1988.

"Response to Fred Dallmayr's paper, 'Critical Theory and Reconciliation.'" Address, October 7, 1988.

"Reformation Faith and American Pragmatism." Paper, 1988.

"Responsibility." Paper, 1988.

"Liberation by Faith: Segundo and Luther in Mutual Criticism." *dialog* 27, no. 4 (Fall 1988): 268-76.

"Programming the Pericope John 18:33-37." Christ the King Workshop, Lutheran School of Theology, Chicago, November 1988.

"When Is God Triune?" *dialog* 28, no. 2 (Spring 1989): 133. Response by Paul Hinlicky and Ann Pederson, *dialog* 28, no. 4 (Autumn 1989): 307-9. Rebuttal by Bertram *dialog* 29, no. 1 (Winter 1990): 60-61.

"Altogether by Faith." Address, March 1989.

"Response to Timothy Staveteig." Letter, July 22, 1989.

"'A Time for Confessing': Recent Confessing Movements in Light of the Reformation." Book proposal, July 1989.

"Lutheran Confessional Perspectives in Today's World." Address, Cabrini Retreat Center, Chicago, June 1, 1989.

"Black Churches in the Civil Rights Movement as a Confessing Movement: Confessio as Disencumbering the Gospel." Address at the Society of Christian Ethics, Notre Dame, Ind., 1989.

"Christ(ening)." *Currents in Theology and Mission* 18, no. 3 (June 1991): 196-97.

"How the Lutheran Confessions Use Scripture; 'Scripture and Tradition' as 'Scripture and Confessions.'" First Draft of Address at the Lutheran-Roman Catholic Dialogue USA, February 1991.

"Is Dialogue Hazardous to Ecumenism?" Address at the Liturgical Institute, Valparaiso University, Valparaiso, Ind., April 10, 1991.

"Abounding in Hope." Address at the 1991 Assembly of the Missouri-Kansas Synod of the Evangelical Lutheran Church in America, Lindsborg, Kans., June 7-8, 1991.

"The Exchange of Peace." Address at the 1991 Assembly of the Missouri-Kansas Synod of the Evangelical Lutheran Church in America, Lindsborg, Kans., June 7-8, 1991.

"Carl J. Peter, Jr. (1932-1991): A Tribute." *dialog* 31, no. 1 (1992): 2-3.

"Response to Michael Hoy." Response article to "The Soteriological Mission of Theology: Robert W. Bertram," by Michael Hoy, *dialog* 31, no. 1 (1992): 52-53.

"A Constructive Theology of the Saints." *dialog* 31, no. 4 (1992): 265-71.

"Luther on the Unique Mediatorship of Christ." In *The One Mediator: The Saints, and Mary. Lutherans and Catholics in Dialogue VIII*, edited by H. George Anderson, J. Francis Stafford, and Joseph A. Burgess. Minneapolis: Augsburg Fortress, 1992.

"Depth in the Faith." *LTSC Epistle* (Fall 1994): 1.

"Infant Communion? Then What Is Communion? Or Baptism?" Paper, February 8, 1996.

"Marriage and Sexuality: Sain Sex (Part One); Approval, Act/Being, and Nature (Part

Two); Marital Uniqueness (Part Three)." *Lutheran Partners* 12, no. 1 (January-February 1997): 8-25.

"He's Got the Whole World in His Hand? Yes, But Which Hand?" Presentation at Bethel Lutheran Church, University City, Mo., October 26, 1997.

"Bulldozed by Baptism: The Better to See You With. A Crossing of Luke 3:1-6." Presentation at the Sebring Seminar, Cape Coral, Florida, December 1997.

"Will 'Full Communion' Include Full Conversation?" Paper, Summer 1997.

"Foretasting 'Full Communion': Tomorrow's LutEpisc Today." Presentation at the Lutheran-Episcopal Workshop, Lutheran School of Theology, St. Louis, May 5, 1998.

"Moving Our Congregations 'from Maintenance to Mission': Is the Jerusalem Congregation at Pentecost (Acts 2) a Model?" Lutheran Professional Church Workers Conference, St. Louis, September 10, 1998.

"Sain Sex." In *The Family of the Future, The Future of the Family: Proceedings of the Institute for Theological Encounter with Science and Technology.* St. Louis: ITEST, 1998.

"Sain Sex: Saving Marriage by 'Crossing' It." Address at Setting Agenda for Lutheran Theology Conference, St. Louis, April 23-25, 1999.

"Telling Time, or, Whose Millennium Is It Anyway?" Address at the Twenty-fifth Anniversary of Christ Seminary-Seminex, Atonement Lutheran Church, St. Louis, June 25, 1999.

"Faithful Teaching, But Religious?" In *By Faith Alone: Essays on Justification in Honor of Gerhard O. Forde,* edited by Joseph A. Burgess and Mark Kolden. Grand Rapids, Mich.: Wm. B. Eerdmans, 2004.

Major Book Reviews

Franz Lau, *Luther.* In *Archiv für Reformationsgeschichte* 55 (1964): 114-15.

Edward Schillebeeckx, *Christ the Sacrament of the Encounter with God.* In *Journal of Religion* 45 (1965): 260-61.

Ludwig Feuerbach, *The Essence of Faith According to Luther.* In *The Christian Century* 84 (1967): 1660.

F. W. Kantzenbach and V. Vatja, *Oecumenica 1968.* In *Journal of Ecumenical Studies* 7 (1970): 346-47.

H. McSorley, *Luther, Right or Wrong?* In *Archiv für Reformationsgeschichte* 62 (1971): 313-15.

David G. Truemper and Frederick A. Niedner, Jr., *Keeping the Faith.* In *The Cresset* 45 (1982).

Roy Rustum, *Experimenting with Truth.* In *Zygon* 20, no. 2 (June 1985): 227-30.

Ronald F. Thiemann, *Revelation and Theology: The Gospel as Narrated Promise.* In *The Christian Century* 103, no. 3 (January 22, 1986): 74-75.

Sermons

"The Better to See You With, Dear World." Concordia Seminary Chapel, May 6, 1969.

"Pardon My Dying." Genesis 3:19; 1 Cor. 15:49. Concordia Seminary Chapel, February 17, 1972.

"The Lively Use of the Risen Lord." John 20:19-31. Concordia Seminary Chapel, April 13, 1972.

"The Uncommon Community." Acts 2:42. Concordia Seminary Chapel, June 12, 1973.

"Who's We?" The Te Deum. Seminex Chapel, September 23, 1977.

"Look Again." Seminex Chapel, February 9, 1978.

"That's Empty, My Son." Philippians 2:1-11. Ordination sermon preached at Grace Lutheran Church, River Forest, Ill., September 24, 1978.

"What Makes the Rejects Sing?" Psalm 118. Seminex Baccalaureate, May 1979.

"Praise to You, O Christ?" Matthew 22:15-22. LSTC Chapel, October 24, 1984.

"God of the Widows." Mark 12:38-44. LSTC Chapel, November 13, 1985.

"The Boast That Is Faith." Romans 3:19-28. LSTC Chapel, Feast of the Reformation, 1986.

"Homily at the Installation of The Reverend William Yancey into the Pastorate of Bethel Lutheran Church." 2 Corinthians 4:1-7. March 27, 1988.

"We Never Know How Healed We Are Until We Hear the Healer Out." Mark 7:31-37. Sermon preached at the baptism of Hannah Davis, September 11, 1988.

"Remembrance, Repentance, Resurrection." Luke 16:19-31. Sermon preached at the Fiftieth Anniversary Reunion of the Class of 1939, Concordia Seminary, at Fort Wayne, Ind. September 24, 1989.

"Be There at Our Homing." Sermon preached at the wedding of Jane Ralph and Peter Rehwaldt, September 29, 1989.

"Clinging for Dear Life." John 20:1-18. Sermon preached at LSTC, Easter 1990.

"Commencement Sermon for D. Min. Candidates." John 16:4b-11. Holy Trinity Lutheran Church, St. Louis, Pentecost Evening, June 5, 1995.

"*In Nomine Jesu.*" Christmas Eve sermon (undated).

Crossings Newsletters

Bertram helped establish the Crossings Community and published several essays in editions of the Crossings Newsletter, beginning with the first issue in 1985. Several of the Crossings Newsletters are available online at http://www.crossings.org/newsletter.htm.

Bibliographies

All resources listed in the following bibliographies have been included in this bibliography.

Robert W. Bertram. "Bibliography, 1960-1980." February 1, 1980.

———. "Faculty Activities and Achievements, July 1981-June 1983 (2 Corinthians 11:17-18)." May 3, 1983.

———. "Publications, 1983-1984." March 12, 1984.

———. "Scholarship." 1986.

———. "Speaking engagements, 1986-1987." 1987.

Steven C. Kuhl. "Bibliography of Robert W. Bertram." In *Currents in Theology and Mission* 14, No. 2 (April 1987): 140-46. This issue of *Currents* as well as the June 1987 issue were Festschrift editions in honor of Robert W. Bertram.

Articles about Robert W. Bertram

Jerome Taylor. "Religion in College." *The Commonweal* 71, no. 18 (January 29, 1960): 483-86.

Thomas Strieter. "The Confessing Movement: A Struggle-Resistance Model Within the Church: Robert W. Bertram and Edward H. Schroeder." In "Contemporary Two Kingdoms and Governances Thinking in Today's World." Diss., Lutheran School of Theology, Chicago, May 1986.

Ralph Klein. "Just Look Around: Essays in Honor of Robert W. Bertram." *Currents in Theology and Mission* 14, no. 2 (April 1987): 82-84.

Edward H. Schroeder. "A Time for Confessing Is a Time for Liberating." *Currents in Theology and Mission* 14, no. 2 (April 1987): 85-93.

"Reflections on a Commuter Marriage." *Lutheran Women Today* 1, no. 3 (March 1988): 16-18.

"1. Bob Bertram Is Retiring. T or F?" LSTC Alumni Newsletter (December 1990): 1.

"Bertram Retires from Faculty." *Epistle: A Newsletter of the Lutheran School of Theology at Chicago* 23, no. 3 (Summer 1991): 2.

Michael Hoy. "The Soteriological Mission of Theology." *dialog* 31, no. 1 (1992): 48-53. With response by Robert W. Bertram.

Index of Names and Subjects

Apartheid, xii, xvii, 1, 26, 57-64, 145-46

Aquino, Corazon, 97, 116-31

Augsburg Confession, xiii, 1-22, 23-38

Barmen Declaration, xii, 65-70, 74-76, 84, 142

Barth, Karl, viii-ix, xv, 37, 38, 69, 70, 73, 74, 76, 101, 142

Basic Christian Communities (Philippines), 98-106, 109, 115, 125

Bethge, Eberhard, xi, xviii, 76, 77, 79, 90, 142

Bonhoeffer, Dietrich, xi, 37, 41, 65-95, 142, 156, 199

Christening (and dependence), 184-205

Civil rights movement (Martin Luther King, Jr.), 1, 39-56

Claver, Francisco, xviii, 96, 98-101, 103-6, 110-16, 127, 129, 131

Confessing Church (Bekennende Kirche), xii, 70, 73, 75, 78, 79, 80, 82, 93, 141-42

Confessing (or confessional) movements: as "ambiguous certitude," xii, 147-49; as appealing for/to the oppressed, 19-22, 96-131; as ecumenical, 8-12, 60-64; as gospel-plus (and adiaphora), 4-8, 39-56; as martyria (witness), 2-4, 24-38; as redefining authority (Law and Gospel), 12-19, 65-95; definition, xvi-xvii, 1, 58, 132-33

Criticism, 150-59

Crossings Community, xiv-xv

Dahlem synod, 72-74

Elert, Werner, ix, 70, 76, 81, 88

Fackenheim, Emil, 2, 58-59

Faith, 105, 106-16

Finkenwalde, xi-xii, 76-80, 88

Gandhi, Gandhism, 52, 53, 54, 124

German Christians (DEK), 67-69, 71-73, 75, 81, 88, 142

Humility, 27-30

King, Martin Luther, Jr., xii, xvii, 39-56, 107, 147

Luther, Martin, viii, ix, 4, 12, 13, 18, 25, 27-37, 39, 44, 45, 49, 67, 81, 83, 87, 92, 101, 105, 136, 140, 152, 154, 166, 178, 183, 200, 201

Lutheran Church–Missouri Synod, x, xiv, 134, 139, 141, 143-44, 146

Melanchthon, Philip, 3, 5, 11-12, 24, 28, 30

Münzer, Thomas, 28, 33, 39

Niebuhr, H. Richard, 11, 58

Philippine (EDSA) Revolution, 96-97, 116, 132

Resistance (to Nazism), 86-92
Revelation, 159-71

Second Vatican Council, 100-103, 106
Seminex, x-xii, xiv, xvii, xviii, 144, 148-49; Internal Governance Document, xii-xiv
Southern Christian Leadership Conference, 54

Tillich, Paul, viii, 46
Tracy, David, 11, 38, 58
Two Kingdoms, 67, 87, 92-95

Universality (vis-à-vis universalism), 172-84

Index of Lutheran Confession References

Augsburg Confession

Superscription	4
Preface	9
Article II	20
Article IV	20, 21
Article VII	5, 132
Article XIV	11
Article XV	5, 6
Article XVI	15, 16, 17, 18
Article XVII	17
Article XVIII	15, 16, 17
Article XX	20
Article XXI	3

Article XXVI	20
Article XXVII	5
Article XXVIII	6, 7, 19

Apology of the Augsburg Confession

Preface	11
Article IV	21
Article XVI	21

Smalcald Articles

Preface	29-30
Article II	12, 16

Article III	12, 20, 21, 22

Treatise of the Power and Primacy of the Pope

	18

Formula of Concord

Preface	11
Article X	xi, xii, 3, 5, 6, 7, 8, 9, 10, 12, 13, 17, 18, 19, 22, 41, 42, 78, 80, 81, 132, 133

Index of Scripture References

OLD TESTAMENT	Luke		5:18	170
	7:50	114	5:18-19	163, 170
Genesis			5:20	170
15:6	114	Acts		6:1	170
		5:29	31	6:2	43
Exodus			6:14	6
34:29-35	156	Romans		6:17	6
		1:18	162	8	198
Job		1:24	162	
13:15	2	4:9	114	Galatians
		4:22	114	1:8	19
Psalms		8:1	136	1:8-9	137
22:1	3	14:23	48	2:4	7, 19
119:46	4			2:5	7, 19, 41
		1 Corinthians		3:6	114
		1:18-25	136	3:23-26	169
NEW TESTAMENT	12:26	xviii	5:1	19, 42, 81
Matthew		2 Corinthians		2 Thessalonians
10:32	132	2–7	xviii, 151	2:7	86
10:32-33	3	3:2	171	
12:30	83	3:7	165	Hebrews
19:3-12	156	3:7-9	171	11	x
27:46	3	3:7-18	156, 164	11:33-37	114-15
		3:13	155	13:17	18
Mark		4:1	171	
5:34	114	4:2	165	1 John
9:20-27	114	4:6	171	5:14	114
9:40	83	5:16	170	
10:52	114	5:17	169	Revelation
15:34	3	5:17-19	167	14:13	xv

CPSIA information can be obtained
at www.ICGtesting.com
Printed in the USA
BVHW081913110820
585982BV00008B/329